THRIVING THROUGH UNCERTAINTY

"This brilliant book is your 'Get out of Fear Now' pass! You have dreams to create and a marvelous life that awaits you. Tama Kieves shares how to be in the middle of all sorts of things and find your way to everything you deserve. She's funny, real, and smart, and *Thriving Through Uncertainty* is essential reading for those who want to live a 'great-full,' authentic, FULLY EXPRESSED life."
—SARK, bestselling creativity author, and coauthor and artist of *Succulent Wild Love*

"Anyone pursuing their heroic dreams faces uncertainty every single day. How you deal with your uncertainty makes all the difference to your bottom line and to your peace of mind. Tama Kieves has written the guidebook for those in the trenches. *Thriving Through Uncertainty* will help you shift your mind-set from anxiety to powerhouse focus."
—Michael Port, sales guru and *New York Times* bestselling author of *Book Yourself Solid*

"Tama writes like someone who has been there before you because she has. She is a qualified and experienced guide. Her words and images land on you like a novel, descriptions that stir the soul as she guides you through a gentle and important transformation. Let this book usher you to a new place where your every wish can get a chance at becoming real."
—Laura Berman Fortgang, author of *Now What? 90 Days to a New Life Direction* and *The Little Book On Meaning*

"We're living in a crazy time where many of us are stuck and afraid to make the wrong move, so we don't actually move at all. With moxie and wisdom, Tama Kieves has written this timely guidebook to help answer some of those daunting questions that continue to keep us running in circles. If you want to unlock your power and laugh your way back to happy, *Thriving Through Uncertainty* is the book you should be reading right now."
—Tammi Leader Fuller, former *Today* show producer and CEO of Campowerment

"Tama Kieves is the perfect tour guide through challenging times. *Thriving Through Uncertainty* is brilliant, funny, practical, motivating, and, most of all, inspiring (like Tama herself). If you are experiencing uncertainty in any area of your life, this book is a must!"
—Joel Fotinos, author of *The Think and Grow Rich Workbook*

THRIVING
THROUGH
UNCERTAINTY

Moving Beyond Fear of
the Unknown and Making
Change Work for You

TAMA KIEVES

A TARCHERPERIGEE BOOK

tarcherperigee

An imprint of Penguin Random House LLC
375 Hudson Street
New York, New York 10014

TarcherPerigee with tp colophon is a registered trademark of
Penguin Random House LLC.

Most TarcherPerigee books are available at special quantity discounts for bulk purchase for sales promotions, premiums, fund-raising, and educational needs. Special books or book excerpts also can be created to fit specific needs. For details, write: SpecialMarkets@penguinrandomhouse.com.

Library of Congress Cataloging-in-Publication Data
Names: Kieves, Tama J., author.
Title: Thriving through uncertainty : moving beyond fear of the
unknown and making change work for you / Tama J. Kieves.
Description: New York : TarcherPerigee, 2018.
Identifiers: LCCN 2017031598 (print) | LCCN 2017051040 (ebook) |
ISBN 9781101992302 | ISBN 9780143109532 (paperback)
Subjects: LCSH: Success. | Change (Psychology) |
BISAC: BODY, MIND & SPIRIT / Inspiration & Personal Growth. |
SELF-HELP / Motivational & Inspirational. |
SELF-HELP / Personal Growth / Happiness.
Classification: LCC BF637.S8 (ebook) | LCC BF637.S8 K46 2018 (print) |
DDC 650.1—dc23
LC record available at https://lccn.loc.gov/2017031598

Printed in the United States of America
3   5   7   9   10   8   6   4   2

I read recently that snowflakes are all alike. However, when they fall through the atmosphere and interact with the elements, they crystallize into their own unique patterns. The way you fall in this life, the way you meet the elements, this is your love song to the Universe. The journey creates who you are. Today, I know that how I respond to my trials, creates who I am.

TAMA KIEVES—from *A Year Without Fear*

Naturally, I have empathy for those with demanding minds—who want to know how to do things, and how to take charge of their lives. I know what it's like to want to know everything up front— documented, certified, and notarized—before you budge a single half step. But, of course, the inspired path is one that asks you to dive into an ocean in the moonlight—when there's no lifeguard in sight.

Then and only then do you understand what you're doing.

And by then, you couldn't care less. Because the love and goodness is overwhelming and you no longer need facts because, let's just say, you've already bought the farm and you're singing to the daisies.

It's a different path, to be sure.

Love is so much bigger than control.

TAMA KIEVES

CONTENTS

AN INTRODUCTION AND INITIATION

I'M HOLDING THIS DOOR OPEN FOR YOU

You may feel like things are challenging at this moment in your life. But let's get this straight right now: It's not because you're failing or broken. It's because your spirit demands soaring—not coping. It's your time.

The Doorway

You're standing at the doorway.

On one side of the door, you can decide that life has not turned out the way you desire. It's unfair. It's too hard. Maybe the same thing keeps happening to you—or not happening.

You might feel anxious or discouraged. It's a young techie's world. Or a blonde's. Or someone luckier and other than you. You don't have real money. Stable true love. The recognition or freedom you deserve. It almost works out sometimes. But then it rains. You lose your ticket. The job is taken away. Your lover turns out to be a tiny bit misleading, what with being married to eight other people and all.

And the disappointments seem familiar, and yet cut you to the bone, because some part of you knows, *it doesn't have to be this way.*

This is a life that is "happening to you." This perspective denies your power. I am not demeaning your feelings of frustration. It's just that I have something more useful in mind.

You can walk through this doorway.

You may have to crawl. You may need to breathe deeper than you have ever breathed. You may do it while kicking stones and cans in resentment, but doing it nonetheless, giving yourself a shot. You may have to grow. You may have to choose to do things in a way that you have never done them before. You may have to become a superhero in your own lifetime. It's what you really want. It's what the deepest part of you desires.

So, are you going through the doorway?

I want you to join me. I want you to step into the life you didn't plan. I want you to loosen up on your control over everything you think needs to happen.

Everything that hasn't exactly worked out in your life brought you to this wooden doorstep. It is the doorstep of willingness. It's a precipice. It's an adventure. It's a choice. It is time to unlock your powers or your destiny. Congrats, you've arrived.

Uncertainty is your new best friend. It will help you discover your certainty. It will help you reach for freedom.

Because when you let go of your plan, you open to a powerful path, the path of being led. It's the end of emptiness. It's the beginning of your True Life, the one of following your inspired instincts instead of your fear.

This takes courage. Or desperation. Or curiosity. Or ambivalence. I don't care how you get here. Let's just do this. Let's begin in this second. Let's give life a new chance. It's the only life you have. I'd say bet your life on it.

Let's step into the greatest life ever, the life we didn't plan.

You are growing beyond where you have been. Your life isn't

diminishing. Your *old* life is diminishing. Your True Life is expanding. It's roaring for your love and commitment.

You may think you're stuck. I'd say you're standing at a threshold.

Are you willing to thrive through every aspect of your life right now—and not just when things change? Things change because you decide to thrive.

Where is uncertainty creating discomfort for you? Making you feel small? Or making you play small in your life? That's where you're getting fooled. You're letting the circumstances of your life define who you are.

Oh, but butterfly, grasshopper, lover of transformation—you are here to define (or redefine) your circumstances. You are the storyteller in your life. And you are here to live a great story with a happy middle as well as a happy ending.

I'm here to teach you how and ease your way.

Here's Why I Wrote This Book—and a Shift I Want You to Have Right Now

This is the secret superpower that successful people have: They can stand uncertainty. They can get past their past and create their ultimate soul-stirring relationship. They can spin a new entrepreneurial venture out of thin air, fail, and spin three more. They can run for office, write a memoir, or trek around the globe even if it seems foolish at their age or level of inexperience. They can stay with things for as long as it takes for their desires to come true. They can hold on where others let go. They can trust instead of trying to control every single outcome. They don't need to have a guarantee in order to succeed.

They already have a guarantee.

Showing up is the guarantee.

Because as you show up for your true desires, life shows up for you. You feel alive when you show up. You feel flattened and hollow when you don't. You may have your "reasons." But it doesn't matter. Anything that keeps you from showing up is poison.

I've seen a Broadway actor belt out a song that practically reshaped the bones of the audience—and helped them remember what it feels like to be redeemed. And I've wondered, what if that singer had stopped going to auditions after a brutal round of rejections? Someone else quit.

And I had a client adopt the Chinese daughter of her dreams after experiencing illness, mishaps, obstacles, and enough paperwork to wipe out a forest. But what if she had closed her heart or stopped jumping through the hoops? I wouldn't get those yearly Christmas cards. And I've met others who were betrayed or faced a major health challenge or other difficulty and they were happier than others I knew in perfect health and with jobs.

Why do some people keep going? Why do some people come up with creative angles that immediately get attention? Why do some people meet the right connection? Or bounce back from setbacks? Find the right doctor? Get funding? Meet that incredible partner? Get the breaks? Enjoy where they are, no matter the circumstance?

They have mastered the art of showing up with love for their lives. Acting with intentionality. Choosing with love. Glowing. Possessing that something extra. They are not forcing their lives. They are discovering them. *Working with their own indispensable spirit, instead of against it.*

I'm sensitive this way, because I have almost given up or settled, lost my own fight with anxiety and frustration too many times. And it's unbearable to me to think of the life I would have missed—and I so don't want you to miss the life that is calling to you.

I know what it's like to have everything change and to have to make up your life out of thin air and fight back tumultuous fears to do it. Years ago, I walked out of an established life into the terror and wonder of transformation. I had been practicing law with an elite corporate law firm. I'd graduated Harvard Law School with honors. Everything looked "set." But while I lived in the illusion of security, that "established, safe life" was crushing and killing the real me, every single day.

Finally, feeling broken and, at the same time, as though I were breaking free, I left everything without a plan for the future or a safety net. I abandoned "conventional wisdom" and followed inner wisdom instead, an instinct, a drive, a hope, and an inner authority that spoke to me about living my life from love instead of fear.

It took a different voice within me to create a different life. I've walked through so many other transitions too, and, always, when I listened to my heart, I experienced a secret footpath through the world, even though I couldn't see this path. And this is the practice of powerful self-discovery I've taught in my workshops, retreats, and programs. At this point, I've written four books, gained a following in the United States and throughout the world, and have been featured in national media. But more than this, I've discovered that I can trust an inner wisdom, and it is more instrumental than anything in this world.

I just couldn't find my way in the world. I had to find *myself* first.

I found myself by learning how to listen to a loving voice inside myself. It's been a quantum shift in how I think about and approach everything in life. When I began, I thought I was just going through a career transition. But that career transition turned out to be an identity transformation. It's been a spiritual pilgrimage of shedding old, limiting, and "rational" beliefs. I couldn't have a different life until I realized I was so much more than who I thought I was. We all are. And that's the journey I'm hoping you'll take with me.

The Pivot Point

I've now been a career, life, and success coach for almost thirty years. I've also worked with thousands in workshops and retreats. Having sat with individuals at the frontiers of their most pressing moments in relationships, work, health, true desire, grief, and every-thing else, I know firsthand the pivotal difference the right support makes. I wrote this book because I want you to have that support.

If you're in transition, the things you decide right now will af-fect your entire life. And because you're going through change, you feel more vulnerable. And when you're feeling weak, it's possible to make weaker choices than you really want to make.

I want to help you choose from strength, love, and the astound-ing guidance of your inspired mind. Because when your plans fail, that's when your real life begins. This is a precious opportunity to create the life that is calling your name right now.

Fears and resistance will talk you out of showing up for your-self in every way you can. But it is showing up for yourself that will end your pain. I am going to help you keep showing up.

My yoga teacher Jen once said, "You think you are hitting ob-stacles on your path. But the obstacles are your path." Now of course she's a yoga instructor and specializes in stretching people into phys-ical torture for a living, while she shares *philosophy*, so there's that. But I've shared this same wisdom with my clients: Whatever is in your way, *is* your way. Because your life is your life. It's not an acci-dent. It's a miracle.

If you and I were working one-on-one together, I would assure you that you have a path. It's already within you. It's better than you imagine. In fact, it's so much more fulfilling, you *can't* imagine it.

It's time to follow your innate intelligence instead of doubt it. In this book, I provide you with ideas, stories, techniques, and tools that dismantle your smallness. I whisper to the strength and creative cur-rent within you. Each piece of this book is designed to call you into alignment. It's not just the words. It's the energy. The truth will speak to the truth in you.

You're not just going to shift your circumstances. You're about to shift your identity. You may be thinking, That's great but can I pay the mortgage? Can I help my son stop drinking? Can I find a publicist for my work? Can I find another job? And I will tell you, yes you can. This and more. Albert Einstein said, "No problem can be solved from the same level of consciousness that created it." It's time to realize you don't have a problem. You have a process. You are in transformation. And that means you're moving forward into the next, best part of your life.

In Praise of Those Who Are Wondrously Stumbling

The famous, wise comedian George Carlin once said, "The caterpillar does all the work and the butterfly gets all the publicity." I am a fan of caterpillars, those who are dissolving their own skins to become who they are meant to be. We who continue to grow, perpetually enter the goop of change, or butterfly soup. It's incomplete. It wouldn't look good on a photo shoot.

As you move along your path, you may feel angry, held back, sad, unseen, or empty. It takes so much courage to be developing or undoing or daring. Yet please don't let the in-between space convince you that you lack anything. Being in transition doesn't mean you're broken. It means you're breaking away from the old, an identity, maybe a set of assumptions or an understanding or a world that no longer fits you.

It's easy to sit on the sidelines in the lounge chair of life and be a spectator, or a critic of those who are facing their lives head-on. But I'm a sucker for those of us who are daring to make something of this time on earth. Real life is always taking place in the middle of things, not just in the polished perfection of an illusion of the end goal. How you live in the middle really is the quality of your life.

In the middle of change, we are consciously engaging with the biggest questions of our lifetimes. *What is this time for? Can I create my reality, and what does that mean? Is there a Higher Love I can count on in life? And if I overeat while I'm anxious, do the calories count?* Many of us don't just think outside the box. We live outside the idea of boxes, in the outposts, in colorful tents, nests, or stations far beyond traditional definitions. We are trying new things. We are thinking new thoughts. We are on our way. We have no clue where it is sometimes. And sometimes we know exactly where—and we're afraid to admit it to ourselves, because it seems as though those destinations are meant for other people, not for us. Oh, the courage to believe. The courage to quest.

We are the ones who are attempting to listen to a truth inside us instead of to the interpretation we hear on the evening news. You can call that unrealistic. I call it creating a new reality. Because it's innovators, artists, messengers, mystics, thought leaders, outliers, and lovers who have always changed the face of the world. It's mavericks in every walk of life. It's always taken someone who believed in an idea more than he or she believed in the situations in which that idea did not yet exist.

We are living in a world of change. Things are moving faster. We are being asked to be more adaptable and fluid. Some will try to find solidity through grasping for an ever-elusive sense of control. I'm hoping you will discover a trust in the creative current of your life.

Sure, you may have just been trying to get through your life without awakening to a shamanic experience or wearing beads. I get it. You just want a job or a boyfriend or a cure. But here you are. This is your life. You have the chance to side with yourself, your deep true self, or turn against yourself. Which choice will you make? Will you choose to be realized or "realistic"? This is your moment, dear one. I encourage you to step into your true power. I encourage you to step into the middle and blaze.

I'm Practicing and Thriving Right Beside You

An inspired life is the result of owning your truth—following your own indwelling authority. It's the intimate landscape of learning how to listen to and trust the precision of your intuition or guidance. This is a life that isn't on any map.

Some days it's frightening, like crashing through the air on a roller coaster. It's that wild and exhilarating rush, too, when life meets you in midair for a kiss.

As I grow deeper in my work, message, and personal life, like everyone who is on a path of evolution, I find myself continuing the "hero's journey," the walk into a mythical forest for the grail. Some days, it's dark and dank and I wonder what the hell I'm really following. Maybe I don't want to be a stupid hero. Maybe I just want to be rescued by some nice knight, preferably one who loves a woman who has an occasional homicidal hormonal mood swing or two. On the worst days, I've feared I'm not following anything except a delusion— and now something stinky, clawed, and *real* is following me.

And then there are those other days. These are the days when you walk through the darkness, resolved. You decide to bet the farm on your own life. You call yourself an inspired pilgrim instead of a fool.

You walk deeper into your life. And then, just a few steps farther from the darkest patch of forest, you come upon a clearing, a meadow, a thousand yellow buttercups, and the sun gleams in a way that paints your name, *your nickname*, on each petal of every flower and you know in an undeniable way that you are exactly where you are meant to be; it's a greater sense of security than any amount of money could offer you. It's hitting the mother of all jackpots, the great sweet Powerball of the Universe.

These are times of knowing that you have been loved and seen and heard. There is so much joy in having trusted yourself and realizing that you were never off-kilter or flawed. You were *different.* You were compelled. You were keeping a promise to yourself.

It is the most extraordinary feeling to have maintained your faith and conviction in something and to be right, to discover the magic, an extraordinary portal that no one else knew. Only you know the secrets you hold—even when they may not yet have risen to the surface of your consciousness. Only you know the potential that beckons you. Only you feel this almost unwanted tug of glory in your bones.

This is the adventure of your lifetime. I don't want you to miss it.

You are a pioneer in your life. It is as though you are discovering the Wild, Wild West. There are no signposts, Starbucks, or convenience stores. GPS has no idea where the hell you are—because, honey, you are so off the map. There is a black, black night with 8 million greedy stars dotting the sky.

And though you feel alone or as though you will never know how to get to your goals, know this: *You have never been less alone.* Without the distraction of the world's answers, you can finally hear your own undivided genius.

Every curve of the road is guiding you. Every tree knows your step. Every bit of sky is whispering clues to you. This mysterious Brilliant Love is drawing you forward, rooting for you, investing in you, chanting for your fruition. It is in the nature of your destiny to lead you to your destiny.

Every circumstance you are in is a chosen conversation designed for your good. There is a scent to follow. The wind is pushing you in the right direction or whispering what is necessary. The rain is a wild, unfettered priest dousing your existence in holy water. Everything is in your favor. The moments of realizing this are worth a lifetime. Really, it's one thing to be alive. It is a whole other thing to be *awake.*

This is what it means to thrive through uncertainty.

This is what it means to show up for your life. I hope you will join me.

Walk through this door.

EVERYTHING YOU NEED TO KNOW ABOUT READING THIS BOOK

I don't believe in accidents. I believe you are reading this book at the appointed time for you. I may have never met you. And yet, here we are. I'm writing to you. Just so you have a visual: I'm wearing my purple glasses, I'm drinking coffee *and* a green smoothie, and my desk is not something I'd ever show you, or maybe I should, because it's proof positive that I *can* thrive through uncertainty.

Just so you know, I don't feel as though I'm talking to a generic group of people called "my readers." I'm here intending to talk to *you* at this exact moment in time. I'm so grateful you care enough about the quality of your life to read a book like this. You are extraordinary. And I believe that you and I are going to open up extraordinary possibilities together.

Now, if I were teaching a class, I'd start by telling you here's the bathroom, we'll take a lunch break at twelve thirty, and other orienting details. Since a book is a journey we're taking together, I want to point out a few things to make your trip as powerful as possible. Once we get started, I don't want to break the trance. So, I'm going to play flight attendant here and go over the safety features of this Boeing 747 before we take off. It's going to be a great ride, and I want to make sure you get the most out of it.

Just Read One Piece. Don't Worry About Reading the Whole Book.

I wrote this book to be read one piece at a time. That means you can jump around. Skip to whatever is important to you. Read out of order. Follow your soul's order. It will still make sense. You may be needing to grieve, so the chapters on finding your answers aren't as helpful. You may be needing to get going and conquer the world. You may have no idea what you need. Feel free to leapfrog. Of course, do feel free to read it all, especially since each piece has more than one message embedded within it. And sometimes, you might not know what you need until you read it.

Because I wrote each piece so that you can read it as a stand-alone, sometimes I repeat a story or context. Also, you may find that a particular piece is one slice of truth, but not a complete answer. To me, each piece is an angle of the prism, and each chapter is the prism.

Wait, but You Said I Should . . .

I'm sharing everything I can with you, to help you shift your mind and choose from strength. Yet sometimes, you might think there are contradictions. For example, in one chapter I'm going to tell you to take time off and rest. And in another chapter, I might tell you that you need to take action to stir up energy and clarity. The truth is more panoramic than any one answer. It's like trying to capture the breadth of a mountain range with one photograph. Likewise, there is never one line of action that is right for everyone in every situation; different approaches work at different times. Use your common sense and your uncommon genius. I'm offering options. I'm leading you to the buffet instead of putting you on a meal plan. Choose what you love.

You Have My Full Permission Here (in Writing) to Skip the Exercises

Do the exercises. Or don't. Whatever you do, do not allow guilt to motivate you. (Personally, I can be horrible about doing the exercises in books.) You do not need to catch up or stay on track in any way. This is *your* journey. If you are doing the exercises (they *are* powerful and fun, and designed to immediately shift you) as you go along, you might also want to jump to the back of the book and read "Three Practices I Recommend."

Trust Me, I'm Writing About Your Issue

I write often about career transition, finding your life's work, and creativity, but don't be fooled. I could have been writing about dating, marriage, health, or financial issues or how to believe in yourself as you learned to salsa dance, pursue a liver transplant, or heal your relationship with your mother. The dynamics of learning to trust your inner voice are the same. Moving beyond fear and the limiting voice in our mind is a universal process. Of course, I *do* include other kinds of stories in this book. I'm just mentioning this here, because I'd hate to have you get hung up on the details. Stories are spells. There is a specific message or gift in each of them.

The Brilliant (Dis)Order of This Book

When it comes to change in your life, it's not a cookie-cutter path. It's not linear. I'd say it's more like a meth lab of explosive power than it is a spreadsheet. So much is going on all at once. Sometimes you don't even realize all that you learned, until much later in the day, or until you write a book.

I did not write this book in chronological order, but in order of significance of what I believe will serve this threshold time in your life. I skip around in time, writing glimpses, scenes, stories, and principles designed to wake up the highest intelligence within you. And I should mention that while I often share my own experiences, this book is not *about* me. It's about all of us who are consciously on the caravan of transition. I use the authority of personal story to liberate the personal truth in you. There's an activating power in intimacy.

Also, I deliberately repeat some aspects of stories or lessons. As a writer and teacher, I trust the instruction of repetition. I find deeper angles or dimensions of teaching in the experience. The "same story" becomes a *new* story.

If you're not familiar with me and my other books (and even if you are), here's some background so that you can understand the context of this book. This quick framework may help shore up some of the information.

I'd been a rule follower earlier in my life, suppressing my deepest desires and doing whatever it took to get approval and be "secure," as I understood security back then. I knew when I was younger that I wanted to write, but I ignored that dream, thinking that the desires of the heart were frivolous. Fast-forward and I graduate with honors from Harvard Law School. I move to Denver to take a job in the litigation department of a top law firm. I'm on a partnership track, receiving accolades and bonuses. Fast-forward again and I'm on a beach in Northern California wondering if I want to live, because having squelched my creative and inspired life, I am empty and suffocating in meaninglessness, and I can't see a way out. I am staring at an ocean when I make the best decision of my life.

Finally, without a plan, another job, a husband to support me, or any significant savings, I walked out of my law firm job, my identity, my safety, to discover who I really am and what might be possible for me in this lifetime, if I followed the pull of my desire. I wrote about this transition and about creating the work you love in my first book, *This Time I Dance!: Creating the Work You Love.*

I spent twelve years writing my first book, healing, uncovering what I really believed and would base my life on, including beginning to study and teach the wisdom path of *A Course in Miracles.* While writing *This Time I Dance!*, I started leading workshops, speaking, coaching clients, and taking people on retreats. I self-published the book initially, but it was soon discovered by my "fairy godmother," a VP of marketing and publicity for Random House who said it was "the best book [she'd] ever read on finding your calling" and promptly got the book to Tarcher, my dream New York City publisher, which was then part of Penguin and is now within Penguin Random House—as in, all the big boys together. This event was an astonishing validation for me, as I had trusted my "inner voice" for years without a contract, publisher, or literary agent.

After *This Time I Dance!* came out, I began taking my dreams into the world in a bigger way. Yet as much as I wanted to succeed, I began to realize that I could not just do "business as usual." I reminded myself that I had not walked out of one conventionally successful, yet incredibly painful, life just to go ahead and create another crazy life. I realized I was still conditioned to believe there was a "right" way to succeed. Now I had to find the courage to listen to my instincts and radical guidance instead of the "experts" (or "experts, schmexperts," as I later called them). I aimed to create *inspired success*—not linear success, but success on all levels, on my own terms, created from the inside out. I believed that the same power that compelled my dreams would also give me extraordinary means. I didn't just want to "make it" in the world. I wanted to remake the world, by teaching other artists, entrepreneurs, leaders, and visionary organizations to create unparalleled success through unconventional means. That's the journey I took in writing my second book, *Inspired & Unstoppable: Wildly Succeeding in Your Life's Work!* I've been traveling and speaking to audiences extensively about this work and it's one of my favorite things to do.

And throughout all these years, I've always worked with coaching clients, helping them stay true to their inner voice. In both personal and business coaching, I saw that clients always wanted to know what to do. I wanted to teach them what to *think*, so that they would always know how to choose from their best instincts. That motivated me to write *A Year Without Fear: 365 Days of Magnificence*, a book of five-minute mind-set shifts that I'm grateful to say has spread through word of mouth and become a morning ritual for many readers.

Finally, I realized that in all my work, I focused on helping people through transitions. I helped them face uncertainty with certainty. I love standing in the middle of the most important moment of people's lives, and helping them discover their own invincibility, core desire, and natural and original next steps. I've seen many simplistic philosophies and programs that not only didn't answer my clients, but actually limited their true potential. That's what made me want to write this book. Of course, while writing this, I've had to deal with all kinds of uncertainty myself. I called it "research," since that sounded better than persecution. Growing and running a business based on authenticity and love sounds nice on paper, but it demands personal growth, which means facing everything that throws you off balance. Sometimes following your bliss seems like anything but. Also, Paul, my sweet life partner, has had ongoing fatigue-type health issues that defy conventional and unconventional diagnosis and treatment. This uncertainty has permeated our relationship and significantly altered our lives. Writing this book helped me find my feet again, my faith, and my wings. I hope reading it does the same for you.

I think that brings us up-to-date. Oh, I do also reference different romantic heartbreaks and breakthroughs in this book, and totally jump around in time. But I'm not even sure *I* remember *that* chronology. You're on your own.

The Whole Truth—and a Little Bit More

In certain parts of this book, especially when I talk about my clients, I have changed the names of individuals or identifying circumstances to protect their privacy. Sometimes in stories, I've also shifted minor facts or details, but nothing that changes the essence of the truth or the point I'm trying to make.

Are Those Your Real Journal Entries?

Over the years, readers have often come up to me in awe of my journal entries. "My journals aren't like that," they say. My journals aren't either. I do lift great wisdom and writing out of my journals. But I leave the petty, whining, repetitive stuff behind. It's what you pay me for.

A Course in Miracles

Throughout the book, you may notice that I frequently quote from A Course in Miracles, which is a spiritual psychotherapy program that has changed the lives of millions worldwide. I've studied and taught it for close to three decades. It's what I breathe. I'm not trying to proselytize. I'm not invested in you studying this path or *any* particular religion or spiritual path. I am fully committed to you finding the way that's right for you. But I sprinkle A Course in Miracles in. I like the seasoning. I like the reasoning. I hope you enjoy it or pick it off your plate and put it aside.

This Book Is Not Medical Advice

I am not recommending that this book replace therapy or medicine if that is what you need. While I write very personally, this is a book and not a prescription. I'm an author. I'm not a psychic or a doctor. I'm sharing my best wisdom at the moment. I may even change my mind as I continue to grow. Besides, dear one, you deserve to use all the resources that can help you have your best life.

I think that's about it. Buckle up. Turn off your cell phone. Listen to your inner voice. And may you have a beautiful flight into the life that is calling to you right now.

THRIVING
THROUGH
UNCERTAINTY

CHAPTER ONE

THE SUPER-POWER

OF UNCERTAINTY

HOW TO MOVE FORWARD IN AN UNCERTAIN LIFE

I hate transition. But I'm black coal and this compression is turning me into a diamond. And as much as I want to conform and just be like every other chunk of coal, I am cursed by my need for a life of meaning. I will walk or crawl through transformation. Because I want a life of diamonds.

TAMA KIEVES (journal entry)

Real change isn't about knowing the right actions to take. Because, really, we all know you should probably eat kale instead of a pail of Ben & Jerry's Rocky Road. Real change comes from

an emotional and spiritual readiness. It's about changing from
the inside, becoming ready to take the steps that arise from our
essence. It's only readiness that makes an action right.

TAMA KIEVES (journal entry)

W here do you crave certainty right now? This, my friend, is where you're growing wings. You are in transition, about to crack open into the next dimension of wonder in your life. I know because you're alive—and that is how life works.

As a life and career/success coach and workshop leader, I've worked intimately with thousands in transition. I've seen every kind of crossroads. And I've often seen this pattern. It's the insistence on *how things are supposed to be* that causes pain. You do not lack the right life right now. You do not lack your path or the absolute best circumstances. You lack awareness.

You are thriving just by being in the fray. Uncertainty is your superpower. It's oxygen. It's necessary. It shakes you awake. It breaks through the shield of habit and exposes you to new options, redemption, and growth. Change is how you discover that you are more than who you thought you were, as you move from one identity to the next. So, yes, awesome one, change, helplessness, frustration—all of it is how we bake this cake. And this is how every extraordinary life is *supposed* to go.

On a clear, bright, high-def day in July, my friend Grace and I walked across the Hudson River walkway in Poughkeepsie, New York. Grace had come with the idea to do a healing ritual. She is my energy-sensitive shaman friend, walking with white owls in one realm and copywriting for marketing executives in another. I love people who walk in multiple realms—and I suspect that you are one of those people. I believe we are the ones who will shift the world.

Grace was going through a divorce. This change was slicing her to the bone, forcing her to let go of a dream and an identity. She was dismantling shared finances, responsibilities, and real estate. And each time her husband, her once-gentle friend, screamed accusations or punched a wall, she felt her heart break again. Yet Grace was determined to thrive, no matter the circumstances.

At the time, I was feeling out of control with my business. I'd wake up in the middle of the night in a panic, worrying that I couldn't get everything done or that I wouldn't ever find the right people to help me, especially since I was now nuts and could offer them something like bubkes as a base salary.

Really, I just wanted to hand someone all of my problems like a bunch of grenades and run. Interviewing prospective hires was like dating, only worse because I might have to pay them, too. I was so overwhelmed that even taking steps to get out of the overwhelm produced more overwhelm. And underneath it all, I was grieving a loved one's health challenge.

In moments of stress that seemed unbearable, I found myself in a haggling mode with God or the Universe or any power on call that day: *Take it all away. Take away the uncertainty, the pressure, make it all go away. Give me an answer. Just take care of it.*

It was the prayer of the tired.

It was the prayer of someone who had forgotten that real peace of mind isn't something you can just pick up at ShopRite like toilet paper. It was the prayer of someone who just wanted this *done* already. I was frantic to be out of pain and I hadn't yet realized that *pushing myself to be out of pain* was causing even more pain. This is one of those mysterious ironies in life that involve something like *acceptance*, and I really hate that.

I wanted to be "there" already—somewhere it was all resolved and I was maybe just a tiny bit wealthy, famous, skinny, and adored and all of it was permanent and guaranteed, and no one I loved was ever going to die, and if possible there wasn't going to be climate change either, because I despise heat.

But, of course, life was asking me to be here. *Be here in the middle*. Because here is where the Milky Way is. Here is where the journey is. Here is where the answers are, and the big payoffs, every single one of them. Here. Not there. The Universe was answering my prayer. It was answering it with the circumstances that would catapult me into change.

Grace had brought with her a woven blue pouch. Within the pouch, there were a small smooth black stone and a small smooth white one. She had gotten this "kit" as a sort of fun personal divination tool long ago. You ask your question about the future, then pick a stone: White is yes; black is no.

She was going to toss the stones into the great beaming Hudson River from high on the bridge. "Good-bye black-and-white thinking," she said, referring to expectations, answers, the mad desire for control. She'd had enough of trying to make her situation just go away or tie it up in a bow. "I'm not looking for definitive answers now," she said. I felt this big space come over us. The truth always has this signature. "I'm done with trying to force solutions or breakthroughs as though I can," laughed my wise friend.

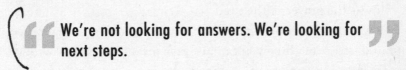

We're not looking for answers. We're looking for next steps.

"So, what are we looking for if not immediate resolution?" I asked her as the tiny pouch with the simple promises twirled its way off the bridge, getting smaller and smaller, finally splashing into the great river below.

The moment I asked the question, I knew the answer. "Next steps," I said. "We're not looking for answers. We're looking for next steps." As if on cue, a breeze rippled the river below. I felt as though a Silent Love nodded with approval.

When I coach clients professionally, I guide these brilliant souls, who are no longer looking to create a conventional life, to follow the bread crumbs along the trail. It's the only path I know to the beckoning "gingerbread house" of the new life, which may not even have a name or definition yet.

There are *always* bread crumbs. This change in our lives isn't just happening to us. It's happening *for* us. That is the bedrock premise of thriving. The caterpillar "dies" so that the butterfly can emerge. And just as in metamorphosis, there is instinctive intelligence that drives the change. Our new life is always conspiring with us, sending us signals and cues.

Sometimes the next step is not an action like going public with your company. Sometimes, it's letting go of an old, limiting belief. Or dying honorably to a time in your life that is passing. Or having that conversation you need to have or picking up that book you heard about. Sometimes it's the decision to frankly accept where you are, even though a part of you wants to win a Nobel Peace Prize already because, well, it would be nice to have *something* to tell your mother.

There is always a next step or focus.

This is how a time of transformation takes place. You are led. You do not lead. This is the free fall and the windfall of uncertainty. You can't plan an inspired life. You can't force genius. It doesn't play by your rules. You may feel anxious, even while you are safer than you've ever been. Yet radical creativity, burning love, alchemy, invention, and the blaze of the wild divine do not fit into ordinary methodology. An extraordinary life is, by definition, not ordinary.

You are walking into the grand unknown. It's scary because anything can happen. It's wonderful because, *finally*, anything can happen.

A life of intrepid original expression requires the willingness to be birthed from within. Buy a paint-by-number set and you are guaranteed to paint a simplistic replica, but never a work of art. True change does not happen through rote execution but through an awakening, a rearrangement of your understanding and abilities. Trust me, when it comes to your real life, your time on earth, you want the work of art.

The writer Anaïs Nin put it this way: "There are few human beings who receive the truth complete and staggering, by instant illumination. Most of them acquire it fragment by fragment, on a small scale, by successive developments, like a mosaic."

You might feel like you want to move faster than one fragment at a time. Good luck with that. Because groundbreaking, foundational changes do not happen in a rush. The 12 steps of Alcoholics Anonymous, the healing program that has enabled millions to do "what they could not do," is based on this simple maxim: "One day at a time." There's reason for that. It works. A spiritual life is not one that is answered in the future. It's the life that takes place in the present, one day, one heartbeat, one filament or breakthrough at a time.

You don't need to figure out your whole life at once. You don't have to know what you're doing. You don't have to know how this will all unfold. You *won't* know, even if you think you do. But you can do what is yours to do in the moment.

Grace looked down at the river that had absorbed her symbolic offering. She said, "I am saying good-bye to the need for certainty instead of authenticity. I am letting go of the need to rush or know what I can't yet know." It was a lovely way to acknowledge that her life was a mess, that all our lives are a mess, a continuous lopsided tango with uncertainty dressed in tight pants and sparkles, impishly encouraging our hearts to beat faster. And that, at times, no matter how much you wish to be standing on solid ground, you are standing in the marshlands between the worlds, hoping like hell you find a clue.

I looked around us on this spectacular day, because somehow all of humanity seemed to be out on that bridge. A big man with a thousand tattoos loped along, listening to a motivational podcast, maybe on how to fix your Harley, or how to love your inner child. Thin, fit women ran by, controlling the calories they burned, controlling *something* in their lives. A shiny dark-skinned woman who looked older than the river itself smiled among wrinkles as she leaned on a cane.

How many of those who passed by secretly worried about a lump they'd discovered? How many knew their lover was drinking again? How many needed to get more clients? How many even feared the promotion or dream project they'd just gotten, wondering if they could pull it off? How many felt lost, as though they didn't even know what they were here for anymore or how to get through the hours?

I smiled inside and thought of the prayer said in yoga classes, "Namaste," the light in me salutes the light in you. I knew we were all made of infinite strength and possibility, even while we felt like we were being jostled in the ocean like seaweed. Our uncertainty made us feel alone. But, actually, it's the one thing we all have in common. Everyone everywhere is dealing with a change in their lives.

Grace and I walked off that bridge feeling brighter. We'd eased some of our pain just by making the decision to stop trying to force the path to freedom to fit into something it would never be. It was okay to feel uncertain and still move forward. "I guess I'm just running a marathon," said Grace. "All I know is that I need to breathe deeply and keep hydrated." It seemed so simple. One damn step at a time.

I felt safer again, too, ironically, the more I committed to journeying into the unknown. It felt good to work with truth on truth's wide-open terms. "We just did something really big," said Grace. "Yes, we did," I said, already feeling myself settle down. I felt a connection to Grace, to myself, to life, to everyone on that bridge, and to everyone who would yet be on the bridge of life—and to *you*—crossing from one solid place to another.

TURNING POINTS:
How to Move Forward in an Uncertain Life

It's the insistence on *how things are supposed to be*
that causes pain.

You do not lack the right life right now.
You do not lack your path or the absolute best
circumstances. You lack awareness.

Change is how you discover that you are more
than who you thought you were, as you move from
one identity to the next.

This change in our lives isn't just happening to us.
It's happening *for* us.

We're not looking for answers.
We're looking for next steps.

You are led. You do not lead.
This is the free fall and the windfall of uncertainty.

You can't plan an inspired life. You can't force genius.
It doesn't play by your rules.

You are walking into the grand unknown.
It's scary because anything can happen. It's wonderful
because, *finally*, anything can happen.

ANY CHOICE IS A RISK, EXCEPT THE RIGHT ONE

Be brave enough to live life creatively. The creative is the place where no one else has ever been.

ALAN ALDA

When you're scared, it's natural to want to get to safety. But keep in mind there is a kind of "safety" that is not safe. There is no safety in denying who you are.

TAMA KIEVES (journal entry)

It's human nature to want to experience the security of having everything under control. It may also be human nature to want to eat a feedbox of chocolate Easter bunnies, so there you have it.

Psychological studies show that we as human beings thrive on "positive stress." You think you want ironclad safety. But you deserve so much more in life than this— because the need for constant control can cause boredom, exhaustion, and hollowness. Like you didn't already know that.

Your spirit craves growth, and growth comes from taking risks. The right risk will offer you more security than holding on to "the devil you know." Because if that devil you know is draining the love out of you, you will meet a devil you don't want to know.

Here's a question I'm often asked: "What do you do when you're trying to choose between the familiar and safe versus the unknown and unpredictable?" I'd say forget about *your* idea of what's safe. Choose a life of meaning. Because perhaps you've noticed, life is transitory. Meaning is the only security in town. And sometimes finding love or even the hope of it, or that which means the most to you right now, requires you to move, voluntarily, *further* into uncertainty.

Where did we get the idea that life is supposed to be safe? What joy of any significance has ever been safe? Giving birth to a child? Taking a road trip? Kissing that dark rogue stranger? Funding a grassroots venture to benefit the world?

There is no risk-free life. Staying inside in your bed is a risk. Taking the bus is a risk. Staying in a marriage or job that crushes your soul but isn't "that bad" is a risk. There is no opting out of taking risks in this lifetime. You only get to choose which risk you'll take.

And my best rocket-fuel expert tip here? Or at least the one at the tip of my tongue?

Bet on the sure thing. Bet on love. Spend your chits on faith. Take the road that makes you stronger. Going after things you want, whether or not you get them, makes you stronger.

A life of thriving requires us to choose between the illusion of safety and the ultimate safety.

The ultimate safety is the life that calls you. Sometimes, you don't even know what you feel drawn to do. Sometimes, you only have exhausting questions. Well, then start here: Begin to move away from whatever steals your spirit.

Let me tell you a story about walking in the direction that seemed more immediately uncomfortable. It wasn't an easy choice. But I'm a logical girl, and choosing life is always a smart call.

Many years ago, I went hiking with a long-haired poetic boyfriend, somewhere in the wilds of Oregon. We scampered along the trail for hours, in the cool green of the forest. Then, we practically fell to our knees and sang the gospel upon seeing the Pacific Ocean at the end of the trail. This is what happens when you live in landlocked Colorado. At the first sight of a body of water, you act like puppies. Giddy as we were, we ignored the time. The sun gradually evaporated from the sky. This wasn't good. It was a time of year that turned very cold once the sun had set.

Just like that, we realized we were in danger.

We'd both dressed lightly, in shorts and T-shirts. We hadn't intended to hike this far. We had no camping supplies, jackets, pants, or milk chocolate, so, really, I couldn't see how we were going to survive. The moment we saw that draining sun, we started hightailing it on the trail back to the car.

The light grew dimmer. We walked faster. My lawyer brain kicked in, seeing possible liabilities everywhere, which is oh so helpful when your heart is already pounding so fast you know the vultures are taking dibs on your body and choosing a wine. Then halfway out of the forest, we heard an unusual knocking noise. A flock of birds squawked and fluttered away. They left a hollowness in their wake. Something didn't feel right. Something didn't feel right *at all*.

The creepy, unsettling noise continued. "Maybe it's a moose," said Kir eagerly, looking around. He was one of those people who thinks seeing wildlife is a good thing. He stopped and dawdled. Type A to the core, I power walked ahead and peered into the trees. I saw darkness behind them, almost a blackness. Then in the hideous slow motion of terror, I realized that the darkness was not some nice woodsy, amorphous darkness, but rather a shape peering at me, the shape of a bear.

Now, for the record, I am not the type of woman who looks at a bear in fascination, even at a zoo. I grew up in Brooklyn, New York. On my best day, I am way more comfortable pressed up against a thousand sweaty strangers in a subway car than witnessing firsthand actual wildlife in a forest. But I was a long way from Brooklyn. And I was a slice of pizza to that bear.

I instinctively walked backward on the trail, cautiously, like a cartoon character. Then I ran farther back until I was at a distance where I could imagine breathing. Kir followed me, wondering what was going on. "It's a bear," I said to him, terror and adrenaline lighting up my senses. "It's a goddamn bear." As though there were any other kind.

Then our negotiations began. We started realizing the horrible Zen predicament of it all.

We had to walk back past the bear to get out of the woods.

We had to walk in the direction of our fears.

Because it just so happened, as it always seems to do, that the direction of our fears was also the direction of our freedom. If we walked the other way, nightfall would set in, bringing its wet ocean breath of cold and death by hypothermia. We were already beginning to shiver.

I imagined being mauled. Hypothermia sounded nice, just going numb forever. I really wanted to avoid that bear. I'm not big on facing things I can't predict or control and knowing they have the upper hand, with claws, no less. But then if we avoided that scenario, we were facing the *guarantee* of a slow, insidious death.

Believe me, the symbolic choice here was not lost on me. At the time, I had only recently left my nine-hundred-hour-a-week legal career to dare my "crazy" dreams of becoming a writer. I had left the "safe" position because I knew it was numbing and annihilating my heart minute by minute. The comfort of that paycheck and validation was seducing me into a stupor in which I abandoned my will and lapsed into a menacing indifference about my own life. It was the hypothermia of having my heart go cold.

But in that scenario, I had decided to fight to save my own life. I chose the terror of a creative, unpredictable, alive life. I faced the immediate risk of not knowing how things would work out. I felt exposed and naked.

Yet I also knew that at least now I possessed the *chance* of something working out. My job had been "safe" in cliché worldly terms. But I knew I had not one shred of hope of living my True Life while there. I was unequivocally dying every single day. It wasn't imminent, savage death. But it *was* certain death.

It hit me then that I would have to walk in the direction of my fear. I would have to walk toward the bear. If I walked by the bear, I might make it to total freedom. It held the *only* possibility of what I really wanted. I'd at least have a chance at life. But I'd have to walk by that bear. I'd have to risk unbearable (no pun intended) uncertainty.

So, yeah, the fact that I'm writing this is a spoiler alert. I lived.

We walked by the bear, slowly, praying silently to ourselves and to the God you pull out of your back pocket when you hope there is a God and you hope he texts. We surrendered to the vulnerability of our desires and the purity of our instincts. Then we ran like hell and, if memory serves, I kissed that rental car's thin tin sides.

That night we ate at a local diner and I told the waitress about the bear and how happy I was to be alive. I have no doubt I sounded like someone who had just seen a UFO. She gave us french fries on the house. I have never tasted better french fries. I know they were probably wilted with grease, ordinary, or even too salty. But I was alive—and everything tasted alive to me.

I suggest you walk by your bear.

> **Sometimes finding love or even the hope of it . . . requires you to move, voluntarily, *further* into uncertainty.**

What action or direction calls to you right now, but might leave you bare or unprotected? Where do you have the best chance of at least moving toward something you desire? A preference for certainty costs too much. There are no guarantees in anything. But love will find you when you go in the right direction. And love is safety.

The right direction can take a while. It's worth it. *It's the right direction.* A sense of integrity is a security all its own; it feels solid to know you are walking your truth. It doesn't matter if it isn't as convenient as Amazon shipping, as few things really are. You don't need to have sound bites or even words yet to describe what you're doing; maybe you don't even know.

Maybe you are crawling away from certain soul death. That's all you need to know. It's worth anything to be moving in the direction of your true possibilities, desires, or growth. This is the purpose of life. And only you can make this sloppy, dangerous, awe-inspired choice.

Pulitzer Prize–winning author Norman Mailer put it this way: "Every moment of one's existence, one is growing into more or retreating into less. One is always living a little more or dying a little bit."

It's okay to be afraid. It's okay to be uncertain. I'm just hoping that you'll choose a direction that makes you feel as though you are staying true to yourself. Because sometimes the dedication to comfort is more perilous than pursuing the mystery.

Recently I read these words from the iconic actor Alan Alda, and I just knew he'd walked by the bear: "You have to leave the city of your comfort and go into the wilderness of your intuition. You can't get there by bus, only by hard work and risk and by not quite knowing what you're doing. What you'll discover will be wonderful. What you'll discover will be yourself."

I have faith in your aspirations and in you. You will make your right choice in your right time. There will always be a bear. And there will always be that within you that can bear anything on its way to magnificence.

TURNING POINTS:
Any Choice Is a Risk, Except the Right One

The need for constant control causes boredom, exhaustion, and hollowness. Your spirit craves growth, and growth comes from taking risks.

Choose a life of meaning. . . .
Meaning is the only security in town.

Sometimes finding love or even the hope of it . . .
requires you to move, voluntarily, *further* into uncertainty.

Bet on the sure thing. Bet on love.
Spend your chits on faith.

Take the road that makes you stronger.
Going after things you want, whether or not you
get them, makes you stronger.

Choose between the illusion of
safety and the ultimate safety. The ultimate safety is the life
that calls you.

Love will find you when you go in the right direction.
And love is safety.

The right direction can take a while. It's worth it.
It's the right direction.

YOU ARE JUST ONE THOUGHT AWAY FROM A MIRACLE

A sloppy mind is no way to create a happy life. If I'm lost in a burning house, I don't want a bellowing, scattered drama queen like my fearful mind leading the way.

TAMA KIEVES (journal entry)

Your entire life is based on the thoughts you choose. The thoughts you choose are more important than the school you attend, the job you get, the wealth in your bank account, the talents you have, the love of your family, or the health of your body.

TAMA KIEVES (from A Year Without Fear)

I don't know about you, lamb chop, but I am a ninja of freedom—one who is dedicated to the right use of mind. That means I slice and dice the thoughts that distract or weaken me. Now, it's not because I'm so together. It's probably because I'm not—and an uncertain life is just way too unsettling with an unsupervised mind.

At the first hint of uncertainty, I turn into Zen Special Ops (though I don't formally practice Zen) and my life becomes my meditation. Because I know I'm either going to focus on thoughts and observations that empower me or I'm going to a dungeon of terror that a part of me calls "being realistic"—though it just so happens to be the darkest room in my mind. This is the gauntlet uncertainty throws down. Wake up and smell the focus.

Uncertainty is going to happen. But crazy-town and electric violins are optional.

You can always choose *how you experience* any experience. And if you want an incredible life—which I know you do—you *must* choose how you experience your experience. Because your response to your life *is* your life.

"I am flipping out right now," said Carol. Her doctor had just performed a biopsy on a vaguely suspicious growth. "I have a lot of cancer in my family," she said on the phone, her voice sounding like it was no longer hers. "I can't stop crying. I'm looking at my little girl and I'm sick inside. Tama, what if I'm dying? I haven't lived. I have more I want to do." The words tumbled out. I didn't interrupt. I hoped my listening would help her steady herself.

Now, I think it's powerful to feel our pain. But that doesn't mean I'm all about letting you become a freak show just because your mind is off to a self-scripted horror movie, buying Milk Duds and yanking your chain saw.

There *are* times in life when we must grieve. But we do not need to grieve *optional*, painfully indulgent, self-selected hallucinations. That's just an unnecessary trip to the underworld without Advil, if you ask me. And I want you to use your brilliant mind for the powers of good—and comfort—instead.

"You do not know what anything means," I said to Carol. It was the only absolute truth I knew. It's the only perspective that's always true. *I don't know what anything means*. This is my go-to comfort thought, like mashed potatoes for the mind. It's one of my favorite lines from *A Course in Miracles*. It's a great big karate chop that silences fear. For me, it's a kind of mini–Zen moment, an instant time-out at the beach, seagulls overhead, finding a gap between my racing thoughts.

Because this is what I've come to recognize about myself and everyone else, too: We do not fear uncertainty. We fear our certainty—as in we become "certain" about what things mean. When I'm in my fear loop, I'm *certain* that I will fail. I will not be loved. I will be stuck. Nothing will ever change. Okay, it will change—it will get worse. I am *certain* that everyone else is drinking champagne, celebrating their plucky, effortless lives, swinging from a Baccarat crystal chandelier—on a *yacht*. And no one else is going through the panic I'm going through.

I don't know what anything means. I tell Carol, "This is your practice right now, sweetheart. Try not to start leaping to conclusions like 'This lump is cancer, stage 4, requiring chemo, radiation, hacksaws, black magic, and nothing will ever work because I am a bad person and God hates me, and now I've wasted my life and these negative thoughts are probably like a grow light to the cancer cells and I'm still thinking them,' or something along those lines. You don't know what's going on. Don't scare yourself with stories. It's just as possible that all is well or *always well*, in ways you don't know yet. You don't know anything. That's the truth."

When I spoke with Carol next, she was relatively calm. "So, dish, what happened?" I asked.

"I did the whole don't-spin-out-of-control and, yo, just-live-in-the power-of-now thing," she said, sounding like Eckhart Tolle meets the Dalai Lama meets Snoop Dogg.

She told me how she had to "get out of her head," so she took her little girl to the downtown Boulder outdoor mall. "We stopped to watch Marvelous Dan, this superfun busker telling jokes and juggling sparkling colored balls. Then he called my daughter out from the huge crowd to do a trick with him. It was magic," she says. "And Tama, I just slipped into the experience. I felt like it was set up for me. I was so grateful to not be thinking about cancer." I smiled inside. I knew that in *that moment* she didn't have cancer. She had fun.

I'm not talking about her cells. But in her *experience of that moment*, which is all our life really is, she was *living* her life, on a Wednesday with a brilliant blue autumn sky in the Rocky Mountains. She was eating raspberry frozen yogurt with her young blond-haired daughter, and they were giggling together as the juggler in the rainbow overalls threw too many balls in the air and strangers gathered together and clapped. This was what was real. There was no diagnosis in *that* moment. She was alive, seamless, and appreciating the time with sudden tenderness.

This is the way we handle uncertainty sometimes. We live. We dare to freaking live in the face of a thousand unknowns. In the face of possible damage.

We have the audacity to watch a movie or to brush our daughter's hair and turn it into silk. Or paint the kitchen table blue or shoot hoops with the guys. We have the ability to thrive right now— even if our lives don't have a guarantee. It's possible to still crack jokes with your friends, even if you're going bankrupt or getting a lumbar puncture in the morning. It's possible to be afraid of what might happen in the future and to show up for love in your life right now. You have no idea what experience can open up for you—as you choose to use your mind in a way that strengthens you.

It's also possible to not allow an uncomfortable fact to become your identity and take over *everything* in your life. You are more than someone with cancer or someone who is single or unemployed. You can always choose another focus or filter.

Carol called when she got her tests back. She did not have cancer. But even if she had, she wouldn't have missed that diamond of
an afternoon of her life. She and her daughter shared a joy-filled
memory together that could never be taken away. It was a *better* day
than her usual healthy and unaware days. Carol's experience taught
me yet again how much unchecked worry ruins more of our lives
than actual difficulties. A ninja chooses a more conscious focus.

> **If you want an incredible life — which I know you
> do — you *must* choose how you experience your
> experience. Because your response to your life *is*
> your life.**

I've negotiated with worry my whole life. I've thought if I consciously prepared for or rehearsed the bad thing happening, like
maybe a hundred times, it would feel less upsetting. But as I've
launched into an off-the-beaten-path life, embracing the unknown,
I've let my tireless rehearsals go. I couldn't afford another moment
in la-la land for the damned. I've never thought of myself as a day-
dreamer. But worrying *is* daydreaming. It's just spinning scenarios
that don't use pastels.

Preparation is useful. Worry isn't. I've driven on road trips by
myself. It's helpful to take a spare tire and your insurance information. It's not helpful to imagine standing by the side of the road alone,
as night falls, near a high-security prison where a serial killer who
prefers brunettes has just broken free and happens to be carrying an
ax to grind—an ax and, naturally, a plump, fresh tire. This is just not
useful. Stress kills. And worry is unnecessary stress. But please don't
worry about that.

A calming thought isn't just a placebo. It's a weapon of choice
that stops fear in its tracks. It can wake you up. By taking direction
of your mind, you can engage in actions that serve you and others,
instead of ones that don't. The Buddhists call this being skillful.

Calm is the new black. It's what you want to wear in times of change, trust me. I want my airline pilots and emergency room doctors calm—okay, not drooling and Thorazine calm, but *centered*, so they can summon the specifics of their training. And I want to be calm, so I can make exquisite choices instead of knee-jerk reactive ones.

Besides, the story you tell yourself is the story you live. It's uncanny how true this is. I have an example that knocked my socks off, though I didn't have socks on at the time.

I remember taking an intense vinyasa yoga class. The teacher started telling us that we would be moving into wheel pose. I swear I could feel my lower back muscles text my brain, "Boss says pain in 5." Then Anastasia, our muscled guru, said something that caught the whole class off guard: "Pretend this is the easiest pose you'll ever do." Wheel pose, the easiest pose you'll ever do. It was such a wildly suggestive thing to say—like pretend doing your taxes is like having sex with your favorite movie star, only better, and audits, oh, you don't even want to know.

Because wheel pose is a nightmare. Yes, it also might be a tiny bit true that I make it like climbing Mount Everest without gear because I resist the pose, when really it's only as hard as climbing Mount Everest *with* gear. Usually, I wait to get it over with in any class. Yup, that's me, tightening with every namaste.

But thinking of it as an easy pose, I softened. *I imagined it could be easy.* It was a preposterous idea. Maybe it was a hypnotic suggestion. Maybe it was Vedic voodoo, calling forth the mercies of noodle-bodied Hindu gods. I think it was a nunchaku to my head, thwacking me with responsibility for my experience of my experience. Because thinking of it as easy helped me to breathe deeper and focus on what I *could* do. My wheel pose that day was so much better. Yes, just in case you're wondering, it's still easier for me to eat my body weight in milk chocolate. But it was freer and that was a miracle.

I invite you to become a ninja of freedom. Take responsibility for your perspective. Step out of imagining the world you think exists. Choose to catch your mental breath. What are you telling yourself that is upsetting you? Can you tell yourself something else? This is a rhetorical question, because *I know you can tell yourself something else.* Think of something that calms you down, even if it's simply that you do not know what anything means right now. This is the right use of your mind. This is the beginning of freedom and directing your extraordinary faculties.

Whatever you're going through, no matter how much fear you're in, this much I can promise you:

You are just one thought away from a miracle.

TURNING POINTS:
You Are Just One Thought Away from a Miracle

Uncertainty is going to happen. But crazy-town and electric violins are optional.

If you want an incredible life—which I know you do—you *must* choose how you experience your experience. Because your response to your life *is* your life.

We do not fear uncertainty. We fear our certainty—as in we become "certain" about what things mean.

You have no idea what experience can open up for you— as you choose to use your mind in a way that strengthens you.

A calming thought isn't just a placebo. It's a weapon of choice that stops fear in its tracks.

> The story you tell yourself is the story you live. It's uncanny how true this is.
>
> Think of something that calms you down, even if it's simply that you do not know what anything means right now. This is the right use of your mind.
>
> Whatever you're going through . . . you are just one thought away from a miracle.

WHAT'S FALLING APART IS WHAT'S COMING TOGETHER

The creative force of change that is impairing my current life is also guiding my expansion. It's the same stroke of the paintbrush.

TAMA KIEVES (journal entry)

What could you not accept if you but knew that all events, past, present and to come were gently planned by one Whose only purpose is your good?

TAMA KIEVES (from *A Course in Miracles*)

Most of us don't relish change. The Persian mystic poet Rumi says that if you asked an embryo why he or she remains scrunched in the dark "with eyes closed," this is the answer you would hear: "There is no 'other world.' I only know what I've experienced."

There is no other world. We have all sung this dirge in one form or another. There is no love for me outside this loveless marriage. There is no money for me beyond this draining career. There is no way to have things fall together now, because if they were supposed to come together they would have; I must be riding on a rickshaw while everyone else caught the plane.

It takes enormous courage to believe that things can be different. Or that there is a life beyond what you can see or even imagine—or a *you* that is whole and inspired.

"There is no other world," says your fear. And to this I say, with great deference to your pain: Poppycock—whatever that actually means.

Because change is always what's for dinner. Buddha said that all suffering stems from trying to hold on to your chocolate mousse. Well, he didn't say *that*. He said we try to make things permanent. The nature of reality is fluid. Real life cracks open, breathes, disintegrates, and expands. It always expands, even when we feel like things are stuck or going in the wrong direction.

Life is designed to shimmy. We are designed to let go of our lobster shells and grow into new ones.

Your true happiness does not come from a stable stock market, a feast of jobs or potential relationships, or climate control. It's about learning how to *thrive* in the times when you lack control.

Boys and girls, we live in dynamic times. And we are *dynamos*. We are dynamos being roused into our powers.

"The voice of eternity within us demands to be heard," says the philosopher Søren Kierkegaard, "and to make a hearing for itself it makes use of the loud voice of affliction, and when, by the aid of affliction, all irrelevant voices are brought to silence, it can be heard." That's a high-class way of saying that pain can awaken you to your big-picture life, and the only relevant voice there is your True Self.

You are not the erratic conditions of this moment. You are a powerhouse. You are a continuous force of evolution. You are a phenomenon, a surprise even to yourself. An inspired life is more than the life you planned. This is the nature of thriving. There is an orchestration, a calculation, sometimes an ambush, yet always an intelligence fueling the "chaos."

I never imagined that my life could get so out of control. But I found myself sitting on a beach in Northern California, staring at the waves, thinking about taking my own life. I couldn't bear to practice law for one more day. And I could not let myself quit. Just the week before, I couldn't summon my usually ferocious willpower and write the brief in front of me. There was *some other will* going on now.

I was so tired. Fighting myself all the time. *I hate this job. You have to stay in this job.* The boxing match that never ended. I thought I was being practical. I thought I was being strong. I look back now, years later, and realize I was fighting against a tidal wave. I was pushing back the hunger to live my full expression—and the most amazing awakening that has ever happened to me. I was resisting my True Life.

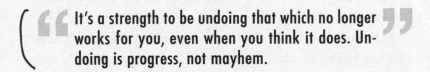

It's a strength to be undoing that which no longer works for you, even when you think it does. Undoing is progress, not mayhem.

I came home from California a mess. A few weeks later, I walked out of my career without a plan or a viable source of income. It was an end and a beginning. Years later, now in a life in which I have taught so many others to awaken their inspired lives, I can't imagine that I could have ever chosen another life, a life that denied my creativity, my essence, my life's purpose, and the wildest happiness I've ever known. But I tried to hold on to what I knew at the time. We all do.

We all have a True Life, the life that does not look like our plans, yet perhaps arises from a deeper wisdom within. This other intelligence sweeps past our conditioning and defies our expectations of how things should go. This life brings us to surrender or acceptance even when we do not yet understand what's going on. It brings us to the truth of our bones. The True Life always prevails. The soul's desires are formidable.

I have seen brilliant transformations in people who have faced addiction, health issues, or the death of a loved one. I have seen these shifts in those who seek to express their life's work or experience true love. Whatever the situation, the shift is always the same: You can't do what you've always done—and then over time you can do what you've never done. And always in the end, you have touched the eternal within you. You wouldn't go back for anything.

This is the gift of uncertain times. Know that it's a strength to be undoing that which no longer works for you, even when you think it does. Undoing is progress, not mayhem.

The artist Pablo Picasso wrote, "Every act of creation is first of all an act of destruction." And the philosopher Nietzsche said, "You must become a chaos before giving birth to a shining star." These are not poetic elaborations. They are descriptions of how a metamorphosis works. First, things fall apart before they fall together.

A mother doesn't have to understand or even trust the birth process to give birth. Your next expression wants to be born. Great and mighty forces marshal their strength around you. It's your time. You're uncovering a new way to breathe and feel safe in the world, even though you can't imagine it. Change may wear a wolf suit. Still, don't be fooled. It's wild, abundant magic come knocking on your door.

It's okay to feel as though you don't know what's going on. You don't. You can't supervise creativity, alchemy, reinvention, evolution, and the divine flower rearrangement of your life. Yet if you trusted the Energy behind this miracle of change, you wouldn't want to control a thing. You'd throw everything you had into the blender and watch it yield a grace beyond all reason.

This is your choice. You can move into co-creation with your life instead of trying to turn the larger forces into something smaller—while continuing to yearn for a larger life.

Here's the work. It's not about staying in control. It's about staying in love.

I know this isn't easy to do. But you can take the fun bus or the misery bus, because either way you're going for a ride. If you want to thrive, this is your practice: Let go of how you think things should go right now. Taste the possibility that something wise and beautiful is taking place. It is.

For right now, I'd like to offer you two simple strategies for embracing the raw juice of change.

Don't Get a Grip: Be Gripped

Do not try to make this transitional time look like what your old life looked like. This is revolution, darling, and it will torpedo your armed guards and old rules.

Lisa left her position as a pharmaceutical sales rep to reclaim her spirit, which she had squelched for years. Initially, she soaked up the newness of time off. That lasted for about six days, which isn't even six seconds in the algorithm of transformation.

Then the mad griffin of responsibility shrieked in her ears, "You're worthless." And Lisa began to realize that she had spent her life in constant activity to fight off this underlying feeling. This is one of the hallmarks of transition. You meet the irrelevant voices that are telling you irrelevant lies.

"I've slept in and I didn't even shower until midmorning," Lisa whispered on the phone, as though the KGB might be on the line, when really it was just her inner critic—which might be worse. "I wore my blue bathrobe for hours," she whined. I couldn't see her, but I was willing to bet she was even making the shape of an L for "loser" on her forehead. "Oh, the transgression," I mock sighed. I was pleased with her incremental freedom. She was gradually shedding old skins, the type A snake molting into a new, unorthodox, available being. Shedding does not feel like building. Shedding does not feel like nailing it. Shedding is not a time for excelling.

I wrote a section called "The Year of Sleeping Dangerously" in my first book, *This Time I Dance!: Creating the Work You Love*, because I wanted all the guilt-ridden achievers out there to know that sometimes breakthrough change requires rest, self-care, and staring into space and middle-earth like your cat. (And at readings, everyone thanks me for this part of the book.) There are secrets and shifts you can't manufacture by scratching things off of your left brain's to-do list. Your True Self is not listless. It's invincible. It's inevitable. It's got bigger plans.

You don't have to get a grip. Be gripped, as in moved from within. I know you think that if you let go of self-control you will turn into a zombie or lag behind the wunderkind cosmopolitan crowd. But I promise you trust is the fast track—it's the *only* track—to your right life.

Fall in Love with the Unknown

The unknown is not the enemy. It's an invitation to become even more alive than you were before. Please resist the temptation to grab at ready-made solutions and definitions too soon. In the haste to end uncertainty, those of you who are impatient—and you know who you are because you've probably skipped to the exercises already—may opt for promises and detours that do not match your essence. In an authentic life, there are no prefab answers. Hold out for the fab ones.

One of my friends tells me she married the wrong man when she was twenty-two because she "didn't want to wait forever." A student once confessed that he knew he was exhausted but took on a higher-level project at work anyway because he wanted to prove to himself he wasn't weak. He ended up on a gurney having emergency stomach surgery. I've also watched clients go back to school for another degree, program, ribbon, bauble, or certification just because "I'm going to school" sounds so much better than "I'm freaking out like a cat in a hat. I have no idea what I'm doing with my life."

What if you're not stuck? What if you're not adrift? What if you're supposed to be right here in the dead center of it all for reasons you can't see yet? Something else is going on. Birth doesn't follow strategy, but it does follow a trajectory.

The unknown offers you an unparalleled life. Trust that your gut and soul have a way. And that a Creative Intelligence only paints in shades of love. The caterpillar must dissolve so that the butterfly can emerge. It's so unbecoming. Yet lean into your becoming.

When our plans fail, our destiny begins. We're off the map. We're on track for an awakening life. Nothing is the same. It's a rite of passage.

If change blows apart your best-laid plans, there's wild magic to be had. It can be painful initially. Yet it's grace that stirs all winds. Remember:

You are not your conditions.

You are your response to your conditions.

You are your strength, love, intelligence, and choices. And you are more powerful than you know. That's why this change is here. You are growing.

TURNING POINTS:
What's Falling Apart Is What's Coming Together

True happiness does not come from a stable stock market, a feast of jobs or potential relationships, or climate control. It's about learning how to *thrive* in the times when you lack control.

The shift is always the same: You can't do what you've always done—and then over time you can do what you've never done.

It's a strength to be undoing that which no longer works for you, even when you think it does. Undoing is progress, not mayhem.

A mother doesn't have to understand or even trust the birth process to give birth. Your next expression wants to be born. . . . It's your time.

Change may wear a wolf suit. Still, don't be fooled. It's wild, abundant magic come knocking on your door.

It's okay to feel as though you don't know what's going on. You don't. You can't supervise creativity, alchemy, reinvention, evolution, and the divine flower rearrangement of your life.

You think that if you let go of self-control you will turn into a zombie. . . . But I promise you trust is the fast track—it's the *only* track—to your right life.

When our plans fail, our destiny begins. We're off the map. We're on track for an awakening life.

IT'S IMPOSSIBLE TO CREATE A BAD LIFE IF YOU'RE GOOD TO YOURSELF

It's amazing to listen to the love within you more than your fear, and to discover a consistent constellation of abundance that dwarfs the scope of any plan.

TAMA KIEVES (from *Inspired & Unstoppable*)

If you listen to your heart and you love yourself, everything good will come from there. Really, it's just not possible to create a bad life if you befriend yourself.

TAMA KIEVES (journal entry)

As a career and success coach, I hear my fair share of wanting to bulldoze through change, especially when life seems to throb like a toothache, turn into the life you never thought you'd have, or slow to a crawl through the rubbery land of powerlessness.

Everybody wants to rush through transition like it's a bad root canal. But transition is a threshold. It's a sacred life appointment—the crossing from one world to another. You will reclaim yourself here, be infused with messages you could receive no other way. This is not just positive mumbo jumbo. I am describing to you a possibility that exists for you, right now, right here, and will not come again, at least, not in this way.

I know, maybe you'd still rather have the root canal.

Maybe your phone doesn't ring with new clients. Or no one calls you back for a second interview. You still can't believe your wife left. The recent diagnosis hangs in the air like a sword, a curse, a question, a dream, not yet admitted into regular life. And there is the terror of feeling as though you're not on solid ground—and may never be again.

Sometimes, the transition is chosen. You're about to become a mother for the first time, head up a new department, or move to a white stucco dream house with an orange grove. Even then you feel the pulses of anxiety. You wonder if you're capable or "worthy." Dread whispers to you that love can be taken away. You clutch your one thin winning lottery ticket, and silently fear every shadow or breeze.

It's natural to feel this way. All growth makes us feel helpless. When life becomes uncomfortable, we are being invited to explore our own personal power and dormant capacities. We have the opportunity to turn scared into sacred and experience a universe of expansion instead of contraction. But it's up to us. It's a choice. It's the opportunity of a lifetime. But only if we consciously choose for it to be that way.

Will you side with your higher intelligence or will you side with your darker fears? Which part of you will create this next part of your life? It takes a life-changing relationship with yourself to create a life-changing life.

The author C. S. Lewis writes, "Now, today, this moment, is our chance to choose the right side. God is holding back to give us that chance. It will not last forever. We must take it or leave it."

What inner voice do you listen to? Is it kind, encouraging, and wise? Does it advocate for your welfare? Does it sound like your hip older sister or your favorite therapist? A mirth-making sorcerer? An earnest lover of your potential? A fervent Jesus? Or a wise guide that calls you to your True Identity?

Or is it *just so bored* with your inadequacy? Punishing like an SS officer? Taunting you like the boys in the school yard who made you wet your pants? Who is your inner traveling companion on this trip around the globe? This isn't about how you present yourself to the world. It's how you view yourself when no one else is around. It's the voice of your thoughts when you're not listening to anyone else.

This adviser runs your life. This adviser *is* your life.

You're listening to either your vitality or your weakness—love or fear. Everything you will ever see and think runs through this filter. The writer Anaïs Nin said, "We don't see things as they are, we see them as we are." Your perception is your reality.

Why would you listen to a voice inside you that shames you? You can spend this next part of your life cultivating and listening to a voice that calls your true name and guides you past every fear or limiting belief. It's worth everything to develop an allegiance to your light.

I'll give you an example from the early years of my career transition. When I left my law firm to write, I wanted to buy myself as much time as possible, so I moved into a postage-stamp-size studio apartment in the middle of the city to save money. While others were financially and socially climbing, I was sliding, downwardly mobile.

My upstairs neighbors seemed to be playing touch football at all hours or yodeling in Spanish, but only when they weren't having wild parties or riots. You know, I'd tell myself, you're just living one of those interesting, artsy "urban" lives. Then I'd get the glossy alumni magazine from Harvard and just the cover of it would make me cry. Everyone looked calm and established and proud. Not one of them looked as though they were lost on the journey of being themselves— or even had a blade of grass out of place on their lawns. They *had* lawns.

At that time in my life, I was still paying more attention to external circumstances than inner experience; hence, I felt like an amoeba on the totem pole of life achievement and success. I also firmly believed that if Harvard Law School could rescind degrees, they'd do a factory recall on mine pronto.

"When will *I* be established? When will I move on? *When will I have what other people have?*" I cried and gurgled these questions to my boyfriend. Mascara ran down my cheeks; I looked like a mash-up of a bad watercolor painting, a raccoon, and a drag queen. Thankfully, the boyfriend looked at me as though I were the goddess Athena. Sadly, he would meet other goddesses later, and send me into another pivotal transition in my life. But that was later.

"One day you're going to feel very sentimental about all this," he said. He had me look around the room and take it in—"the writer's early years." Never mind that "the writer" (that would be me) wasn't that young, wasn't living in a garret in Paris—and wasn't even *writing* on a regular basis. Still, as I imagined a future of publishing a book, I looked upon this renegade nest more softly. I came to see the choice to downsize not as one of embarrassment and failure, but one of courage. I was a woman who was willing to stalk her dreams and potential at any cost.

> **Will you side with your higher intelligence or will you side with your darker fears? Which part of you will create this next part of your life?**

It's your choice how you hold your experience. And what you see now will often determine what you will see later. You get to decide how you tell your story—which often *creates* your story. This awareness is worth the price of the journey.

I did end up becoming a successful, published writer. It turned out to be true in "real life," because I continued to see it as true in Real Life, the inner chambers of my being. It was a practice. It was a discipline. It was the choice to side with myself instead of against myself, every single day of every single year.

Believe me, there were days I didn't get this right. I fizzled. My worries played Ping-Pong with each other in the tight ship cabin of my brain, drinking whiskey and trading mentally ill scenarios. But I always returned to the knowing-sense that I needed to befriend myself. I needed to parent myself. I needed to champion myself—hopefully for the rest of my life. I wanted to grow. And I knew that I would flourish more from love than from pain.

When my second book came out, I found myself in another transition. It was a new world and I wasn't sure what to do. Some people thrive on the unknown. But I felt like I was handling explosives while tiptoeing on a tightrope and desperately trying to reach into my pockets to find instructions—or horse tranquilizers.

Yet I knew more this time. I knew that no matter what the alarmist in my brain screamed, this transition was not just about taking action. It was also about creating a safe space for myself. I knew that transition made me feel vulnerable. And in my vulnerability, I needed encouragement more than I needed a screaming inner maniac.

So, I swore in my journal: "I will bless myself. I will trust myself. I will tell myself, 'You're doing fine. You're where you need to be right now. This confusion is not your identity. It's only a mist between the worlds. You will grow dormant abilities, vision, and muscles.'" And this focus helped me focus.

It turns out that unlike what my inner critic railed, my own encouragement didn't coddle me into becoming a pathetic sloth who would end up living on Purina Cat Chow or out of Dumpsters, desperate and unwashed, not to mention *unpublished*, though quite well versed in the rationalization of affirmations. No, indeed. Encouragement got me off my own back, off the couch, and pounding the distance with a quiet fire that wouldn't quit. It was just easier to fight for myself when I wasn't fighting with myself.

If you're in transition right now, it's a kind of an emotional checkpoint. It's not just a time when the train got stuck in the tunnel, or the Universe dropped your call—*all your calls*—and suggested you try another carrier. It's a time behind the scenes that sets the stage for what is to come.

When the illusion of a guaranteed result or situation falls away, you have the opportunity to expand. It's time to discover who you are now or who you've always been deep in your core. This may require that you unconditionally accept yourself, even when you do not look like the image of yourself you prefer. You may need to shake loose of how you think things have to be in order to be okay. This is an initiation to uncommon freedom.

The ways of transition are training grounds of mysterious powers. You leave behind the protection *and the hindrance* of the familiar. Sometimes you are stripped of worldly comforts, casual identities, and chances to just coast or make do. These times may bring you to raw knees.

You will not be comforted by platitudes. Or even "commonsense" strategies. You search for the unnameable truth and homecoming that only you can find. You may hunger now for a new influence or paradigm. This soul-searching may bring you to the self-help section of the bookstore, an expedition to Peru, the silence of the woods, a rabbi, or a woman in New Jersey who talks to angels but doesn't take Discover cards. Your search will bring you to yourself.

Transition makes you question everything, which will give you real answers.

When conditions change and old assumptions fall away, you will seek and discover the truth in the quarry of your depths. Your depths will bring you to your heights, because when all the props are gone and you connect with your quiet soul intelligence, you find a strength and love that knows no limits. *Sometimes it's only limits that can teach us how unlimited we are.*

As you cross a threshold, it's *your* chance to decide *who you are*, instead of allowing the world to decide for you.

Once you really know the ardent love that inhabits you, the love you are here to give, the love that walks beside you, and the love that will bring you all the way, then there is no longer a transition. You've arrived. And the circumstances won't matter a fig.

TURNING POINTS:
It's Impossible to Create a Bad Life If You're Good to Yourself

Will you side with your higher intelligence or will you side with your darker fears? Which part of you will create this next part of your life?

It takes a life-changing relationship with yourself to create a life-changing life.

You get to decide how you tell your story—which often *creates* your story.

I knew that transition made me feel vulnerable. And in my vulnerability, I needed encouragement more than I needed a screaming inner maniac.

The ways of transition are training grounds of mysterious powers. You leave behind the protection *and the hindrance* of the familiar.

When all the props are gone and you connect with your quiet soul intelligence, you find a strength and love that knows no limits.

Sometimes it's only limits that can teach us how unlimited we are.

As you cross a threshold, it's *your* chance to decide *who you are*, instead of allowing the world to decide for you.

Do Try This at Home: Jump-starts, Inquiries & Exercises

Some of these suggestions are just right for *you*. Others, not your cup of latte, or at least at *this* moment. Follow your gut. Feel free to adjust to your liking. Do what's right for you rather than what's written here.

Pick three Turning Points from this chapter. Write them out for yourself. Post them where you will see them. Meditate on them. Journal about them. Do a Freewriting exercise. (See page 252 for more about Freewriting.) Create a piece of art. Pay attention to your thoughts, memories, dreams, and "random" ideas and incidents. Inspired thoughts spark inspired responses. My words begin the conversation, but what do these truths unlock in you?

1. **Journal or meditate about this principle of thriving.** "Change in our lives isn't just happening to us. It's happening *for* us." If you could get behind this statement, what could it mean for you right now? Can you act "as if"?

2. **Do a "stay-awake" daily check-in this week.** Notice each day: When and how do you avoid risk? Where do you feel sluggish or hypothermic? Is there a risk you can take in these areas of your life? As for waking up: What road will make you stronger? ("Going after things you want, whether or not you get them, makes you stronger.")

3. **Grab your "I do not know what anything means" sword and slice through negative assumptions.** What are you "certain" about that causes you pain or fear right now? Where are you spinning a story that has you feeling constrained? What if it didn't mean that? Pay attention to how you interpret the behavior of others or your own behaviors.

4. **Do an Inspired Self-Dialogue** (see page 248 for directions). Will you side with your higher intelligence or will you side with your darker fears? Which part of you will create this next part of your life? Also, begin to pay attention to what your negative voice sounds like.

5. **Tell a new story: Remember, how you tell your story *creates* your story.** Tell a story right now about what's going on in your life, from the point of view of you being *heroic* and life being fully on your side. You are *always* unconsciously making up stories. Why not consciously make up a story that feels good? Notice how it feels to think this way.

6. **Write out "I am willing to . . ." and fill in the blank five times.** Consider this: "It's worth everything to develop an allegiance to your light." If it were worth *everything* to you, what would you consider doing? Five minutes of meditation a morning. Fifteen minutes of journaling. A daily walk. Scheduling an appointment with a coach or therapist. What are the first thoughts that come to your mind? Write out "I am willing to . . ." and fill in the blank five times.

Do you have a question about this chapter? I'd love to know what's on your mind! *I may just get wildly inspired and answer you immediately.* Send me your thought or question at www.TamaKieves.com/uncertainty-question, and you can also register for a **FREE** Thriving Through Uncertainty Coaching Call designed to shift your mind-set and bring you immediate clarity.

CHAPTER TWO

FINDING FAITH WHEN YOU'RE FREAKING OUT

EVERYTHING YOU NEED IS HERE

Another name for God is surprise.

BROTHER DAVID STEINDL-RAST

Are you willing to trade in your "reality" for Unbridled Reality? True desire is the chute to a path of surprises.

TAMA KIEVES (journal entry)

Henry David Thoreau said, "Your religion is where your love is." And it's true—we sense a larger presence whenever we love anything. But sometimes we have to give ourselves permission to love what we love, or want what we want. The brain often has untrustworthy brain rationale in the way.

True desire is where everything begins. It's going to be your clue to unraveling the ball of yarn tied up in knots, otherwise known as your current life. Now, you might view your heart's desires as irrational. But that's the point.

This is an awakening experience in your life. It's time to go past your "rational" mind and activate your heart's authority, the uncanny abilities of a nonlinear intelligence. Because when you stop blocking what you really want, you stop blocking the inexplicable, unthinkable good that already awaits you. Apparently, the Universe loves an irrational desire.

I have a story to share with you about decorating my living room that isn't really about decorating my living room, so bear with me if you have a few more pressing catastrophes on your mind. It's about a miracle. It's about getting unstuck. It's about finding your way out of a paper bag and realizing you were standing in the bull's-eye all along. It's about listening to your foolproof guidance. It's about your career, your marriage, your weight, or maybe your living room.

I had been looking at my living room for months, feeling *meh* on the high end of the spectrum, to "maybe my brain has turned into that white fuzz on your tongue" on the other. I just felt stuck in a life that didn't represent me anymore. My living room seemed like a daily symbol and advertisement of the paralysis I felt in other areas of my life.

Hoping for interesting ideas, I started looking at houses online, even homes in other states. It felt a little bit like scoping out Match .com while your husband gropes through the refrigerator, commenting on how you really should arrange the shelves more efficiently. *Romantic walks on beaches.* I'd be checking out the dimensions of *that* living room, then noticing my own. I quickly learned that every living room looks great with nine-hundred-foot cathedral ceilings. Wall-to-wall windows with an ocean view and whales also do the trick. I live in Denver with neither.

Paul, my partner, started dreaming about ripping out the ceiling and creating a loft above. Awesome, but way beyond what my overwhelmed mind and bank account had in mind. Realizing that *really remodeling* was just creating stress, Paul offered magic words: "What if there's just one simple thing you can do, just to change the energy? What if there's one thing that starts moving us in the right direction?" So, I started looking around and imagining a different shade of paint, a new couch, or an unusual light fixture. But nothing clicked.

I felt tangled and impatient, two feelings that should never date each other, much less hold each other close, when you're looking for new insights and breakthroughs. I wanted change, but I didn't want to put real time into it. I wanted change, but I didn't want to put money into it. I wanted change, but I didn't even have ideas as to what I wanted to do. I wanted it to be easy. But everything seemed impossible.

So, I returned to my original desire: I want this room to feel great to me. That's all I knew. Sensing my frustration and helplessness, Paul suggested, "Don't think about this room as it is now. Just think about something that would feel like what you want."

I started thinking about what *did* feel great. My house was built in 1908. And one of the owners, back in the 1920s, had created an extra room by putting an extension on the back of the house. I love this special room, where we have an Italian oak table and have hosted potlucks, business meetings, Thanksgiving, and other gatherings. This part of the house has a quirky, formidable, black cast-iron woodburning stove on its own little brick platform. But the best part of that room is an entire wall of exposed brick, uneven texture and happiness, worn solidity and a poetic karma you can't find in new construction. I fell in love with that room years ago, as it winked its old-house charm at me. It's why I bought the house.

"I'd love something like that, an exposed brick wall," I said to Paul, as though he could magically order one out of a *House Beautiful* catalog and have it shipped, or maybe blink his eyes like a cartoon genie. It was preposterous and pretty obvious that this desire was cooked.

Yet the heart's desires are often like this. They defy logic. That's why I've come to believe that following what you genuinely want will take you to your radical spiritual power. Because your answers are in you. Yet you don't see how they could happen. And that's the journey. Because the part of you that is intuitive enough to know the exact truth also knows the way to translate that truth into reality.

Anyway, you know how when you start to focus on something you want, you start to notice all the reasons you want it? I began to notice movie scenes with people who had cool lives and living rooms. They often had exposed brick walls. Naturally this meant they had marvelous conversations, cheeses, sex, iPads, and income levels. *Exposed brick*. It was just subliminal shorthand.

One day, standing in my living room, I was again talking to Paul about painting the walls. He looked like he wasn't listening (which, by the way, would never happen to people who lived in cool living rooms). He was staring at the fireplace in the living room and the large plaster wall (which I'd painted purple—"blueberry yogurt," says a friend) above it. It jutted out from the rest of the blueberry yogurt walls. "You know," he began, "that wall that juts out is probably plaster over the chimney to the fireplace." He stared intently.

"Mmm," I said, as though he was beginning to explain the periodic table to me, when, really, I was more interested in end tables.

"Well, if it is the original chimney to the house, then it's probably brick." I still didn't follow his thinking, because there is the small possibility that I was too busy judging him. So, he spelled it out. "If we break off that plaster wall, you might have part of an exposed brick wall."

What? Had my dream been here all along? Could it be? I was afraid to get my hopes up. But even the thought of the possibility was a rush. We decided to try our theory. We have a large wooden Buddha face from a Thai temple hanging on the wall above the fireplace. We decided to poke a tiny hole in the plaster wall, figuring that even if we were wrong, Buddha could hide the emptiness and imperfection. It seemed metaphorically appropriate, so I was all in.

Paul chipped away a hole, kind of like a baby bird pecking through a shell. Sure enough, there was a tiny hint of red brick, a rustic ruby, peeking back at us from the hole. It was like a bindi, the holy red dot on an Indian woman's forehead, and to me, it was every bit as devotional. I gasped. My crazy, improbable desire might actually come true.

The next day, after an all-day meeting, I came home to find Paul covered in the white dust of plaster. He looked like a crazed baker. He smiled at me as I beheld his "cake." We had an exposed brick wall above the fireplace. Worn-out brick. Textured brick. Brick that changed the whole vibe of the living room, even more than I had imagined. I couldn't believe it. Who needed a fantasy genie or a stinking catalog? Real life was the real miracle.

> **Yet the heart's desires are often like this. They defy logic. That's why I've come to believe that following what you genuinely want will take you to your radical spiritual power.**

The answer had been there all along. It had always been there. I'd lived in this house for more than seventeen years. *It's always been there.* This house is more than a hundred years old. Really, it's *always* been there. But I never would have discovered it if I had only looked at the room I thought was there.

In *A Course in Miracles*, there is the teaching that a miracle is about "undoing the blocks to the awareness of love's presence." In English, that means a miracle—the existence of a loving perspective or resolution, which is the signature of Spirit—is always present. But you have a belief in the way. You have an assumption or "reality" in the way. *You have a way of seeing in the way.* I had a thick purple plaster wall in the way.

But more than the plaster, I had a blind spot. I was trying to decorate the room I believed existed.

Yet it was only when I asked what I *really* wanted that I found a direction that had wings and leverage. It wasn't about fitting a solution into my existing circumstances. It was about finding an answer or direction that *changed* my existing circumstances. So, are you ready to design your life? Never mind your current situation, or what you think about your current situation. What do you really want?

In my coaching practice, I see this repeatedly. I ask people, "What do you love to do?" They tell me, "I have an MBA and I'm in advertising." Or "I'm the manager of a home association." They tell me what they've been. The ten years they put into one direction. What they're trained for. Their age. The market. Their pained beliefs about the market. They do not tell me about the destiny that is hunting them down.

They do not initially admit that they'd like to leave it all and ride an elephant in India. They do not mention the movie script that thrums in their veins. Or their instinct to adopt a child, be a ski bum in Aspen, or start a foundation.

"What do you love?" I ask. Each one treats me like I'm pretending to be Santa Claus, despite the fact that I'm Jewish, and as serious as chicken soup about this question. I stand strong. I know that real desire is the only way you will ever find your truth. The truth awaits you. The truth has the power to take you into the life in which you belong. Every limit you believe in will bow before the *real truth* within you. *There is always a real truth.*

In my case, there was always a brick wall underneath the plaster. It's such a great metaphor. Because there is always the presence of everything you want—though it's veiled by the mental hurdle of a familiar story. It's waiting for you. It's been there all along. There's an astonishment beneath your confusion and habitual way of thinking. There is another way to see this situation. Let go of your grip on what you think the situation is.

There is always love awaiting us, beyond every single fear.

TURNING POINTS:
Everything You Need Is Here

When you stop blocking what you really want, you stop blocking the inexplicable, unthinkable good that already awaits you.

Apparently, the Universe loves an irrational desire.

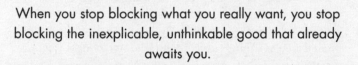

The heart's desires are often like this. They defy logic. . . . Following what you genuinely want will take you to your radical spiritual power.

Your answers are in you. Yet you don't see how they could happen. And that's the journey. . . . The part of you that is intuitive enough to know the exact truth also knows the exact way to translate that truth into reality.

It was only when I asked what I *really* wanted that I found a direction that had wings and leverage.

It wasn't about fitting a solution into my existing circumstances. It was about finding an answer or direction that *changed* my existing circumstances.

Every limit you believe in will bow before the *real truth* within you. *There is always a real truth.*

There's an astonishment beneath your confusion and habitual way of thinking. There is another way to see this situation. Let go of your grip on what you think the situation is.

NOW TAKE A VOW: I'M NEVER GIVING UP

That is the real spiritual awakening, when something emerges from within you that is deeper than who you thought you were. So, the person is still there, but one could almost say that something more powerful shines through the person.

ECKHART TOLLE

I saw a young man in Trader Joe's wearing a black T-shirt that said, "The ego is not your amigo." I don't believe in a devil, but if I did, it's the voice in your head that talks you into giving up on your dreams. It's a voice that lies to you, shows you scraps of things, only half truths. It whispers to you, Never. Always. Stuck. Forever. Loser.

TAMA KIEVES (journal entry)

Sometimes in transition you have to say, "Enough," to your demons, as in, I will not listen to your stupid voices for one more second. You have to remind yourself that inner voices that exhaust you do not have your best interest in mind. There comes a time to decide you are going to believe in a higher strength within you, *no matter what.*

We all spiral down at times. One of my friends once drawled in an exaggerated Texas accent, "Lord, life is plaguing me. It's everything but the locusts." During these times, we feel lost or like life is not worth the pain. We may start giving up on moonlight. Our hopes turn to stone.

These are times of initiation. You are being asked to make a choice to love and advocate for yourself in a more powerful way than ever before—enough to choose faith in your own good life.

When uncertainty feels like a monolith of pain, here's what thriving looks like: Breathe deeper. Be kind to yourself. Put one foot in front of the other. Keep going. Resist devastating conclusions. Fight defeatism; don't fight yourself. And make this vow: *I will not be taken down.*

My parents' house, in the Mill Basin neighborhood of Brooklyn, had burned down. It was a tragic, unreal, unholy, and holy time. My father, who had been ill, had died in the fire. My mother had been injured but lived.

A year or so later, still grieving, my mother and I visited our tiny summer country cabin in Lake Peekskill, New York. The property had drifted into complete disrepair, and with my father's death, we needed to sell the place. That morning, still an unpublished writer, I'd gotten another rejection letter from a literary agent telling me there was no chance in hell that anyone would ever want to publish my pathetic writing or read my words. Really, the letter wished me "best of luck" in my "endeavors." Same thing.

As we pulled up to Cherry Place, I was shocked. In my memory, the "country house" was a magic cottage, an outpost of innocence. It was the seat of our happiest, sanest family times, swimming in the nearby lake, breathing in sweet grass, beady-eyed, Monopoly games rich with paper money. We'd flee Brooklyn's pounding August humidity. My father, away from his office, lost his rage, and played baseball with my brother. The portable radio aired the Carpenters or the Bee Gees. I played with Barbie dolls on the screened-in porch. It was the nectar of my childhood.

I wasn't prepared to see the place destroyed. Shreds of cloth from the curtains stuck out, like a home-and-garden magazine that had gotten nauseated and thrown up on itself. The grass was tall like battered wheat, neglected. Bushes and trees that had created a natural fence line had been hacked away, leaving the property exposed and brutalized. It felt as sickening as rape. I'd already just seen this same crazy dismantling of everything I knew when I'd visited the remains of my childhood home in Brooklyn.

It was all too much. The rejection. The death. The house I'd grown up in devastated. And now this, the crown jewel of my childhood, shattered. I felt myself sinking into a haze of despondency, where nothing mattered. I know I wanted to leave my body. I wanted to leave this moment. I wanted to leave this lifetime. I wanted to give up, float away on an endless wave. I didn't want to have to face anything anymore. I just wanted to disappear. If I wasn't in my life, I wouldn't have to deal with my life, I thought. Vacancy sounded like a plan.

And then the finale. That same damn day, my mother began saying things like "Did you love this country house?" which was kind of like asking *sincerely* if I knew somebody named Tama. My mother knew how attached I'd been to that tiny house. But this mother was showing signs of early dementia, triggered by her own trauma.

Everything but the locusts. And in the dark middle of it all, it didn't seem as though "everything happened for a reason," or that things would get better. It was just a parade of pain.

Sure, I'm what they call moody. But when it came to the big picture, I'd always been buoyant. I believed my future would work out somehow, no matter what was going on. I'd come to trust in an inexplicable flow that would gradually untangle life's knots. I believed in a benevolent Universe, even one that favored you like a special aunt. This unseen love had always peeled my oranges for me, spoken to me via synchronicities or license plates on the highway.

But now it didn't seem like enough. My nuances couldn't stack up to the reality before me, this onslaught of continuous devastation.

Something about seeing my personal symbol of happiness destroyed, unglued me. This was ripping up my sense of well-being from its roots. This was breaking a promise I didn't know existed. And I was tired. I could barely carry the weight of my own eyelashes. A wild woman raged within, someone let out of the attic, waving her manacles, someone who could not take another minute of enduring.

Then through my silent tears, I felt this other presence take hold in me. It welled up like a wrath, only it was a wrath of self-love. In retrospect, I've called it my will. It said, "I will not let you take me down."

I am not a biblical girl. I am not someone who uses words like *evil*, other than in a good way, like "You look evil in that dress, girlfriend." *Wicked* is a compliment in my book. But this was like something from another place and time. This presence roared within me in quiet. *I will not let you take me down. I will not let you take me down. I will not let you take me down.* It was as though I'd been drowning, and finally I started fighting with everything I had to save my own life. I would not give up.

Sure, I'd have "good" reasons for giving up on my dreams of writing. I could abandon my views, too, my reliance on a life-affirming intelligence stamped into every aspect of life. I'd just be considered realistic. Hell, bitterness is always considered brainy. And I was tired of seeming naive, as though my faith made me sunny and lamb brained, without much going on in the critical-thinking department upstairs. Like I should be so lucky.

But I knew active faith *wasn't* weakness. Faith is proclaiming the undiluted power of your own mind—like a ninja employing unshrinking focus, even when the locusts do come. It doesn't get me off the hook. It puts me on it. I know I'm responsible for what I believe and that my beliefs determine every action I take in this lifetime.

Still, on that really crappy day, it was tempting to believe that there was nothing to believe in except my failure and pain. But this presence within me, my Inspired Self, the one who is the keeper of my dreams, said no—do not let the distortions of self-deception take you down.

It drew a line in the sand. It brandished a sword of integrity. I didn't know how I would heal. I didn't know how I would soar. But in that moment, I held myself with heroic tenderness.

I was making a vow. I was not giving up on myself or my belief in some intelligent grace in this life. I would never give up. I knew I would face doubt and disappointment throughout my journey. Yet this would be my wild, courageous practice. I would return to the light that fueled me. It sounded hard. But the alternative was a butchery of meaning. I chose to fight for my life.

Something transcendental within me knew that all houses will crumble. All memories might have tears in them. All lives will be littered with rejection and ridicule and the ripping up of our own private scripts of how things should go. Yet we are more than what's in front of us. We are what's inside us. I trusted in an infinite spirit. I believed my Essential Self would generate new possibilities. *I will not let you take me down. I will not give up on who I really am. I am born to rise.*

> " These are times of initiation. You are being asked to make a choice to love and advocate for yourself in a more powerful way than ever before — enough to choose faith in your own good life. "

I made a choice in that moment. I ripped a piece of curtain from the pile to place on a small altar in my home. (Later my sweetheart decided to wash that strip of curtain and it was so old, it disintegrated, so I didn't even have that.) I chose to put my faith in life. Something within me had pushed back the dangerous current.

I imagine a tap-dancing preacher yelling out, eyes bulging, sweat pouring, skin dancing with electricity, "Get thee behind me, Satan!" And I was that preacher that day. I was a daughter of the way. I stood up to the self-denial that threatened to have its way with me and trample all my chances. I trusted I would find a way. I trusted that somehow the way would find me. I did not give up. I allowed myself to ache deep down. But I did not go down.

"Freedom is what you do with what's been done to you," said Jean-Paul Sartre. There is a moment when you have to resist the temptation to believe in powerlessness. You have to resist the lure to see yourself as a victim, instead of as someone who can still choose to create a new life with heart, integrity, mud, spit, and whatever else you've got in your emotional cupboard. You are not the story of your conditions. You are unconditional freedom.

My definition of *evil* is the reverberation that makes you believe you are forsaken. It makes you believe that this is it. This negativity denies your chances by convincing you to deny yourself of chances. Don't do it. Don't believe the lie.

Let appearances crumble. But do not give up on yourself. Things will shift. Everything changes. The sun will pierce the cloud cover. There will be other houses, people to love, and opportunities to thrive. We as human beings have the tremendous capacity to reinvent ourselves. We can leave behind countries, former injustice, physical abilities, betrayal, and more. We can cry. We can grieve. But we do not have to die to who we really are.

You are meant for good. You are meant to thrive. You have love inside you always. Love can always create new life.

TURNING POINTS:
Now Take a Vow: I'm Never Giving Up

Inner voices that exhaust you do not have your best interest in mind.

These are times of initiation. You are being asked to make a choice to love and advocate for yourself in a more powerful way than ever before—enough to choose faith in your own good life.

Resist devastating conclusions. Fight defeatism; don't fight yourself. And make this vow: *I will not be taken down.*

Faith is proclaiming the undiluted power of your own mind. . . . It doesn't get me off the hook. It puts me on it. I know I'm responsible for what I believe and my beliefs determine every action I take in this lifetime.

We are more than what's in front of us. We are what's inside us.

I will not let you take me down. I will not give up on who I really am. I am born to rise.

Negativity denies your chances by convincing you to deny yourself of chances. Don't do it. Don't believe the lie.

You are meant for good. You are meant to thrive. You have love inside you always. Love can always create new life.

FINDING FAITH WHEN YOU'RE FREAKING OUT

The magic is not gone because you hit a bump in the road. Infinite deep love is with you. There is no world apart from love. This essence is all around you, and has always been. The bumps are challenges to your ego, but not to your destiny. There is only one power.

TAMA KIEVES (from *A Year Without Fear*)

Essence is eternal and absolute. I'm connected to this Love. That means nothing changes, even when everything changes.

TAMA KIEVES (journal entry)

As you travel down the dirt road of this one wild life of yours, I have a bumper sticker for you: TRUST OR BUST. It's that simple. Yes, and that imperative. I have no idea how you get through the nettles of real life without having a feeling that things are working out for you, even if they do not appear to be cooperating at this second.

Anything else seems like a harrowing acid trip, which just might involve gym in junior high, snakes, rats, and bad Wi-Fi. Believe me, I find it hard enough, even when I know there is a silky genius within every fiber of this life. That said, I've had to work at cultivating this big trust. I work at it consistently. But I'm willing to do this work night and day. Because I don't do well when I'm drowning. And I drown fast when I lack trust, like a truck in a lake.

"But how do I have faith when things don't work out?" my clients ask. "Where does Spirit go when I'm freaking out?" This is the perennial question. It has haunted mystics, saints, stockbrokers, grocery clerks, and little ones who know there is a fanged slime monster just tweeting away in the closet.

I am not a theologian or guru, especially since my go-to prayer might be as enlightened as "If it be thy will, please let me eat another maple scone and not have to wear Spanx." But I don't believe that the Love that steers the stars, spins the planets, and inspires cable TV ever leaves the building. I'm convinced we abandon ourselves. You will no doubt work this big-ticket item out for yourself. Meanwhile, I'll share an experience with you.

Years ago, I facilitated a workshop at a women's retreat held at an eco-resort in the breathtaking Riviera Maya, in Mexico. At the time, among other issues in my life, I suffered anxiety around flying. While other airline passengers ate salted peanuts and solved sudoku puzzles, I'd lock on to the faces of the flight attendants to determine when we would be inevitably crashing. The minute they stopped laughing, I prepared for impact. If they laughed a lot, well, then it was obvious they were snorting nitrous oxide and things were worse than I thought. The flight droned on like the drill of a dentist.

I remember the moment I finally arrived at the eco-resort. It was like stepping onto holy ground. I stared at this remote beach of glittering aqua water and untouched white sand. I began to cry. My whole body went limp as currents of tension dissolved. The beauty stung me. It rattled me and stilled me. My travel sweat evaporated. I felt naked and robed at the same time, emptied and filled. And most of all, I felt very, very loved. I felt loved in that moment, loved in the past, and loved for all time—because that's the nature of real love.

Before arriving, I'd had another week of ragged confidence. I felt weary inside, tired of giving myself constant pep talks just to function in an ordinary day. My business was faltering, like someone trying to sing an opera with a stutter. Daily, I wondered what I was doing wrong. I secretly felt defective, like, clearly, I was not the type of person to be running her own business.

I'd always had this sad, persistent feeling that other people knew how to get through a day without questioning their entire existence. They'd check off perfect to-do lists and live in remodeled kitchens with happy families and talk about soccer practice and dinner parties and all throughout their conversation there would always be the hum of *I am normal. I am normal. I am normal.* It would just be there, like the whirr of their deluxe French-door refrigerator.

But standing in that hypnotic warm water, I recognized that my inner voice had brought me here—I was, after all, being paid to be here. It was this perfect moment in my life. I felt whole and safe and I remember having this thought come to me: "I am always cared for." It just suddenly seemed logical. And then it was global and universal, too. I could not be this loved in this moment and forgotten in the next. The nature of this love was all-encompassing. I realized, then, a truth that has empowered my life: *Sacred love is consistent.*

See, the Universe isn't like a rotten boyfriend who loses interest in you if, say, you let your hair go gray or gain some extra pounds or chins. Spirit never forgets your birthday or any day in which you exist. The love of the Goddess, God, or Christ is not fickle, narcissistic, passive-aggressive, or dependent on you counting the exact number of mala beads or hairs on a saint's head. Infinite intelligence isn't petty.

A Higher Love does not ever suddenly abandon you. You may have abandoned your relationship to your connection because you felt disappointed.

I know I didn't always recognize this unwavering love in a fluctuating life. If I experienced a loss, a bad meeting, a bad bill, an unwanted situation, or didn't immediately get what I thought I needed, I decided I wasn't loved by this all-loving Spirit *at all* and, in fact, it hated me and now I hated it. But if you have ever grabbed a pack of matches out of a toddler's mouth, you know that you are not "taking away" the good. You are not abandoning your loved one. You are loving with abandon.

I am that toddler, without the dinosaur-patterned outfit, and I don't always perceive my own best interests. Let's face it: I'm the one who longed for and schemed to date a guy who later robbed a bank, but that's another story. I've come to believe that while I'm always loved, my spirit supports the bigger me, the me I am becoming, not so much the me in this moment who maybe wants to swallow a matchstick but calls it cotton candy.

There is a line in the wisdom tradition of *A Course in Miracles* that says, "God has not changed His Mind about you. You are His beloved child in whom He is well-pleased." The problem is that we change our mind about God or whatever you call the infinite, kind, spacious undercurrent in your life. The sun still shines. It's not the end of the story. It's just that sunlight can't shine through brick. I've met people who have turned harder than bricks. They've stopped loving. They've stopped dreaming. Maybe they lost something they valued. But now they didn't lose just the one thing. They lost everything. They lost their sense of trust. They lost their connection to themselves. They stopped showing up. It breaks my heart.

At one of my retreats, I did an exercise with the group I called "Forgiving the Universe or Forgiving God." I asked everyone to write down things that made them stop believing in a present, loving, intelligent energy in their lives. Together we explored our illnesses, accidents, deaths, bankruptcies, betrayals, and all that had bruised or blighted our innocence. I suggested that we look again at these situations to see if there was a place where we needed to forgive ourselves or let go of any unkind conclusion we had drawn about our own worth or future.

It was amazing to hear the conclusions we had drawn. It was also interesting to see how these chosen conclusions—things like "I'll never find love again" and "Good things will always be taken away from me"—had caused even more harm than the original loss. Then we looked at everything else we had come to experience because of our heartbreaks—and how we had been strangely gifted. Pain had brought perspective or a meaningful offshoot in our lives, a road we might not have taken any other way, and a new experience of our own strength.

Whatever happened to you, you can still decide to turn your broken heart into a deeper vessel for love and purpose. Or you can numb out—or embitter yourself into a poisonous presence. I urge you to choose more meaningfully. Yes, it takes crazy bravery and a hunger for sanity to work with forgiveness. You have to want to be free and in love with your life, more than you want to be "right."

Many of us have believed that if there's a loving Infinite Intelligence, then everything goes our way. It's a rookie mistake, a misperception of what I call Transformational Love. Transformational Love is an agent of soul that stretches us, grows us, dares us to be the most potent expression of ourselves that we can be, and deeply assists us in silent, extraordinary ways. It's kind of like the coach who trains you for the big game when, really, you'd rather play small.

I have lost the "love of my life" to another woman, lost other loved ones to death, and suffered numerous heartbreaks in business. Believe me, I've got street cred in keeping a broken heart open. But I'm going to share a vanilla example of how what we think we need might not be what we need. I want to be quick and generic, and I want to spare you the details of processing my psyche. You can thank me later.

When I was eight years old, I believed I would drink Hawaiian Punch for the rest of my life. I worshipped that sweet red beverage with all my heart, and would never desire another. I swore my allegiance. But as I grew up, my tastes changed. There was Tang, which even astronauts drank. And then Black Russians in singles bars on the Upper West Side. And today, bottled spring water after yoga. I'm grateful I couldn't shape my life from that part of me that was certain it *knew* what I wanted for all time. A limited self will insist on a limited desire. Our unlimited self has boundless versatility and capacity for growth. You get the idea.

Just try on the idea that *sacred love is consistent*. Think of a time when things worked out for you. The same supportive, astonishing intelligence is with you now. The Presence hasn't changed. I remind my clients, "You're on the bus, headed in the right direction. The scenery outside the window changes, but the bus driver doesn't. Brilliant Love is at the wheel."

You might lose something you wanted, but you can never lose the source of all good. An infinite grace resides within you. Maybe you lost a job. But you haven't lost the intelligence, persistence, or other abilities that got you the job in the first place. Or if you've lost a loved one, you can never lose the light you've already experienced with that individual, or the qualities in you that helped to create the beauty in that relationship.

You have this opportunity in life to discover that you are more than who you think you are. Where have you allowed a disappointment or crisis to *become your identity* or block your awareness of other possibilities or resources? I'm not saying this is easy. Yet you know that if you break a lamp in your house, you still have electricity. The light is not in any one job or person or situation. It's in you and in your connection to a Greater Intelligent Love. Ernest Holmes, founder of the Religious Science movement, said this: "Since there is but one Spirit and this Spirit is in me, then everywhere I go, I meet this Spirit."

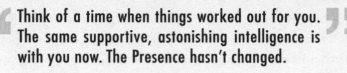

> **Think of a time when things worked out for you. The same supportive, astonishing intelligence is with you now. The Presence hasn't changed.**

Sacred love is consistent. It hasn't dropped the ball. It hasn't forgotten your name. It hasn't gotten distracted watching *The Real Housewives of New Jersey*. What if the Universe is not capable of diminishing its love because love is its nature and only possible expression? Yes, what if, indeed. A brighter what-if, if you ask me, than what if the plane is going down at record speed.

On that same magical trip to Mexico, I decided to get a temporary henna tattoo inked onto my ankle. I'm a mild-mannered Jewish rebel, after all. I picked a Chinese symbol that represented the word *always*. I wanted to remind myself that the same loving force that had helped me experience this women's retreat was the same loving force that blessed me always, even in times of bewilderment and strain.

Of course, that tattoo faded from sight, just as my comfort and trust has washed away many times since, maybe even a week later. *But always is always.* I am always loved, whether or not I see it or feel it. If I have been led or loved once, that same presence is with me now. And it is with you.

TURNING POINTS:
Finding Faith When You're Freaking Out

I could not be this loved in this moment and forgotten in the next. The nature of this love was all-encompassing. . . .
Sacred love is consistent.

A Higher Love does not ever suddenly abandon you. You may have turned away from your connection because you felt disappointed.

I've come to believe that while I'm always loved, my spirit supports the bigger me, the me I am becoming, not so much the me in this moment.

Whatever happened to you, you can still decide to turn your broken heart into a deeper vessel for love and purpose.

Think of a time when things worked out for you. The same supportive, astonishing intelligence is with you now. The Presence hasn't changed.

You're on the bus, headed in the right direction. The scenery outside the window changes, but the bus driver doesn't. Brilliant Love is at the wheel.

Where have you allowed a disappointment or crisis to *become your identity* or block your awareness of other possibilities or resources?

Always is always. I am always loved, whether or not I see it or feel it. If I have been led or loved once, that same presence is with me now. And it is with you.

DARE TO EXPERIENCE HOW LOVED YOU ARE

I like to think of thresholds as times when the veils part and angels and ancestors hover near. You may be slim on worldly resources, but you have unworldly helpers, secret beekeepers and fire starters who light the world.

TAMA KIEVES (journal entry)

A sense of separation from God is the only lack you need correct.

TAMA KIEVES (from *A Course in Miracles*)

There are two ways to live, said the Nobel Prize–winning physicist Albert Einstein. "You can live as though nothing is a miracle. Or as if everything is a miracle." You probably know where I stand. And let me tell you, I've worked to get here.

I've spent more than two decades learning how to listen to my inner voice and follow it past every statistic, convention, or limit into a life that is unthinkable and breathes within me. And I want to open a door for you.

Because no matter where you start, you can develop an elegant bond with your own mysterious powers.

And it's worth every awkward silence, coarse granule of distrust, and feeling of disconnection.

You don't have to have a religion or a robe. You might believe in God or you might believe in pixies. You might subscribe to an unseen good or a higher dimension of the neuropathways of mind. I'm not here to tell you what to believe. I am here to tell you to believe in something, even if you wobble. Cultivate an inspired connection. This sacred intelligence will move you through every patch of uncertainty and expand every dimension of your life.

Find your brand of connection. Find your language and your way to a bigger reality. Chase goose bumps, visions, mala beads, or hawk feathers upon the trail. Take a damn chance. Don't be so smart; it will make you stupid. This life is bigger than your brain. There is so much we don't understand. Yet there is more we *know* without having the data beforehand. It's love or energy. You can't quantify it. And it changes everything.

I started my spiritual journey being mocking and skeptical, but these days I use my connection, kind of like I depend on Wi-Fi. My relationship is as real to me as jury duty, only it's not obligatory or dull. The more I cultivate a relationship with my own inner voice or intuition, the more I step into a precious, responsive, just a bit larger-than-life life. I no longer care if it's weird or if it's gifted. It works. And I'm a fan of *anything* that works.

For me, the most important thing is that I feel less alone, even when I'm in transition, at the edge, and I don't know what to do. I sometimes feel as though I'm walking with an unseen friend, a playful, quirky, mojo-powered force that infuses my life with meaning, strength, and tenderness, even on the days when the rain just won't quit.

One summer I went home to New York and spent some time with my mother, who had just turned eighty. She weighed no more than a graham cracker. She was tired. She didn't even want to eat at Red Lobster, her favorite restaurant. I couldn't help but observe her shedding her enthusiasm for life. Her conversation, world, and size seemed to shrink every time I blinked my eyes. I wanted it to stop. I felt as though she was dying in front of me—in slow motion.

It is so hard to watch someone who has been such an archetype in your life, a pillar in the story of you, start to turn into a memory before your very eyes. I experienced a riot of feelings. I had so much crazy compassion for her fear and frailty, a reckless love, even though I had spent much of my life seeking and finding mothering elsewhere. We had a complex relationship. But in these later years, I felt so

much tenderness. Chalk it up to therapy, forgiveness, cosmic intervention, raw necessity, and growing up.

On my last day of my visit with her, I feel helpless saying good-
bye, knowing I can't hold back the tide of time. While, logically, I
know my brother lives nearby and can help her, it's still upsetting to
know that I will fly thousands of miles away, and a medical emergency
could demand a response time of minutes, which I could never meet.

I also feel small and exhausted myself, having ziplocked all of
my emotions inside myself, so that I can show up as my mother's
bright and resourceful daughter, the one who can tap-dance on a
pinhead and never stumble or weep. I feel heavy knowing I face a
long train ride to Grand Central Terminal, where I will hop a shuttle to JFK airport, and then a plane back across the country to
Denver.

Then this: I feel stupidly helpless because I have ninety minutes
to wait until I can catch the shuttle. It's not enough time to see more
of New York City, as I'd hoped, or go shopping, as I'd really wanted
to do while here. Those ninety minutes feel like some vestiges of
yarn. You can't knit a blanket or even a cap with them, but you don't
want to throw them away. For some stupid reason, those ninety
minutes make me feel even more helpless. They represent running
out of time *again*, as well as one more thing I'll have to figure out in
a life that feels as though there are already too many buckets and
pans to fill.

The minute I board the Metro-North train and wave good-bye,
the tears come. Passing olive green lakes and willow trees outside
the window, everything blurs. I cry because I am tired of holding it
all in, swallowing a big rubber ball for a week, while watching *Law
& Order* and the evening news with my mother. I cry knowing that
my mother is going home alone to eat her microwave dinners, and
that so many souls feel alone in this life, and that all of us deal with
scary, incomprehensible junctures that make us feel like gauzy
leaves in autumn, waiting our turn to be swept up in the astonishing
unknown.

Then I do something brilliant. I ask Spirit to be with me, to let me know that I am not forsaken and that none of us really have to ride the train alone. To be honest, it feels like a dry gesture—not a true-hearted invocation, but more of an across-the-board cry or croak for help, *any help* available anywhere.

When I get off the train, I walk through majestic Grand Central Terminal and out into the street looking for something to do with my "extra yarn." I am thrilled to see a cluster of street vendors selling leather goods, T-shirts, sunglasses, and other items. I love the street vendors of New York City and feel so grateful that I have at least a few moments of shopping before finding a Starbucks to sit in to pass the time.

But as I walk, I begin to notice that it isn't just a cluster of vendors on one block, it's a cluster on *every* block. With sheer delight, I see that there is no end in sight, that the vendors span for miles with every kind of ethnic food, designer cosmetic, silver jewelry, and leather good, all available for discounted prices.

I ask you, how can you doubt the presence of God amid an infestation of bargains? I mean, come on, I even have my choice of Estée Lauder lipsticks. I am tickled. Almost everything I wanted to experience in New York City is right here at my feet. Fantastic people-watching, endless cheap Italian, Indian, Thai, and halal food, live music, and the Chrysler Building towering and winking at me like some urban genie granting my commercial indulgences. There's even a slight breeze, in August, and not one ounce of humidity. Everyone is relaxed, as relaxed as New York gets, a summer Sunday afternoon vibe washing over all of us like jazz.

I feel new tears in my eyes, tears of abundance and gratitude, for the grace of this spontaneous experience, and for ninety minutes to enjoy it. I ask a large Italian man selling rock music T-shirts if this street fair takes place in this location every Sunday. "No," he says. "It's special today. Only now." I feel as though one hundred doves burst out of my tight rib cage. He might as well have said, "No, the Beloved did this just for you."

Yes, I understand that not everyone will look upon this as a miracle. It's not exactly the presence of the Virgin Mary (though she was for sale at the street fair), or the turning of water into wine. But that's the thing about having a relationship with the Infinite Friend. The language of spirit is exquisitely personal. It doesn't have to be religious, filled with dogma, stemming from a specific form of meditation, or even what you think of as "spiritual." The Sufis say that "God is the Great Beloved who kisses the individual on the inside of the heart."

I felt known. I recognized a signature feeling. I felt soothed and answered, as though I was walking on rose petals set down just for me, below a soft, bright canopy of all-encompassing generosity.

Suddenly, I felt cherished, even though I still felt sad, and there was still litter on the streets, and time would still march on. But even so, I felt as though I would always be okay, my life would have big love, and that my mother would be okay under her own canopy, and that we'd all be okay, because the Presence was within us and we all find meaning, sweetness, and inexplicable liberation in our own time and way.

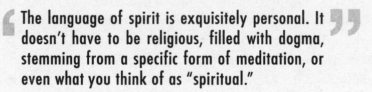

> **The language of spirit is exquisitely personal. It doesn't have to be religious, filled with dogma, stemming from a specific form of meditation, or even what you think of as "spiritual."**

Go ahead, play with it. Ask the Sacred Friend or the Beloved One, or your Inner Teacher to join you, guide you, and help you open to the love that surrounds you. If it helps, pretend that you're held dear and guided, and see what you notice in your experience when you do so. I've seen that when I call upon a higher wisdom, I often open to the direction, beauty, and surprises all around me. The legendary spiritual teacher Ram Dass says, "The next message you need is always right where you are." It's true. You are never separate from the consciousness or energy that provides your greatest comfort and sense of expanded possibilities.

Dare to live an awakened, irrational, happy life. Dive into your own intimate relationship with the Presence, the spaciousness or tenderness in between the broken moments, the nudges, the co-incidences, and uncanny, joyous juxtapositions.

Of course, your "logical" mind will discount this communication. But I urge you to go beyond your safe, rational mind. Try on an alternative source of information. Let go of your smugness or your persistent self-doubt, both of which impair your natural connection.

Dare to experience how loved you are.

TURNING POINTS:
Dare to Experience How Loved You Are

No matter where you start, you can develop an elegant bond with your own mysterious powers.

Find your language and your way. Chase goose bumps, visions, mala beads, or hawk feathers upon the trail. Take a damn chance.

Don't be so smart; it will make you stupid. This life is bigger than your brain.

The language of spirit is exquisitely personal. It doesn't have to be religious, filled with dogma, big, erupting from a specific form of meditation, or even what you think of as "spiritual."

Ask the Sacred Friend or the Beloved One, or your Inner Teacher to join you, guide you, and help you open to the love that surrounds you.

> If it helps, pretend that you're held dear and guided, and see what you notice in your experience when you do so.
>
> Dive into your own intimate relationship with the Presence, the spaciousness or tenderness in between the broken moments, the nudges, the coincidences, and uncanny, joyous juxtapositions.
>
> Let go of your smugness or your persistent self-doubt, both of which impair your natural connection. Dare to experience how loved you are.

YOU ARE BEING GIVEN THE CHANCE OF A LIFETIME

I'm making changes in my business and life. "Reinvention" is a lovely term. It sounds like I know what I'm doing. Like some Lexus engineer in a white lab coat, retooling designs based on crash tests, forecasts, and a genius's scratch pads. I don't even have scratch pads. I've got scratch.

TAMA KIEVES (journal entry)

May your trails be crooked, winding, lonesome, dangerous, leading to the most amazing view.

EDWARD ABBEY

Feeling safe is, sometimes, just about having the right perspective. When we're in transition, we often lose perspective. Well, to put it mildly—mildly as mashed potatoes. Because if you're like me, you're freaking yourself out with thoughts that are not mild, but wild as wasabi.

It's a bit discouraging to feel like your whole life is up to you, when, really, you'd like to hand it over to someone more capable or maybe even get a refund. Every coach and therapist tells you about self-responsibility, as though this is a good thing. How do you take action when there are so many of them to take? Ants crawling on a pinhead, so many choices and implications, and they all mean so much. And you feel tired, dazed, clearly ill-equipped and unfit to choose.

I don't know about you, but sometimes I can't help but feel like a contestant on a game show, where it's all on the line. Choose the wrong thing and you're buzzed off the show, kicked from the candy store of what could have been, in front of millions of people who groan about your mortifying and irreversible loss, while eating barbecue potato chips.

Damn, I want to wake up in the nice palace of safety already, where life is handled and Hershey bars are served at four p.m.

Some days, I just don't want to be a heroine or someone who has to floss her teeth even one more day. I want a butler. I want the life of my cat. I want opiates. I want it to be spring.

I don't want to find my secret strength, survive an expedition, have an Oprah-worthy moment, kiss the hem of Sir Richard Branson's garment, or take steps toward enlightenment—even if some people swear it's better than a spa vacation or retirement. I want to watch reruns of Grey's Anatomy. I know you know what I'm talking about.

It's not always easy to be really alive, feeling like your world is foundering no matter how much you prop it up or pay your therapist. Or feeling like you know something meaningful calls you, knowing you can't hide or just stay where you are, and knowing you don't always feel up to the assignment of being great or even being in the room.

And as if saving your life isn't enough, there's also the constant growing. Believe me, I've left certain limitations and several identities in the dust about a thousand years ago. I've experienced freedom and establishing myself in a new field of work. I've published books, spoken at leadership conferences, appeared on national TV, and even gotten some of my relatives to stop worriedly asking, "But what does she *do* for a living?"

And I still don't get a free pass from growth or uncertainty. I sometimes share this in the retreats I lead. I can feel the collective groan, except for the one or two adventure freaks who get all glittery at the idea of new leaps. But it *is* good news. It means I'm discovering more of my True Self. I am still increasing wingspan.

Real life goes on. All of life, if you're fully living it, entails growth. You encounter hurdles or resistance through which you uncover hidden capacities. You discover new goals, free yourself of guilt, fear, regret, scarcity, and obstacles at every stage of the game. It's kind of like a spin class or lifting weights. The workouts don't end. Maybe you take the weekend off. But it's not like you're done. Strength and fluidity require movement. Believe me, it's not like I came up with these horrible rules. Sure, this can feel tiresome at times. Yet on other days, it's an electric dance party and you have all the moves.

Because you don't want to be done. Done is boring. Done is when there is no juice left. You didn't come here to be static. You came to be ecstatic.

> **I know you just want to get through this time. But I want you to woo this time. Don't rush. . . . Because nothing that is yours is a matter of harried timing.**

One day, seeing as the *Grey's Anatomy* life plan was out, I wrote a "letter of perspective" to the frightened part of myself. I wrote it from my future, brilliant, confident self—because I believe we have all of ourselves within us already, and, really, because when you're anxious, you do what you need to do. I'm going to share it with you. You can think of it as a letter from Divine Presence or Obi-Wan Kenobi or your Aunt Betsy or a Wise Self. Maybe it's the words you'd say to your three-year-old daughter or best buddy in the world. Except these words are now directed at you.

I wrote it to my own fearful self—and to all our fearful selves. I wrote it because I am committed to living my full potential. Likewise, I want you to run your race. And while you're running this race, I want you to not just "get through it." But maybe to let this appointed time *move through you*. Don't miss the chance to absorb and integrate the nutrients of this healing recalibration.

Dear Alive One,

I know you just want to get through this time. But I want you to woo this time. Don't rush. Take your time, because nothing that is yours is a matter of harried timing. It's going to work out. It always does in its own inexplicable way. And everything occurs in its own right hour; you simply can't breach the laws of reality.

I am proud of you. You will make all the decisions that are right for you. And you will make new ones on the spot with new information. As you create this life, you will have a thousand chances. This isn't a multiple-choice exam in which you can fail. Take your time. Slog through whatever you need to go through in order to grow, even if it feels like cement. You are being given this chance. And it is a worthy one, followed by nothing but more avenues for your good. There is no scarcity of opportunity.

Step out of linear time into inspired time. Let padlocks burst off ancient doors, dried rivers flow again, and payments, contracts, healing, relationships, creative ideas, and sudden shifts in your favor come in ways you can't imagine—and know that anything is possible for you and for all of us. Discover this path you can't possibly foresee by following your desire, even if that desire is faint or seems as likely as a chocolate factory or maybe the Easter Bunny himself in the middle of the desert. It's real. It's there for a reason. Use desire as a compass.

Stay as close to your true desire as you can, and do not concern yourself with *how* it could ever happen. If you really want to grow and experience all that life can offer you, let go of calculation. This is a path of revelation. It's the journey of becoming who you did not know you could become.

The censoring voice that tells you that you only have one chance to get this right is a voice of smallness and powerlessness. It's got sour dinosaur breath—it's of the old regime. It's the voice of limitation, asking you to die to your birthright of choice and possibility. It only has one agenda, the agenda to make you wrong. Really, do you think any voice is protecting you by shaming and threatening you? Any advice that limits your spirit is not advice. It's damnation.

I am here to tell you that you are made of astonishment. You are finding your way, even when you are losing it. You may feel as though you're struggling or lost. You may ache for resolution, because it's human nature to want to skip steps and watch Netflix. But here's what I want you to know. *It is working out right now.* That's the nature of life. It works out. A spiritual journey happens when we open our eyes to see it this way, no matter what.

Your Essential Self—not your smaller, demanding, insecure self—will prevail. You will always end up where you belong. It's in your soul's DNA and the programming of every particle of life dust. It's not about the facts of your situation. It's about how these facts serve as the catalyst for your transformation.

You are learning to tune in to the signal that will take you all the way; you are learning to listen to nothing in this life but that which strengthens you.

So will you—right now—thank yourself for everything, everything, everything, and I mean *everything*, past, present, and to come, no matter what? Now, that's a viable prayer. You can decide right now how you will view this time of uncertainty. You may not be able to choose different circumstances. But you can choose to thrive in every circumstance. This isn't positive thinking. This is positive incarnation. It's your minutes on earth. It's your melody. And it's your choice how you play the song.

Besides, there are an exponential number of outcomes that will help you thrive. There is no outcome that will not gift you. You bring the light with you. You're the homecoming queen or king thinking you need to win the school's election. You've already won. You're already chosen. It's already done. The whole world is simply waiting for you to choose yourself and the perspective that most sets you free. It will wait forever with baited breath. You are that valuable and necessary. We all are.

No matter where you find yourself, you can always choose again. As long as you have breath, you can start over. There is no complexity except in the mind. There is only this simple moment. There is no promise in the distance. The promise is here. It's everywhere. If you are feeling lack, it is because you are not appreciating yourself and your journey. You are not forgiving yourself for things you imagine you should have done or been.

Choose to be here. Know that this moment in your life has a purpose and this purpose is essential to your deepest happiness. This is a choice of mental focus that activates the power of the mystery. You're not thwarted or in a maze. *You will be in amazement when you realize your freedom to choose and how extraordinary you truly are.*

Do take in the privilege of being alive and having choices, drama, and desires. There are those who are dying right now. They would give anything to be where you are.

And there are others who would give anything to have your "problems." They ache to have the chance you have right now. And there are others, still, who are fondly looking back on times in their lives when they stood where you stand right now. The times you are trying to run from, some say were the best in all their lives.

Acknowledge your courage. It is not easy to be born strong and to crave higher ground. You may feel as though you're lacking. But truly, it's because you're burning to be who you really are. You have a bird of passage within you. You are made of quester fabric. You would never be happy at the end of your days having played it bulletproof safe, never knowing where your expression could have gone—especially because you *do know* deep down where the power of love is meant to take you.

Part of you knows that this world is not quite what it seems. It's not solid, made of mortar and brick but of ideas, thoughts, and choices. Your vibration can change the electromagnetic composition of the molecules around you. Everything can change. And you long to discover the powers of your mind.

Likewise, your suffering deepens your compassion and connection with others. You will be available to this world in a different way. So as much as part of you longs for ease, another part of you welcomes this candid encounter. Because real life isn't about just buying a nice car. Real life is about having a ride.

Of course you're frightened—but it's because you're in the game. Your blood pumps and your breath quickens. You'll bleed if the knife cuts, and that's a good thing. It means you haven't given up. You're still invested.

You didn't come into this lifetime to avoid desire and risk and get to the finish line without a smudge, a scar, or a difference in your point of view. You want to have put everything into it. You won't look back and wish you'd given up. You won't wish you'd sat it out and watched others on television live fascinating lives. You wanted to get wet. You wanted to know. *You did know.*

Yes, dear one, it's good to be afraid. It's important that you're living a life that matters.

That's what I wrote. That's what I know. That's what I'm holding for myself—and all the awakening hearts who are gathering in this unglued revolution of transforming their lives. We are many, by the way.

TURNING POINTS:
You Are Being Given the Chance of a Lifetime

You don't want to be done. Done is boring. Done is when there is no juice left. You didn't come here to be static. You came to be ecstatic.

I know you just want to get through this time. But I want you to woo this time. Don't rush. . . . Because nothing that is yours is a matter of harried timing.

Any advice that limits your spirit is not advice.
It's damnation.

It is working out right now. That's the nature of life. It works out. A spiritual journey happens when we open our eyes to see it this way, no matter what.

It's not about the facts of your situation. It's about how these facts serve as the catalyst for your transformation.

You've already won. You're already chosen. It's already done. The whole world is simply waiting for you to choose yourself and the perspective that most sets you free.

Acknowledge your courage. It is not easy to be born strong and to crave higher ground.

You would never be happy at the end of your days having played it bulletproof safe, never knowing where your expression could have gone.

Do Try This at Home: Jump-starts, Inquiries & Exercises

Some of these suggestions are just right for *you*. Others, not your cup of latte, or at least at *this* moment. Follow your gut. Feel free to adjust to your liking.

Pick three Turning Points from this chapter. Write them out for yourself. Post them where you will see them. Meditate on them. Journal about them. Do a Freewriting exercise. (See page 252 for more about Freewriting.) Create a piece of art. Pay attention to your thoughts, memories, dreams, and "random" ideas and incidents. Inspired thoughts spark inspired responses. My words begin the conversation, but what do these truths unlock in you?

1. **Leave the room.** In a situation that you would like to shift, where are you trying to "decorate the room that currently exists"? Think about what you really want. Pretend you aren't dealing with "what is" in the situation. You can have anything. What would you love to experience? What's as crazy as wanting an exposed brick wall that doesn't exist?

2. **Now make a vow.** Where have you been tempted to give up on yourself or a situation? What vow will you make to yourself? Do a Freewriting exercise (see page 252 for directions) with this prompt: *I am never giving up.* Can you imagine calling forth a wrath of self-love?

3. **Release a past disappointment.** Where do you feel as though you don't have "big trust" because fill-in-the-blank happened? Are you willing to see this differently? List the gifts that came from this experience. Create an altar or light a candle. Give this situation to your higher wisdom for re-calibration. Remind yourself that you are willing to see this differently. You don't need to know how or when.

4. **List your touchstone experiences.** List the times or experiences when things worked out for you. Or a time you knew you were loved or that there was a Presence. Recount these experiences often. Remember, if sacred love is consistent, the same love that was with you in that experience is with you now.

5. **Do an Inspired Self-Dialogue** (see page 248 for directions). Ask your Inspired Self for the best ways to connect, deepen, or begin this ultimate relationship. Make this Presence your best friend. You might want to collect images that inspire you. I have a picture of a young African boy sitting next to a leopard. It's my feeling of being side by side with a Greater Presence. Or imagine a "guide" you wish to consult. (For years, I loved Dr. Crusher from *Star Trek: The Next Generation*. She was smart and kind.)

6. **Write a letter to your fearful self from your future self.** Let it begin: "Dear One, you are being given the chance of a lifetime." What does your future self want you to know? Make it up. Write for fifteen minutes. Go.

Do you have a question about this chapter? I'd love to know what's on your mind! *I may just get wildly inspired and answer you immediately.* Send me your thought or question at www.TamaKieves.com/uncertainty-question, and you can also register for a **FREE** Thriving Through Uncertainty Coaching Call designed to shift your mind-set and bring you immediate clarity.

CHAPTER THREE

TRUST YOURSELF AND YOU WILL KNOW WHAT TO DO

TO THINE OWN SELF BE TRUE

Don't be trapped by dogma—which is living with the results of other people's thinking.

STEVE JOBS

The individual has always had to struggle to keep from being overwhelmed by the tribe. If you try it, you will be lonely often, and sometimes frightened. But no price is too high to pay for the privilege of owning yourself.

FRIEDRICH NIETZSCHE

Shakespeare, the dude, wrote, "To thine own self be true," and I think he would have made a fine life coach or business guru. Because moving in the right direction requires astonishing independence. You thrive when you become attuned to your own rhythms and desires, not when you follow others like a sheep to slaughter.

It sounds great on paper. But if you're like me, it means you have to go against the very thing that made you successful in the past. I was a poster child for the American education system. I learned how *not* to think for myself, so that I could do what I was *supposed* to do and score higher. I knew how to jump through hoops. I didn't know how to *choose* the hoops.

So when I first walked out of my high-status legal career to reinvent my life, I was a virgin to listening—and I was a mess. You might be, too, even if you think you're not—because truly listening to yourself is a path of throwing out the window what you think is lucrative, spiritual, appropriate, responsible, generous, and every other prepackaged idea you have.

This is a path of following your own arriving wisdom and inspiration, not education.

And inspiration doesn't always arrive smelling like sandalwood or frankincense. Sometimes it arrives like a drunken rebel in a library shouting at you and ripping pages out of books. It may not be a tendril growing up a garden trellis hitting the light just so. Instead it's a raw insistence—a mule braying for all its worth, making you pay attention to a direction or suggestion you *do not want to hear*. And paying attention to ourselves is the price of admission to a genuine life.

If you know me, I learn and teach from experience. So, here's what I'm talking about. Years ago, I worked with a "complicated" woman I'll call Laura, who hosted me in her sexy international city. Laura decided hosting gave her rights to my life, and apparently I had agreed. I spent a full day theoretically going over "event details," but really bearing Laura's scary snarky judgments about everyone on the planet, except her peerless, adorable self. Then we embarked on her manic tour direction of every sight I *had to* see, and finally she suggested we walk this labyrinth in a church downtown. When I say "suggested," I mean we were already parking.

Laura explained the labyrinth dynamic to me. "The labyrinth

is a walking meditation. Just follow the paths to the center and back out again. Go your own way and be with the experience," she said, sounding all peachy Zen, when really, we both knew she'd be much better suited as den mother for a pack of Nazis.

At the time, I just wanted to go back to my hotel room and cry, maybe catch an episode of *Law & Order*, the kind of show that is always playing on TV in absolutely any hotel room. I longed to eat takeout Chinese, bathe in the grease, and slide my way into numbness and comfort. Lo mein therapy for just $8.95. Yes, this was before I'd grown a pair of authenticity. It was times like these that helped me get there.

But back to the story. When we arrived, the event was larger than I'd imagined, and crowded. I dutifully stepped in line with the herd of seekers to follow into the mystical maze. Once walking, I found myself wanting to jam into a fast lane. But it didn't feel right to push past people who were being *really contemplative*. Maybe they weren't just slow thick-skulled cows. Maybe they were listening to angels. Hell, I'd walk carefully if I were listening to divine dispatches. But I was in a hurry. I wanted to do this spiritual thing, get it done, get my answer, and get out of here.

"I don't want to do this," said a voice in the back of my mind. I heard it like I heard so much of myself, like a radio playing a song you don't really listen to. You know the words, can repeat them, but they haven't landed, haven't melted into you yet, like warm butter on an English muffin.

I carried on putting one lead foot in front of the other. I felt exhausted on every level. It takes a lot to ignore your truth. In that hushed hall, my mind spoke as loudly as an American in Europe. "I don't want to do this," I heard. "Of course you don't want to do it," said another voice, the mean one within that always kept me doing what others thought I should do. "You're a sissy. You can't commit like the others. You're bailing." I trudged forward, not yet seeing the irony of walking in shame and burden toward enlightenment.

Of course, what really kept me going was this: I was terrified that I'd miss something, that maybe I was "supposed" to be here, that maybe if I took just one more step, I'd have a revelation or divine intervention. Maybe a wizened monk or even a tooth fairy who looked like Lady Gaga would enter my consciousness with a message that could change my life, if only I stayed the course.

Besides, everyone else seemed to be blissful, vibrating in a sea of open chakras, mantras silently streaming from their lips, no doubt realizing staggering inner truths. I looked around. It was obvious that *they* were receiving lifetimes of soul healing or, hell, maybe even dictated insider stock trading tips. I did not want to be the loser in the crowd that just felt tired.

"I don't want to do this," the voice insisted again. And for the first time, I thought about it rationally. *Would I really hear inner wisdom if some part of me were hurting and begging me to leave?* Was it inner wisdom to listen to this exhausted part of myself? Who said it was inner wisdom to ignore my pain? What if this voice screaming for freedom *was* my inner wisdom?

"I just don't want to do this," the voice said again with everything it ever had, everything it would ever have, demanding, pleading, begging, knowing, chanting, being reasonable and unreasonable. And just like that, my truth became clear. I wanted an experience of liberation and clarity. But I didn't want to walk this damn labyrinth. I wanted to go back to my hotel and tuck myself into bed.

Immediately, new negotiations began. "Well you can't just walk out of the labyrinth. You can't just cut across people's path or move diagonally. You have to stay in the lines," my inner Follow-the-Rules Girl said emphatically. She'd be a great IRS employee.

Then I remembered the real rule of the labyrinth: find my own way to the center. Who said *my* way couldn't just be to leave and take my center with me? Yes, it felt like crying uncle, or abandoning a peace rally. It seemed heretical, like spitting out a Communion wafer.

But self-love is heretical. Freedom requires bold choices.

And really, nobody in this conglomeration of clumpy self-contemplation gave a fig. I bolted. I walked out of the labyrinth and held my own hand. I held my own soul like a soft, wounded bird. I walked in the direction of comfort, self-care, mercy, and, ultimately, redemption. I walked in the direction of love.

I didn't know it then, but I wasn't walking away from Spirit; I was walking toward Spirit. I was listening to myself. I was honoring my own timing and capacity. On my way out, I told someone there who knew Laura to let her know I'd taken a cab back. When I arrived at my hotel, which seemed like the real shrine to me, I got into a hot bath, cried, and slipped into the velvet of inner peace. Apparently, I'd found my way to center.

> " **Self-love is heretical. Freedom requires bold choices.** " \

I had to abandon what others thought was "spiritual" to listen to my Spirit.

You will, too. Listening to your inner voice requires honesty, integrity, and courage. There are no formulas. It's all fresh chemistry every second. Many of my coaching clients seem to trust their inner voice only when it suggests something like studying for an MBA or saving the whales. That is to say, only "virtuous" things count, things you could tell your Austrian aunt Helga and make her pat her dress in pride.

But I tell them and I'll tell you, you do not know what is most productive on this path. You have no idea how much creative progress you can make when you listen to your own unconditional genius, that within you which is not conditioned by society. Why would you attempt to create a life of unbounded freedom by listening to the advice of the bound one within you?

Of course, I'm not advising you to simply follow the part of you that always suggests relaxation. You and I both know the voice of cruel self-limitation can sound kind and concerned. I've had a cunning voice tell me for years that I shouldn't "strain" myself by writing, exercising, forgoing my beloved Diet Pepsi, or doing any of the things that would take me across the bridge into a new world. Resistance can mimic compassion. And the results can stagnate you.

So how do you discern which instincts to trust inside you?

Here's a quick rule of thumb: It's not what an inner voice advises that matters. Pay attention to the motivation behind the suggestion. Are you listening to love or fear? I didn't leave because of fear. I was *staying* because of fear. For me, leaving that walking meditation wasn't a reflection of my weakness. It was trusting in my strength. The desire didn't come from boredom, petulance, or an unwillingness to go past my smaller self. It stemmed from self-respect, self-awareness, mercy, a sense of timing, and self-loyalty. No single action is always right. Guidance is exact, original, and unduplicated. There are no mechanical rules. Staying true to yourself requires receptivity and experimentation.

Dare to listen with respect to your emerging truth. Your truth may not look the way you wish. It may have you make "undesirable" or unpopular choices. You don't get to decide what freedom, clarity, or success should look like. You will only know how sweet a truth feels.

TURNING POINTS:
To Thine Own Self Be True

Truly listening to yourself is a path of throwing out the window what you think is lucrative, spiritual, appropriate, responsible, generous, and every other prepackaged idea you have.

Inspiration doesn't always arrive smelling like sandalwood or frankincense. Sometimes . . . it's a raw insistence—a mule braying for all its worth, making you pay attention to a direction or suggestion you *do not want to hear.*

Self-love is heretical.
Freedom requires bold choices.

I had to abandon what others thought was "spiritual" to listen to my Spirit.

Why would you attempt to create a life of unbounded freedom by listening to the advice of the bound one within you?

No single action is always right. . . . Guidance is exact, original, and unduplicated. There are no mechanical rules.

Dare to listen with respect to your emerging truth. Your truth may not look the way you wish. It may have you make "undesirable" or unpopular choices.

You don't get to decide what freedom, clarity, or success should look like. You will only know how sweet a truth feels.

NO ONE HAS A BETTER LIFE THAN YOU

Through fear of knowing who we really are and what we want we sidestep our own destiny which leaves us hungry in a famine of our own making.

JOHN O'DONOHUE

At the end of my life, I would be very sad if I had been compar-
ing the privilege of my singular days here to anyone else's experi-
ence. If I had wasted one teardrop, one glance, one errant
thought on how someone had something better than me, as
though that was ever possible, as though I wasn't loved com-
pletely. This would make me sad, as I realized I'd been throwing
the bouquet Life had selected for me back into its face, stomping
my tiny, uneducated foot, demanding something lesser in the
name of demanding something better.

TAMA KIEVES (journal entry)

Here's a crazy little law of life, I've discovered. It's really hard to trust yourself when you don't want to be yourself.

But dear one, you do not know who you are.

There's a cartoon in *The New Yorker* magazine that says it all. Two cavemen are drawing figures side by side on the wall. One of them is rendering some perfect-looking Leonardo da Vinci–type drawing. He peers over at his neighbor, who is scratching the stick figures of a five-year-old. The Leonardo character groans, "Man, I wish I could learn to loosen up like you."

And there it is. It's always going on. Comparison is a blindfold, not a lens.

Some years ago, I attended a wedding and met Risa, a younger woman who had attended not one but two Ivy League schools, bagging her doctorate and a husband with buckets of money. Before our Caesar salads had even arrived, I'd learned that she had run marathons, hiked in Cambodia, had an electric sense of humor, owned a raging side business, and could belt out hip-hop at the karaoke bar.

Clearly, she'd gotten quite the package deal from the big cosmic travel agent in the sky and I would have to change my seat. And if you're anything like me, you will meet someone like this at your most bloated, hormonal, horrible moment possible. One moment you're feeling fine-ish and then suddenly you have to win a Pulitzer Prize or do a TED talk that goes viral just to justify your existence. It's exhausting.

A *Course in Miracles* teaches, "Love makes no comparisons." It says this because comparison is impossible. You do not ever know the real story about someone else or yourself. Because if you did, you would choose your life again and again and again. In fact, many spiritual traditions teach that on a soul level, you have chosen this life.

But let's just stick to simple logic: Since this *is* your life, it's better if you choose it. So, I'm going to ask you to consciously and wholeheartedly "pick" and embody your own good life. Because the only reason you could ever want to be in someone else's life is because you're not *really* in yours.

I remember seeing Natasha and Steve at a conference. They were the "perfect" couple. They would have made Barbie and Ken turn plastic green with jealousy. She had long flying blond hair. I am not even kidding. Let's just say that when life wants to show you something, it pulls out the Hollywood movie props.

Natasha was wispy in a soft blue cotton top. Steve, also blond, was stroking her hair, whispering in her ear. I was watching like a stalker, but nonchalantly, of course. He was the singer at the event, funny and quick-witted, and moving us to tears and laughter with each of his original, offbeat songs.

They had met at another conference and had been traveling together since that time. They meditated in the arroyos at dawn in New Mexico and drank goblets of wheatgrass. They had strolled on moonlit beaches in Kauai and ate farm-fresh papaya on the balcony of a condo lent to them by friends. They read each other's auras, palms, and astrology charts. I wanted to puke. I wanted to touch them.

"We're twin flames. We're soul mates. This is everything you read about," gushed Steve about Natasha. They were disgusting. And, of course, time-consuming, as I had suddenly lost complete track of my own life and why I'd come to this conference. Obsession hit me like a hurricane.

I was having issues in my relationship life at the time, as in I didn't have a relationship. I felt injured every time he looked at her or she giggled, because I was lonely for love and didn't believe I'd ever find it. I didn't want to keep looking, but it was like a bad car accident on the side of the road. Don't look, I told myself. I gaped. At one point, she saw me, so I smiled a forced, gooey, spiritual, I-am-beholding-your-love kind of smile, before I slithered off.

Later in the conference, she came over to me and asked if she could partner with me in one of the sharing-in-communication exercises. Oh great, I thought. *This is exactly what I need.* Only I didn't know how true that was.

Her yoga-type ensemble hung loosely on her body. She was a stalk of wheat lit by sun. I was her opposite, being short, dark haired, intense, and with meat on my bones, junk in my trunk.

I realized I was afraid of her.

I just didn't want to hear how great her life was. Sure, I wanted to be "enlightened" and happy for her success. But on the car ride here, I'd cried for half the trip. I was raw with pain. I was fragile. I had been left by the man I loved and I was having trouble breathing and my taste buds had gone numb for life. That's why I had decided to come to this conference in the first place, looking for a filament of hope. I found it hard to be joyous for others when I'd just had my heart crunched and broken.

But it was too late. Natasha sat cross-legged before me. Cross-legged with long legs. And we began the exercise.

We were supposed to share what was going on without fixing one another or editing. I started first and blurted, as boundaries are not so much my thing. I don't remember what I said, but I no doubt shared about my insecurity about relationships, career, or life, or how unfortunate it was that I had not been born blond like her.

Then perfect, nimble Natasha shared with me. "I hate my life," she said. "I'm so scared. Steve is hanging all over me night and day and I need to get out of this relationship. I don't know how to tell him. I'm scared to tell the truth. I don't want to hurt him and then I'm sick to death about how I don't tell the truth ever. I am living a lie again."

Natasha looked at me with these clear blue eyes that could skewer you into Sunday if you didn't blink. Then she said the unthinkable: "I wish I could be like you. You're so honest. You would never let this happen to you. You're so real. I could never be as together as someone like you." I swear to God she said those words. She was my guru, come down from the mountain to gently usher me back into reality and an appreciation of my own flawed and phenomenal life.

Borrowing again from *A Course in Miracles*, "You are altogether irreplaceable in the mind of God. No one else can fill your part in it, and while you leave your part in it empty, your eternal place merely waits for your return." This is the work of trusting ourselves and our lives on the deepest levels.

It's time to own a greater story of your life than the one you hear from your yapping ego. Here's the nutshell version, which, if you're like me, could just keep you from being a nut. You are a promise and a vessel like none before you. You were born on the day crafted for you in all of time. You will always draw to you what you require for your True Life. You haven't yet fully lived your story. It's the only reason you pine for someone else's story.

I remind myself that when I live my undiluted life, I will want no other. I'm on a journey of healing. It's not a race. It's not about external appearances. It's a story of how I break open my own heart and discover the pomegranate seeds and red juice of magic. It's a story of what I bring to the table. It's a story of coming home to my own astonishing capacities. But I will never come home while I long to be where I am not.

I once heard about a little girl who was at her family's Christmas celebration. Her brother opened his present and pulled out an electronic game. "I want what Johnny got!" the little girl cried out. Her mother stroked her head and said, "But darling, you don't even know what you got yet." The little girl was inconsolable. I don't know the end of the story. I just remembered that part, because I am that longing little girl at times. I don't really know what I have yet, so I crave what I think others have. And the irony is this: The more I focus on what others have, the more I have no idea what I have.

> **You haven't yet fully lived your story. It's the only reason you pine for someone else's story.**

Yet we are all in the right life.

It's blasphemy to diminish yourself. It's not just an attack on your own abilities. It's an attack on the mysterious integral forces of the Universe, the committee of the unseen that whisper stage directions here and there. I often write to a voice within me I call my Inner Teacher. It's part of the Inspired Self Dialogue technique I teach, and not a Sybil moment, just in case you're wondering. This Brilliant Love once answered in my journal, "Do not limit my destiny with your feeble opinions of yourself." I love it when my guidance talks clean to me.

And when I get out of the way, I get back to the simplicity of reality. I did not create myself or my inherent inclinations. I'm a creation as much as any design in nature. There is a blueprint for my natural expression. A wild purple iris knows when to poke through the dirt in spring. A robin knows when to molt. I'm going to trust my own pokes and seasons.

I am learning to trust myself the more I lay claim to my life. This is my practice. Can I stay loyal to myself? It costs too much to long for someone else's life. I don't want my heirloom roses to wither because I'm so busy looking over my shoulder at my neighbor's roses that I neglect to water and feed this beauty before me. Nothing grows without love and attention.

Likewise, nothing given love and attention remains the same.

TURNING POINTS:
No One Has a Better Life Than You

It's really hard to trust yourself when you don't want to be yourself. But dear one, you do not know who you are.

Comparison is a blindfold,
not a lens.

It's time to own the greater story of your life. You are a promise and a vessel like none before you. You were born on the day crafted for you in all of time.

You haven't yet fully lived your story. It's the only reason you pine for someone else's story.

The more I focus on what others have, the more I have no idea what I have.

It's blasphemy to diminish yourself. . . . It's an attack on the mysterious integral forces of the Universe, the committee of the unseen that whisper stage directions here and there.

I don't want my heirloom roses to wither because I'm so busy looking over my shoulder at my neighbor's roses that I neglect to water and feed this beauty before me.

Nothing grows without love and attention. Likewise, nothing given love and attention remains the same.

DARE TO BE UNFAITHFUL, SPORADIC, AND UNUSUALLY TRUE TO YOURSELF

Sometimes I know I can do more. I know I can be more. This haunts me when I'm taking a baby step or coaxing out a new behavior. But lately it's occurred to me that I don't want my potential to rob me of my potential.

TAMA KIEVES (journal entry)

It is better to begin in the evening than not at all.

English proverb

One of my coaching clients was talking to me about not being able to stay with a Zen meditation practice—so she gave up meditating altogether. "I'm either gung ho all the way or I don't show up at all," she said with self-disgust.

We were talking on one of the unfortunate evenings when she "hadn't shown up at all." To listen to her, you would have thought that she had just hacked up Checkers, the family's cocker spaniel. Things were a tiny bit morose. Clearly, she needed self-forgiveness more than self-discipline. Actually, I'm thinking she might have benefited from a good old-fashioned head-spinning exorcism. But that's just me.

I understand the desire to make changes in your life. I am a believer in enthusiasm. I also believe in commitment. But I'm more of a fan of incremental, organic, *natural* commitment.

That means I invite you to be inconsistent and unreliable. I dare you to break promises to yourself and I dare you to make fresh new ones. This is what it takes to be on the courageous path of learning to reinvent, hunt down your bare heart, and discover and trust yourself.

You are here to follow an unpredictable light wherever it leads, not to wrangle unfathomable power into a silly, stupid box. This isn't rationalization. It's strategy. Because a realistic and sustainable path doesn't come from obligation or hostility. If you want something to go the distance, it needs to come from love.

Commitment is bold and wondrous. Still, let your intention breathe instead of suffocate you. You're learning how to commit from something deeper than willfulness. I'll call it willingness. This willingness arises from an inner summons. Authentic success springs forth from irrepressible desire—not impatience.

"I never follow through," said Sandra on one of our afternoon calls. I knew this wasn't true. She is a bright, passionate woman who has raised children, which, if you ask me, is quite the follow-through. In fact, she's still feeding them, last I heard. "I get it. You've got to stare resistance down sometimes," I said. "But honey, believe me when I tell you that rigidity will create more problems than it solves."

Following through is so much less important than following inner guidance.

It's not effective to stay true to a faded goal. Stay true to your gold. Your intuitive guidance is the gold. I am a coach who happily turns the term *accountability* on its head. But Ralph Waldo Emerson, leading the transcendentalist movement in the mid-nineteenth century, beat me to this. He said: "A foolish consistency is the hobgoblin of little minds." Now don't get hot and bothered. Your inner wisdom is never going to ask you to abandon your integrity. It may ask you to abandon your hobgoblins. And give yourself room to grow.

Being flexible doesn't mean you have a problem with commitment. It may indicate adaptivity, which is so much sexier than being erratic. Really, what if who you think you "should" be is keeping you from the fire of who you are becoming?

For example, I've worked with many high-powered, successful

individuals who "don't follow through," because while something might be a good idea, it's not an idea that sets its fangs into their jugular. It's just a good idea. Good ideas are a dime a dozen. "I know I'm wildly creative," says Rhonda, a writer with several books to her credit. "I don't waste time on good ideas. I'm waiting for the *great* one. I'm waiting for the whale. I need a whale to carry me out to sea." It takes emotional honesty to explore and stay true to your instincts. It takes enormous courage to *not* follow through.

> **❝ Following through is so much less important than following your inner guidance. ❞**

Maybe you think you're just a quitter. Yet I've met many intelligent authenticity seekers who refuse to settle. They kept moving on. It wasn't because they were flighty, but because they had already taken flight. When you move on to the eighth grade, have you quit seventh grade? No. You're not quitting; you're evolving. When you've grown, it's healthy to move forward. Sticking with something isn't always a sign of strength.

There's also a divine timing, when something just takes hold as it has not done before. My partner, Paul, tried to get sober three times before he got sober for life—or at least for two decades and counting. It wasn't ever a mistake for him to try to get sober. It wasn't a failure to take a run at it, even though he didn't follow through. It's never wrong to move toward health. It also wasn't wrong for him to fall down. It wasn't time yet. You can't force yourself to be ready. But you can keep taking steps in the right direction as many times as possible.

To me, there's beauty, intelligence, and grace in showing up lopsided, showing up fitfully, showing up sporadically. *Showing up is showing up.*

The dream basher in you pushes you into airtight commitments. But real change is about breathing, coming in and going out. Daring to live the authentic life that calls you is a path of invitation, not obligation. If it's right for you to make a deeper commitment to something, you will move into this grace. But you will make it in your own time and not a second before or afterward.

The Persian mystic poet Rumi, the absurdly free and expansive spirit, writes, "Come, come whoever you are, wanderer, worshipper, lover of leaving. . . . Come, even if you have broken your vow a hundred times. Come, come again."

A Course in Miracles echoes this philosophy by telling us to "choose once again" whenever we have made a choice that has felt painful. It doesn't say crucify yourself, throw in the towel, and, by all means, go ahead and create your *identity* out of all that hasn't worked out yet. No, it instructs us to save time. Just begin again.

Choose the new behavior or belief *now*. Give birth to a different experience this very minute. This kind of freedom isn't irresponsible. It's the ultimate responsibility. I believe we each have a mandate in this lifetime to give ourselves every chance to be healthy and true.

When I first began writing in hopes of turning it into a career, I suffered from my own blame and shame, kind of like bad cop and worse cop interrogating me about my creative whereabouts and lack of productivity. I'd work up all kinds of writing schedules. Then I'd ignore my own intentions and, seeing as I was on a roll, eat my way through muffins and chocolate, too, a screw-you etched in sugar. I absolutely couldn't trust myself. This was mortifying.

Of course, I *did* make progress as a writer. But I didn't get there by finding a nice, harmless chemical to paralyze my legs from the hours of twelve p.m. to four p.m. so that I'd sit still and focus—and yeah, maybe I *thought about* researching manacles on the Internet. I didn't get there by calling myself a string of names that would make a marine drill sergeant call home and cry to his mother. No—get this, I was kind. I learned to coax myself to dare what was most important to me.

In my first book, *This Time I Dance!: Creating the Work You Love*, I wrote, "Only the tender can breed the fierce." This was a revelation to my alpha-trained type A brain. Like my nonmeditating client, I thought that if I had "misbehaved," I deserved an electric cattle prod, not a bubble bath.

But my deeper wisdom reflected, "Be even kinder to yourself when you feel fear. Love, not anger, inspires right action." It was true. Part of me avoided writing because I was afraid to face a new challenge in the bright, blinding light of my own self-cruelty. I quivered with the pressure to perform.

Every minute of writing was like having NASA monitor a launch, not to mention the panel of Olympic writing judges in my head, forever irritated that I wasn't Proust or a senior editor of *The New Yorker*. They'd dispute every word I wrote: *Really, you're writing about that again? Do you think this material is scintillating enough to promise you a career? And you're going to use a comma there?* With cheerleaders like these, I didn't need hit men.

Let's just say it's hard to take the biggest risks of your life in front of your greatest enemy. I was my greatest enemy. That's why gentleness rocked my world. It led to *inspired* action. And these actions generated traction. And finally, getting deeper into the work invigorated my heart's commitment—which is a whole different beast than a commitment from your head.

Sometimes, we have an ill-advised idea of what showing up looks like. In a creative life, many people confuse rigidity with purity. But remember as we dedicate ourselves to wholeness, we may have many loves and devotions. And this is not distraction or avoidance. This is self-expression.

When I lived in the mountains outside Denver and was writing my first book, I drove into the city weekly to teach classes and because I loved to hang out at bustling coffeehouses downtown. Ralph, an older gentleman in a writing group, lambasted me one night, yes—in a *support* group. "If you were serious about that book, you'd just stay in the mountains and write," he barked. I immediately felt like a wannabe, someone who lacked the emotional grammar to go the distance. I didn't know then that allowing myself to do what I really wanted to do was what was going to help me sustain the distance. I wasn't creatively flighty. I was discovering the idiosyncratic mechanics of how *I* took flight.

Having more than one interest or responsibility doesn't make you less faithful to your dreams. I love writing, and consuming great literary novels, but I'm also an extrovert and a teacher and I love to share my experiences with other people in passionate conversations. I love both lives. Just as I have clients who are parents, and they are not only going to sculpt or work on a product launch for their business—another part of their lives is going to soccer practice and picking up bananas. They are not abandoning their passions. They are claiming more of them.

I've also known dedicated people who work "regular" jobs to pay their rent while they steal scraps of time to devote to their souls' goals. They may never feel like they're doing enough. That's only because they're focusing on what they're *not* doing.

Focus on all the steps you *do* take to live your true desires. That's how you maintain self-trust and progress. Focus on the behaviors you wish to encourage, not the other choices.

If you are trying to lose weight, don't agitate over your failure of will on the third day of your program. Celebrate the first two days of motivation. *Only the wins count—if you want to win.* In 12-step program lingo, "It's all about progress, not perfection."

I know the sticklers will tell you that taking one exercise class or spending one hour with your camera won't help, but I disagree. *Every act of love for yourself makes a difference.*

That one time can boost your self-esteem, help reveal the heavens, stretch a muscle, or send a rush of dopamine to your brain, which, believe me, will increase the likelihood that you'll return.

Go ahead, stumble into grace. Start and stop a million times. Get there late and leave early. Whatever it takes. So what if some think you look spasmodic? You are an extraordinary truth seeker, an inspired explorer, or as Rumi says, a traveler in a "caravan of joy." And that works just fine, because you're moving in the right direction.

TURNING POINTS:

Dare to Be Unfaithful, Sporadic, and Unusually True to Yourself

I invite you to be inconsistent and unreliable. I dare you to break promises to yourself and I dare you to make fresh new ones.

You are here to follow an unpredictable light wherever it leads, not to wrangle unfathomable power into a silly, stupid box.

A realistic and sustainable path doesn't come from obligation or hostility. If you want something to go the distance, it needs to come from love.

Following through is so much less important than following your inner guidance.

It takes emotional honesty to explore and stay true to your instincts. It takes enormous courage to *not* follow through.

To me, there's beauty, intelligence, and grace in showing up lopsided, showing up fitfully, showing up sporadically. *Showing up is showing up.*

Every act of love for yourself makes a difference.

Go ahead, stumble into grace. Start and stop a million times. Get there late and leave early. Whatever it takes.

THINK TWICE BEFORE YOU TAKE ADVICE

Don't follow any advice, no matter how good, until you feel as deeply in your spirit as you think in your mind that the counsel is wise.

JOAN RIVERS

Never take advice from unhappy people.

TAMA KIEVES (journal entry)

When it comes to living an inspired life, we are charged with learning how to listen to our own instincts. That means we allow ourselves to be uncertain and muck around, which makes most of us feel like failures—even while we are practicing the most heroic discipline of all.

But here's the thing. Uncertainty attracts advice- -kind of like a cantaloupe on a picnic table attracts ants and blackflies. Everyone is suddenly an expert or knows one. Everyone knows just what *you* should do, even if they don't know what you want. And let's face it, they might not exactly be specimens of a life with wide-open happiness chakras or stellar finances, but—and I say this with sheer amazement—that doesn't stop them from suddenly deciding they are the perfect consultants for you.

Sometimes you may need to fight for your right to stay uncertain, because you are giving yourself time to move in the ways you need to move. And the only way to discover your own inner voice is to stop listening to the tired myths, patchwork or irrelevant data, and transitory solutions that others offer.

I sat in a print-patterned booth at Panera Bread with Kate, a lovely woman who managed a premier health foundation and who listened with a heart that took you in, like a relief worker in a war zone. Recently, I'd started falling into an old trance of mine, the "I don't know how to . . ." and you can fill in the blank. This time it was around business. Well, hell, it was always around business. But yours might be different. I mentioned my concerns about marketing and hiring team members to Kate, the wonder listener.

"Oh, but you know how to get the right advice and results," she said, sipping her soup. *Bam!* I felt suddenly hot. Here we go, I thought. Here comes the lecture on hiring brand experts, networking with colleagues, yadda, yadda, you should . . . And I felt sick of all of it. Kate had stepped on an emotional land mine. I'm sure every peace-loving Buddhist in a five-mile radius felt the shock waves of my reactivity. I folded my napkin carefully, as though it was an explosive.

I waited for the spiel on obvious business practices. *Hire a marketing firm. Hire a PR person. You could do so much with social media these days. There's a program I saw where this woman tells you how to . . .* This kind of information made me crazy because I knew "normal" folks would just dive in and be done. But I didn't seem to be able to do it. Yes, I wanted results. But so much of what I'd researched just didn't click for me. The information made me feel tired, not inspired.

Kate was in my Inspired & Unstoppable Life Tribe, the group support program I run for anyone who is daring their dreams, and I liked her, so I risked being vulnerable and headed her off at the pass. "Wow, I'm on edge. I know you're trying to help. But right now, I feel resistant to working with business consultants, gurus, and online courses, et cetera." I left out the part where I wanted to throw my soup in her face. She was a student of mine and all. Pace yourself, I thought.

"No, I wasn't going there," she said softly, her eyes, dark coffee beans, radiating wisdom.

"You know how to get the right advice," she said again. "You know how to get *your* answers. You know how to get them *here*," she said, pointing to her heart. *Oh*. Well, somebody had been listening to my coaching calls after all—thank goodness, since I obviously wasn't.

And damn if that heat within didn't just cool right down. I felt this wave of knowing roll in. And Panera Bread got all glittery, or I just felt that way because I had been blessed, as though a high priestess had opened up the top of my head and poured in wild lavender and starlight, or maybe rich espresso and a muscle relaxant. It was safe for Buddhists again, and maybe a baby guardian angel or budding psychotherapist got her wings. I felt answered. This woman called me back to power and freedom in my own native tongue.

She gave me back my way.

It seems that I have to learn to trust myself about a thousand times a month. Clearly, I have spiritual amnesia. Or, more to the truth, I'm daring to live a different paradigm, uncovering and defining happiness for myself. That means that popular advice, often based on others' values, can lead me astray from what I really want.

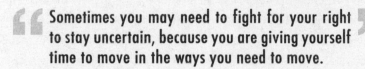

Sometimes you may need to fight for your right to stay uncertain, because you are giving yourself time to move in the ways you need to move.

When it came to running my business, I didn't have the exact answers. Still, I didn't feel secure with the "experts" who promised to whisk me into better results in seven quick steps. Sure, their promises feel wildly alluring because they give you the *illusion of control*, or the illusion that *someone else will do the work for you*.

But too often, I'd seen that real life demanded a deeper commitment, especially if I craved excellence. Prepackaged answers often just skimmed the surface, providing shallow information without transformation. I knew I had to get my hands and heart dirty.

I love learning from anyone and everything. Yet I know that my inspired answers have always demanded patience, integrity, and a powerful direction born of experimentation, fermentation, self-understanding, and readiness. I didn't need more information that felt good to my brain but left my soul parched and wandering in the wilderness. Experience had taught me I'd eventually abandon all the "good ideas" and return to searching for the truth.

"That's because you're a lazy baby," the foul voice within hissed. "You don't want to grow up. You don't want to do what it takes. You want to stay a dreamer, thinking your answers will fall from the sky like shooting stars in a Disney movie, which by the way is formulaic and making people billions of dollars, because *they* are listening to sound business advice. You think your answers will float in on butterfly wings."

But really, I wasn't motivated, not because I'm lazy or elitist, but because I'm honest. I can no longer force myself to squelch my instincts and go along with a program that doesn't move me. I'm too far in. I'm too far gone. I'm too in love with the possibilities that have opened up when I've stopped beating myself up and embraced the path of listening to intuition instead. In the business world, they call the creativity of doing things a totally new way the "power of disruption." It's a gift, not a curse. I guess some of us are called to live, love, and work in ways that don't fit into the textbooks—yet.

I'm not saying I don't take advice. Far from it. I am saying I do take advice, but only when I'm feeling excitement or the draw of my own integrity rather than insecurity.

Julia Cameron, author of *The Artist's Way*, says that an artist's laziness is not a lack of discipline but a lack of enthusiasm. I love the word *enthusiasm*. It stems from *entheos*, meaning "divinely inspired, possessed by a god."

So, there it is. I am stirred by fireflies, a fire in the belly, and a tingling around my head more than by promotional promises. I am moved by divine instruction or the genius of the gut check. Unlike Coca-Cola it *is* the real thing. There's a quieting or an electricity. It's intrinsic communication. It's not obligation or "should." I am numb to "good ideas" because I require ideas that are good *for me*. It's uncomfortable sometimes, but I have to wait for the real thing. True power has its own note. And the truth yields uncanny results. I've lived them; I can't go back to ordinary.

Do I crave immediate progress or solace? Of course I do. But I won't end uncertainty on a head level anymore. I want to end my questions on a gut and soul level—a *knowing* level. That's been the only thing that has given me stamina and moxie to do this wild life of following my creativity all the way into the national and international realms of speaking and business, on my own terms, knowing a peace of mind no one else can give me.

So now I'll ask you, why settle for the illusion of relief? That's the junk food diet of the mind. You deserve the real thing, the kale and grains that feed your blood and bone. Easy answers are like french fries: We crave them, but they do not help us in the end. And french fries have certainly never done anything good for my rear end, but I digress.

So, I beamed at Kate as we continued to talk and I slurped my chicken soba noodle soup. (Oh, that kale and grains thing—just a metaphor.) I basked in remembering how good the right advice feels.

Not everyone has advice for you, though they will surely give it. Mind you, you may receive "sound" advice—brawny, data-packed, *New York Times* or Harvard PhD advice. Yet it still may be inadequate for you. It depends on your values and what you need in this moment in time. I worship results, don't get me wrong. But I've also spent too many years of my life listening to "excellent" advice and achieving ill-fitting "tangible results." Those tangible results broke my heart and left my spirit to float on the ceiling looking down at my bored, busy, aching, results-filled life.

Remember, when you're looking to thrive, you're not looking

for "credible" direction. You're forging an *incredible* life. And if, like me, you're daring to live from inspiration more than fear, then you are tasked with discerning the aliveness in everything you choose. Pay attention to advice. *But pay more attention to how advice lands for you.*

When someone says something that's right for you, your shoulders relax. You melt into the moment. You can't fake it or force it. Even if it's hard advice, something speaks to your gut or marrow. There have been times in my work life when I've felt drawn to do something that didn't feel like bliss, but it felt *right*. I've also used many conventional business techniques or shortcuts because they worked and I could make them authentically my own. And I've hired experts. I'm not living off the grid just because I'm living with awareness. I'm just taking the extra measure to choose consciously.

You know what is right for you. You know when you feel love and you know when you don't.

When you receive an answer that is not right for you, you say yes but your voice is high-pitched or flat with disconnection. The reason you don't move forward is because it's not your way or it's not your time. There is a holy stubbornness in you. You are obedient to your cue. You are waiting to be called.

Yes, sometimes you're refusing to hear the truth because of fear of pain or change. But even then, you will eventually hear your answer when it is right for you, and that is all that matters.

Kate and I finished our lunch and conversation. I left behind an unfinished roll and any guilt or doubt I'd felt from ignoring conventional wisdom. I stepped back into magic.

TURNING POINTS:
Think Twice Before You Take Advice

Sometimes you may need to fight for your right to stay uncertain, because you are giving yourself time to move in the ways you need to move.

I'm daring to live a different paradigm, uncovering and defining happiness for myself. That means that popular advice, often based on others' values, can lead me astray from what I really want.

I didn't need more information that felt good to my brain but left my soul parched and wandering in the wilderness. Experience had taught me I'd eventually abandon all the "good ideas" and return to searching for the truth.

I am numb to "good ideas" because I require ideas that are good *for me*. It's uncomfortable sometimes, but I have to wait for the real thing.

I won't end uncertainty on a head level anymore. I want to end my questions on a gut and soul level—a *knowing* level.

Easy answers are like french fries: We crave them, but they do not help us in the end.

Pay attention to advice. *But pay more attention to how advice lands for you.*

The reason you don't move forward is because it's not your way or it's not your time. There is a holy stubbornness in you. You are obedient to your cue. You are waiting to be called.

Do Try This at Home: Jump-starts, Inquiries & Exercises

Some of these suggestions are just right for *you*. Others, not your cup of latte, or at least at *this* moment. Follow your gut. Feel free to adjust to your liking. Do what's right for you rather than what's written here.

Pick three Turning Points from this chapter. Write them out for yourself. Post them where you will see them. Meditate on them. Journal about them. Do a Freewriting exercise. (See page 252 for more about Freewriting.) Create a piece of art. Pay attention to your thoughts, memories, dreams, and "random" ideas and incidents. Inspired thoughts spark inspired responses. My words begin the conversation, but what do these truths unlock in you?

1. **Create a despair repair strategy.** Whom do you compare yourself to? Can you stop finding out information about this person? Disconnect from his or her Twitter account? Immediately focus on doing something good in your life. You don't want this person's story. You want yours.

2. **Move from rote to real.** Pay attention to what you're doing this week because others think it's the right thing to do, someone else expects it, or you're afraid to miss out. Go rogue. Practice *not* doing one or more of these things. See how good it feels to give yourself the time. What's your labyrinth, the thing you'd really like to get out of? Go for it!

3. **Write a permission statement.** Give yourself permission to begin something and then quit, or to do it badly. Make sure to shock your perfectionist.

4. **Adopt a "choose again" practice.** Fire the "past police." Forgive yourself for what you haven't finished or accomplished. Call a truce. Clear the slate. Do you need to make

amends to yourself? What do you need to do to let this go? Let it go. Choose again. Start now. And when you forget, choose again.

5. **Do a Win List.** (See page 250 for instructions on Win Lists.) Take a project or emotional goal you want to encourage. What would you like to stay true to? Do a targeted Win List every day this week.

6. **Take an inventory.** When do you tend to listen to other people instead of yourself? What do "they" say? Pay attention to how advice lands for you. Do your shoulders relax? Or do you feel tense? Are you making decisions from obligation instead of inspiration? In a situation in your life in which you're feeling frustration, fill in this blank quickly and repetitively: The "assumed right thing" for me to do here is . . . Discover the assumptions that might be blocking your instincts or truth.

Do you have a question about this chapter? I'd love to know what's on your mind! *I may just get wildly inspired and answer you immediately.* Send me your thought or question at www.TamaKieves.com/uncertainty-question, and you can also register for a **FREE** Thriving Through Uncertainty Coaching Call designed to shift your mind-set and bring you immediate clarity.

CHAPTER FOUR

ACTION ISN'T THE SHARPEST TOOL IN THE SHED

HAPPINESS IS AN ACTION

"But you could make more money if you just . . . [fill in the blank]," says Rhonda. It's a reasonable idea. And it takes every fiber of resolution I possess to not act. I keep telling myself, Just because you could, doesn't mean you should.

TAMA KIEVES (journal entry)

It takes courage and discipline to turn your face to the sun. Getting happy is an action and an act of revolution.

TAMA KIEVES (journal entry)

It takes practice to stay inspired. Real life is an opponent that won't quit. We are barraged with facts and influences that attack our confidence. Peace of mind is not an opiate. It's an act of heroic self-compassion and dedicated concentration.

But most of us have been conditioned to believe that happiness is an indulgence, like doughnuts. It's not the main entree. And it's definitely not as "virtuous" as working hard, the fish and leafy greens of life choices.

My father, a self-made businessman, had a high-strung, judgmental temperament, which is a nice way of putting it. He also had the Eastern European Jewish mandate to be a "good provider" for his family, and he worked hard. He disdained those who relaxed. I remember him seeing a middle-aged man sitting on a bench in the sun in Central Park, smiling casually to himself. "Look at that guy," my father snarled with condemnation. "Nothing on *his* mind." My father's implicit message weighed heavily on *my* mind. Be worried, cynical, and constantly in motion all the days of your life. This was the subtext for success. Stress meant you were responsible, a "thinker," someone to be counted on, and who could achieve results. You were "on the ball."

Yet these days I know how imperative it is to remain calm in a world of frenzy. My best decisions and outcomes do not come from agitation. This *isn't* when I'm on the ball. This is when I'm on the hamster wheel, pacing and spinning. And let me just say that just because you're on a roll doesn't mean you're getting somewhere.

In my own life transitions and through working with others, I know that self-possession requires focus. I work with creative individuals, meaning seekers, and people on fire with a mission. They must face the brunt of uncertainty daily. And I know that the power to help yourself feel centered, connected, and confident no matter what is one of the most important skills I can offer them. Often, it's the difference between those who can stay focused on getting through unsettling times and creating rich, authentic lives and those who can't.

It takes action to be happy, but not the kind of busy work a driven Western-values culture advances. Happiness requires the action of paying attention to your mood, your internal landscape, and your thoughts and reconnecting with your soul.

This isn't "fluff" work. It's the real work. And it can be harder than lifting a dumbbell over your head. It's the magic of *getting out of your head* and into a quiet state of strength. When you're in the throes of transition, feeling good is not a casual happenstance. It's the feat of a ninja.

Of course, I'm not talking about being unconscious or ignoring human suffering. I'm not talking about skipping out on your federal taxes or taking a break from feeding those pesky children. I'm not even saying you *shouldn't* take action. I'm talking about *also* valuing the kinds of actions that help you stay aware, awake, and in alignment with your true desires and potential.

I remember when I lived in the mountains writing my first book. I was good and depressed, like every other stereotypical writer on the planet. I was ambling around the house, smothered by a matted gray woolen blanket, only I didn't really have a blanket on me; the self-inflicted shame just felt that way.

I was in a mood, heading down the psychic sewer. I had decided that I was a terrible writer and an incompetent entrepreneur and quite possibly a human being who was just damaged, in some squirrely, deep-down way. I could never wrangle the purple octopus of all my creative ideas into a coherent book or seminar. I'd never "get there"; I wouldn't make a living. I'd definitely screwed up my whole life by leaving the established status of working for a big law firm. My God, I had to eat everything in the refrigerator just to stay sane.

But that day something uncanny happened. I did a meditation or journaling exercise or both and I changed the direction of my thoughts. Like a school of fish, they started swimming in a positive direction. I started feeling hope, maybe even confidence. I held my own brave little hand in the middle of the day. I broke through the gate and got to see the wizard.

I felt amazed. *I had changed my own mood.* I hadn't paid a life coach. Or listened to a podcast. Or chanted with a guru. I hadn't swallowed some white capsule. I had control over my own mind. This was fantastic news. *Because I damn well knew my mind controlled my life.*

To take yourself from misery to hope is a miracle. It's like parting the Red Sea, only without the audience and publicity. It was like finding a Diet Pepsi machine or a Whole Foods in the middle of the desert. I know you know what I mean. One minute I was aching. And in the next, I'd brought peace to the Middle East just by humming inside myself, "we can work it out," until a million voices sang along and drowned out all the ache and strife. I wasn't just a pair of empty boots after all. I was Madame Curie, Nelson Mandela, and Lady Gaga all rolled into one superhero in the middle of a Wednesday afternoon. My small worn flowered couch shimmered like a holy man's cave in the mountains of Nepal.

But later that day, a quasi-friend called. Susan was rapid-firing through tasks at her sleek office downtown. She was Athena, Conqueror of the To-Do List. "Wha'd ya do today?" she chirped, computer keys clicking in the background. Believe me, I understood the menu of acceptable answers. Long gap. "I changed a thought," I wanted to croak and glow with reverence. *I changed the neuroplasticity of my brain and opened to a whole new trajectory for my life.*

"Nothing," I demurred instead. Because I had done nothing *she* would recognize.

She was looking to hear that I'd cleaned the pantry and hauled out three full Hefty bags of trash or donations. Or attended a webinar on logo design. Or maybe made a cool mil by day-trading futures while getting an acrylic pedicure. To her and most everyone else in my life at that time, it was far more productive to organize your shoe closet than to organize your mind. She wanted nuts and bolts. I had stardust on my tongue. Which meant I said nothing and felt dull.

There's a societal bias toward doing. It's the cult of action. But don't be fooled. You will not win yourself certainty by ignoring the status of your own mind.

I see this with many of my coaching clients. They are embarking on a business or life transition and they're scared and quaking with newness. So, they do a thousand things, anything to avoid the terror of inaction.

Yet you can never take enough actions to feel safe. Because it's not actions that make you feel safe or get results. It's mental focus.

It's learning how to use your mind-set appropriately. Otherwise you're the sock puppet of fear. You're a chicken without a head. You might be running in all kinds of directions, but it doesn't mean you're moving toward anything you truly want.

> " You can never take enough actions to feel safe. Because it's not actions that make you feel safe or get results. It's mental focus. "

We live in a culture of staying busy. But an inspired life will ask you to look at what part of you is coming up with the tasks. Is it your strength that motivates you? Or is it your desperation? Where you come from is where you'll go.

It takes daring work to be in your strength. It takes focus to be happy. I'm here to tell you, go ahead and take that "Awaken Your Inner Druid" workshop if it speaks to you, even if you dare not speak it aloud. Take a Centering Prayer or Tibetan meditation retreat. Chant along at a kirtan or sign up for the mindfulness program run by your favorite therapist.

There may be grief you need to feel. Beliefs you need to unpack. Or parts of your life where you are needing to sort things out and heal, which is an inward "doing." Feast on books that feed you. Journal. Pray. Get to know yourself from the inside out. Devote yourself to the intangible power you possess. It will yield you tangible results. Your mind-set is your most powerful resource. No plan or eight-step strategy to success will offer you as much peace as knowing how to center yourself.

You are not empty-headed, because you are dedicating yourself to being levelheaded when there are alligators circling your feet. The masses will tell you to get out of danger, that only an idiot remains still in dangerous waters. But you know that being in the middle of a change is where you need to be. For you, the shore may be a more dangerous place, because it could be a step backward. You are not oblivious. You are awake.

Dealing with your feelings is not a popular choice. Likewise, ig-noring statistics and choosing to believe in what you cannot see is also shunned. So, if you're choosing to be happy or believing in your dreams, you may be labeled "unrealistic." Yet everyone who has ever moved beyond the status quo, the ordinary bulk regimen of the ev-eryday "real world," was once considered unrealistic. Those who make a difference will always be different. It takes work to safeguard your difference. It demands courage, focus, and mind-set.

It takes little faith or bravery to clean the kitchen, serve on the board, or go back to school when that's what others expect of you. The rat will always push the lever where the pellets are. But it takes human consciousness and choice, the strength of a warrior or lioness to stay true to yourself, to walk in the park in the middle of the work-day, let go of an image that brought you security, launch a venture that mocks mediocrity, or tell your lover what you really want. There are no guaranteed pellets in courageous actions. Yet some of us have learned that pellets leave us hungry. We hunt for more.

The times are changing. The concept of an inner journey has moved beyond the fringes into more public awareness. Neuroscien-tists are studying the irrefutable benefits of peace of mind. And quan-tum physicists are diving into the dynamics of thoughts and energy. Peace of mind has infiltrated the mainstream conversation.

I've seen the *New York Times* run articles on mantras and mind-fulness at work. More CEOs are bringing meditation and yoga into the workplace because mindfulness measurably increases produc-tivity, employee retention, employee health, and profitability. And Arianna Huffington, cofounder of the *Huffington Post*, has coined the term "the third metric," a way of redefining success. She says that typically success has been defined by money and power, but now we need to discern and acknowledge the feeling of well-being, and an individual's access to intuition and love.

Mark my words. Someday, someday soon, you will tell most any-one, "I changed a thought," and he or she will bow down before you like the hero you are.

TURNING POINTS:
Happiness Is an Action

My best decisions and outcomes do not come from agitation. . . . This is when I'm on the hamster wheel. . . . Just because you're on a roll doesn't mean you're getting somewhere.

When you're in the throes of transition, feeling good is not a casual happenstance. It's the feat of a ninja.

You can never take enough actions to feel safe. Because it's not actions that make you feel safe or get results. It's mental focus.

What part of you is coming up with the tasks? Is it your strength that motivates you? Or is it your desperation? Where you come from is where you'll go.

Devote yourself to the intangible power you possess. It will yield you tangible results. Your mind-set is your most powerful resource.

Those who make a difference will always be different. It takes work to safeguard your difference.

It takes little faith or bravery to clean the kitchen, serve on the board, or go back to school when that's what others expect of you. The rat will always push the lever where the pellets are.

It takes . . . the strength of a warrior or lioness to stay true to yourself, to walk in the park in the middle of the workday, let go of an image that brought you security, launch a venture that mocks mediocrity, or tell your lover what you really want.

HOW TO BE UNABASHEDLY ALIVE

Sometimes, I sat in my sunny doorway from sunrise till noon,
rapt in a reverie, amidst the pines and hickories and sumacs,
in undisturbed solitude and stillness.

HENRY DAVID THOREAU

There are "opportunity costs" for getting things done. Are you
rushing to an appointment and missing one your instinctive self
has in mind for you? What if you don't take time to unwind and
process the argument with your daughter? Or write that song
that came to you in a dream? Presence is a time-saver and a
lifesaver.

TAMA KIEVES (journal entry)

The ego, or the self you imagine yourself to be, has a thousand
goals. But are they really yours? And are they your sweetest goals
right now?

A whirlwind Western world worships productivity, as defined
by how much we "get done." Still, I invite you to consider *becoming*
undone, connecting with the fullness and presence of your inner being in the present moment. It's a shift from unconsciousness to rap-
ture. No one can do this for you. And yes, it's disconcerting at first.
But trust me on this: Learning how to be unabashedly alive is a very
productive goal.

I want you to be free. Freedom doesn't mean you'll run away to
Istanbul or forget to pay the rent. It's a remembrance, not a forgetting. It's remembering who you *really are*. It's too easy to lose sight of
your nimble, guided self in the everyday tasks and habits, not to
mention the self-talk that has you feeling crippled, haunted, and

behind, even before you've made your morning coffee and remembered your name.

It's preconceived ideas about what we "should" be doing that prevent us from listening to our hearts in any given moment. But you can stop this "virtue" in its tracks. Set down the laundry or report, even for a minute. Become vulnerable and *present* to your present life. Your deep self wants to talk to you. Do you want to listen?

A *Course in Miracles* teaches, "The miracle comes quietly into the mind that stops an instant and is still." You might think you're just being "responsible." But you have a higher responsibility to listen to the part of you that honors the higher promise of your life. Why would any of us choose a routine instead of a miracle?

We don't always realize what we're *not getting done* by "getting things done."

One day in the middle of a busy month of a busy year of a busy lifetime, I decided to give myself a mini-retreat on the plump sofa of my back porch. Actually, I'd hurt my neck. And the pain was distracting me from answering e-mails. It was bad. You could say it was a pain in the neck. So, I resolved to put aside my tasks and spend the day listening to my body and myself.

Immediately I heard a perky voice within dictating glamorous, *acceptable* ways to relax. *Maybe you should go to a spa and get a hot stone massage. Hey, you could read that new book about scaling your business. Since you're not on the computer today, why not organize your meditation space?* I was horrified to see that even in the domain of my "time off," I had a brisk checklist waiting to devour me.

I spent the day in my favorite ratty T-shirt instead, resting on my couch, "doing nothing," meditating by not even trying to meditate, just being and receiving cues from a tired and pained body. It was one of the most productive days I'd had in a while.

I didn't meet with friends. And I didn't watch television or listen to an audiobook. I met the silence, big as a bear. It held me. I couldn't remember the last time I'd given myself space to just be. I allowed myself to be bored and awkward at times, like I was on a *really* bad date, the kind where you're maybe hoping for a tiny stroke so you can leave—but I wasn't bailing and calling a cab. I remembered again, in tiny bursts of raw self-acceptance, this is what my soul *needs* to experience, and it's not on any to-do list.

I *always* hunger for real life, not the mass-marketed "get real" life. I want to see the dawn caress the Taj Mahal and *feel* the spices, centuries, and love in the air. I want to smell the wild honeysuckles taking over the wooden fence, knowing I only have a bucket full of summers here on earth. I want to taste my life, seize moments that will live inside me forever. I am a jewel thief greedy to collect rare and shiny moments. And for me, it's not just about going to interesting places. It's about cultivating a sense of presence, becoming aware of the infinite in a finite moment. I don't just crave a change in scenery. I crave a shift in consciousness.

In rebellious chunky penmanship, I wrote in my journal, "I am not going to answer e-mails today or get back to clients. I want to know, witness, and love myself. This day of self-care will get more 'done' in my life. Because I may not know everything I want to experience in this one mad life of mine, or what I want to be remembered for, but I do know it isn't this: *She always got back to people within a day. And with such excellent grammar!*" Yes, I know. I'm no Malcolm X when it comes to insurrection. Still, this was a Rosa Parks, I'm-sitting-down-and-you-can't-stop-me moment for a responsibility freak like me.

I was experimenting with taking a spontaneous day off: off-line, off-limits, and off my own back.

That day, "doing nothing," I ended up journaling, resting the cells in my body, forgiving myself for forgetting myself in any way, cradling a part of me who'd suffered disappointments, and not pushing myself to do or be anything.

And when I least expected it, another part of my mind woke up. It felt like the stone had been rolled away from the gate. In the quiet, self-love and creative ideas deluged my mind. I couldn't write fast enough. I chased the bursts of illumination and ideas that flew at me like a pack of butterflies, and forced my "practical" mind to take a backseat.

Then, later, I even wrote the newsletter for my business, the main task that I'd set aside that day. It was suddenly easy. Everything felt like mind candy. Work that would have taken me hours took minutes and came out better. No, I was not on drugs. But the lack of self-judgment is intoxicating. And if I could bottle this mystical superpower I would.

I felt like Thoreau, who wrote in *Walden* about his time just being still and in reverie: "I grew in those seasons like corn in the night, and they were far better than any work of the hands would have been. They were not time subtracted from my life, but so much over and above my usual allowance."

Checklists, shmecklists. *It's so much more productive to be inspired.*

Believe me, I know about inspired space. I work in this realm with others.

I've been leading retreats in nurturing, scenic places for years. I am the one who encourages others to let go and trust the process. Participants arrive tired, excited, and some slightly frightened with faces white as goat cheese. I sometimes wonder if they think I am going to make them call their bosses, quit their jobs, and run away with me to follow their bliss—or maybe join a new age circus. Some may be secretly hoping I will.

Naturally the bright-eyed overachievers want to get their money's worth. They are hoping that in the opening circle I can start giving them exercises to figure out their lives *now*, before they unpack their luggage. I feel the need pulsing within them to attack the problem at hand. I tell them we are going to spend the weekend relaxing, undoing conditioning, and receiving what is already within. I am setting them up to be guided.

Some look at me with relief in their eyes, as though someone has finally invited them to stop running a decade-long marathon and sit down in the shade, wipe their sweat, and sip lemonade. Others look at me like this better not be a trick. *I better get an answer by Sunday*, their body postures threaten. And I want to assure them that they will be answered by Sunday. They will receive the juice, resurrection, and clarity they do not even know they crave.

I'm not being arrogant. It's just that through the years, I have come to trust the wild efficiency of the Universe, which uses these intentional "time out of time" occasions like one of those Japanese chefs at a Benihana restaurant, tossing knives into the air, carving carrots into roses, then handing you sustenance in the wink of an eye. It's like Anne Lamott writes: "Even a moment's transcendence changes us."

I know that emotional safety and relaxation are the most critical ingredients in creating inspired time.

As a facilitator, I am trying to sweet-talk my students into releasing expectations of themselves. I am escorting and training them into radical receptivity. "The more you relax, the more you will receive from this time," I say. I'm not interested in lecturing their know-it-all brains or their ordinary identities —the surface level of who they really are. I am beckoning the extraordinary within them. I don't want to ask the most important questions to the least literate part of their brains. I don't want to engage their tired, angry, habitual selves in a dialogue about joy, meaning, and desire.

I need the daily self to take a nap. I want this self to bathe, to scrub off the layers and veneers of disillusionment, resentment, and toxic self-talk. I am eager to engage their Inspired Self, the one with an unlimited love that lights up memories, inclinations, and clarity. I know that if I can engage this self for even an instant, the real work is done.

Inspired time is indescribable. It's like skipping steps in a long, cumbersome equation. It's as though you're suddenly on the moon, where concrete boots and money issues are weightless; it's easy to move or to change anything. Believe me, it's constructive.

And it's a magic I want to experience as much as possible in my daily life. This is what it means to be productive to me.

Just like my students and everyone else, I have had to understand the rites of the realm.

When I want unpredictable and unprecedented healing and abundance in my life, I know I need to feed myself time and space. Orchids don't grow in sand. My revelations require the loamy earth of love, space, time, meandering, and permission. So do yours. Some of you might think taking time for yourself is impossible, with kids, jobs, deadlines, making payroll, and dependent relatives. It's a tough choice to make. Yet an exquisite life requires exquisite choices.

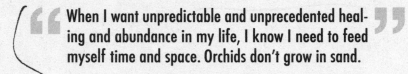

When I want unpredictable and unprecedented healing and abundance in my life, I know I need to feed myself time and space. Orchids don't grow in sand.

I get it. You have so much to do. But that doing may be about sustaining a life that may not be sustaining you. Or you might want to rush the process, take an express train to your expressed life. My clients often want to just "get there" as they traverse the middle of a life that is changing. They do not easily trust the idea of "meandering," allowing, or resting, though they are gung ho for receiving. "It takes an intermission to find a mission," I say, then wait for the groan. I also know I'll hear a sparkling voice when we next speak.

Take some time to consciously do less. Rest. Be. Get yourself to a lake, a park, a beach, some nature if you can. But a flowered couch will do. Let go of self-judgment as it arises. See what wants to happen. You may want to paint or walk or write or cry. Be still. Be moved. Be forgiving. Be curious. Breathe. This is important work to do. It's the most important work you can do.

TURNING POINTS:
How to Be Unabashedly Alive

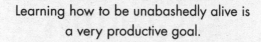

Learning how to be unabashedly alive is
a very productive goal.

Freedom doesn't mean you'll run away to Istanbul or forget
to pay the rent. It's a remembrance, not a forgetting. It's
remembering who you *really are*.

It's preconceived ideas about what we "should" be
doing that prevent us from listening to our hearts in any
given moment.

You might think you're just being "responsible." But you
have a higher responsibility to listen to the part of you that
honors the higher promise of your life. Why would any of us
choose a routine instead of a miracle?

We don't always realize what we're *not getting done* by
"getting things done."

When I want unpredictable and unprecedented healing
and abundance in my life, I know I need to feed myself time
and space. Orchids don't grow in sand.

An exquisite life requires exquisite choices.

You have so much to do. But that doing may be about
sustaining a life that may not be sustaining you.

DROP YOUR DEMANDS, RAISE YOUR POSSIBILITIES

Being overwhelmed does not come from too much to do. It comes from lack of clarity. When you're clear, you know you don't need to do everything. You just have to do the right thing. The right thing is always the one step that you feel guided to do right now.
TAMA KIEVES (from *A Year Without Fear*)

I am working on accepting myself where I am. It's okay to be someone who is, at times, on fire in her life, and someone who is frightened, paralyzed, and feels broken. I am all of it. And in the end, if the gurus and philosophers are right, I'm sure I'm none of it. But either way, I'm going with it.
TAMA KIEVES (journal entry)

I know I'm not alone in feeling overwhelmed at times. While the White Queen in *Alice's Adventures in Wonderland* says, "Why sometimes I've believed at least six impossible things before breakfast," I believe we're expected to *do* at least ten of them now. We're pelted by the Internet and media. Forget about raising a healthy child. That kid needs to be on *America's Got Talent*. Be tweeting by the time she's seven. Getting ready to leave a legacy.

And when we're in transition, that squishy, vulnerable place, that's when expectations swarm like killer bees. The more disempowered we feel, the more desperately we hope to shoot out of the gate like a prodigy or a silver bullet.

Yet these high expectations do not come from abundance. They come from scarcity.

Expectations of scarcity assume that we are not enough the way we are. And that when we achieve more, our value will increase. It's a setup for failure. Because an inspired life does not come from self-improvement. It comes from self-acceptance and expansion.

Mind you, I want you to feel like you're moving forward. But I want you to achieve your true goals, your reason-to-be-here goals. With all due respect to your intellect—heart-stopping desires do not come from the head. Your most essential direction comes from love.

I've had to continually learn how to let go of my ego's plans so that my soul's plans could make their way through to the light. Sometimes everything I think I need to do actually keeps me from the *only* thing I need to do. The only thing I need to do is to diminish fear. Because when I let go of fear, I feel my light. And when I'm in my light, I know what to do in each moment.

It doesn't matter what the overwhelm is about. Really, *a sense of overwhelm is a dire lack of self-love*. I know this turf. I have a graduate degree in overwhelm from Punish Yourself University.

I felt ridiculously tense before launching my second book, *Inspired & Unstoppable: Wildly Succeeding in Your Life's Work!*, into the world. I wanted to "make up" for everything I "didn't do right" in the past, which is the cardinal ingredient in a recipe for disappointment. My mind teemed with tasks. One night, I noticed that even in my yoga class I'm churning with fear.

The teacher guides us into downward dog, and a pack of stray mangy dogs begin yipping in my head. "You're never going to get everything done," they bark. "Here you are stretching, when you should be writing stellar convert-to-cash website copy. You're going to fail big time now." Then Yoga Dog interrupts, "Shhh, you're not in the present moment," and I swear Achievement Dog bites his ear and goes for blood. Namaste, it's a party to be me.

Later that night I journal about the things I'm thinking I need to do. It is even more sickening in print. I have a new website to design, workshops and online products to create, a book launch campaign, tour and media appearances to schedule, or more accurately, to beg from the powers that be. Each of these projects triggers my sense of inadequacy. There are learning curves I will never master in this time frame, even if I had the desire, which I don't, which makes me feel like the big fat loser lunkhead my ego tells me I am. Do more, more, *more*, screams my ego, while also making it abominably clear that even if I pull it off, it will still never be enough.

I feel so behind. I always feel so behind the smart, together, on-top-of-it-all crowd. Basically, I feel like I'm being asked to run up a spiral staircase that leads to an ocean to swim across like I'm in an Ironman competition or something—just to get to the dusty starting point, where everyone else took off so long ago, their grandkids are starting with me. It's that old Pink Floyd song where I missed the starting gun. Plus, I'm old and know the old Pink Floyd song.

I begin to cry and sort of pray or intend to listen to a higher voice within me, while melting down. Mucus is the prelude to all my miracles, by the way. And when I finally feel my feelings, just cry with helplessness, my inner voice speaks with authority and self-advocacy: "Lower your expectations." Whoa, this is not my ordinary self-talk. This is a life raft. I am a bit stunned, suspicious, and radically comforted.

Suddenly I remember a therapist from many years ago telling me, "I want you to think about doing less." Her eyes were wise and bright like a chess master's. "If the goals are less threatening, you will show up with more joy." What a concept. *Showing up with enjoyment.* "You don't want to work from effort," she said. "You want to work from effortlessness." She assured the achievement freak within me that I'd accomplish more in the long run. The woman was smart; she knew who buttered her rolls.

I can only imagine the eye roll I gave her at the time. Yet over time, I grew. The lack of pressure allowed me to breathe and embrace my own rhythm. It was as though sunlight fed my veins. And working from alignment, I experienced real progress. I didn't achieve my urgent, flustered, maniacal goals, most of which had come from a fearful mind generating an unrealistic wish list. But I moved forward elegantly. I also discovered this lesson: Simplicity encourages mastery.

I remembered this experience as I approached creating a new website for my book and more. "Lower your expectations," reiterates the sane voice in my mind. "Design the website adequately. Pick one section and do what you can. You can improve it later. Choose a simple target. Don't try to do everything at once, or maybe ever. Give yourself time to grow or express in stages. Drop your demands. Raise your possibilities."

> **Sometimes everything I think I need to do actually keeps me from the *only* thing I need to do. The only thing I need to do is to diminish fear.**

That night I journaled: "Fear will never take you where you want to go. You cannot be afraid and soar at the same time. You will not hear the bell ring inside of you, the place where you are whole and all is well and everything comes together—the only success there is on this planet. You will not remember your true name when you're anxious. And if you don't remember who you *really* are, you cannot express your full potential. Flying is the path of undoing fear, not increasing it."

I have to say, this wisdom was better than a thousand downward-facing dogs.

I want you to give yourself permission to not catch up, to not blog, to not eat vegan this week, to not please your boss, your needy sister, or your narcissistic father. Or maybe to acquiesce to a humbled, tired body. What would be unthinkable to you? Unforgivable? This is the part of you that requires acceptance and love. Yes, I get it. You'd rather bake cookies for Hitler. *But what you cannot allow yourself to be holds you back from being everything you want to be.*

This is what the Buddhists call attachment, a form or condition you think you need more than freedom. I'm not asking you to give up what's important to you. I'm asking you to give up the idea that you have to do these things to be okay. I'm talking about moving forward toward your desires, while feeling good enough no matter what. Otherwise, your expectations aren't just "standards"; they're conditions on self-love. And when you limit your self-love, you limit your spirit's oxygen.

Give yourself permission to be—acceptable, blessed, and unstoppable—no matter what. Unconditional acceptance pulls the plug on anxiety. This is better than an elephant tranquilizer, friends. It is this acceptance that allows you to breathe when everything is changing or nothing is changing and it seems you lack control. It stops you from fighting yourself and draining the life out of your life. This acceptance is *divine*, and emboldens you to show up as much as you can, instead of focusing on what you haven't done.

The world is asking you to run faster. I'm asking you to breathe slower. I'm asking you to be truly great, by allowing yourself to do less than what you think you have to do to be great. Allow yourself to be led instead of threatened. This is the beginning of effortless accomplishment.

I see this wildness in my clients, a desperation to get things done. I know their healing comes from undoing the old programming that has them wanting certain results at the cost of attaining other results, inner shifts that may be far more important. Of course, I'd never ask you to let go of your dreams. I am asking you to let go of your idea of how you need to get there.

Life is more expansive than your constructs or timelines. Soften your expectations, and allow the freed-up energy to surprise you with support. Don't ever give up desires; give up your scarcity thinking and need. Really, I am asking you to *give up reasons for withholding love from yourself.*

Nothing you think you need will give you the freedom you already have within you but deny yourself. Be gentle with yourself. Start anywhere. Do what you can and allow this to be enough. Follow what makes your heart feel full, not what alleviates a sense of guilt—because guilt does not belong in the equation of radical freedom. You are never failing by being who and where you are.

If you think you're behind the eight ball, you'll always be behind the eight ball. Yet there is no eight ball. There is no behind. There is now. Do you want to go forward? Take the most easeful action possible. This is not complacency. This is agency.

I've always been afraid of "settling" by being less than I could be—but now I think it is a form of settling to succeed, if you do it in ways that exhaust or emotionally bankrupt you. I'm finally realizing this, late in the game: Striving *is* settling, at least for people like me. Being driven by unconscious ambition isn't, as I've imagined before, being someone who refuses to accept less. It's being someone who *always* accepts less—because it's aiming for the achievement of my smaller self, which is far less than I am meant to be.

I am meant to succeed through wild love, not fear. I am meant to take inspired direction, not control every detail and pound out results. I am meant to fly, be lifted by something dynamic and true, not to crawl and fight for every crumb. I don't want to succeed because I'm a superior monkey who can jump through more hoops while still living in chains. I want to succeed because I'm free of chains, free of guilt, and trusting in a higher power, the power we all have when we're listening.

I am no longer interested in living a hollow life, even if it looks good on paper or to others. It is unholy to ask myself to be other than what I am. I choose love instead of force. It's not about getting everything "right." It's about knowing everything is already all right and choosing to act from there.

At last, there's no guillotine hanging over my head. I'm just following bread crumbs and rose petals.

TURNING POINTS:
Drop Your Demands, Raise Your Possibilities

I've had to continually learn how to let go of my ego's plans so that my soul's plans could make their way through to the light.

Sometimes everything I think I need to do actually keeps me from the *only* thing I need to do. The only thing I need to do is to diminish fear.

If the goals are less threatening, you will show up with more joy.

Flying is the path of undoing fear, not increasing it.

What you cannot allow yourself to be holds you back from being everything you want to be.

Nothing you think you need will give you the freedom you already have within you but deny yourself.

Do what you can and allow this to be enough. Follow what makes your heart feel full, not what alleviates a sense of guilt—because guilt does not belong in the equation of radical freedom.

I am meant to succeed through wild love, not fear. I am meant to take inspired direction, not control every detail and pound out results.

MOVE ON WITH LOVE

For many years, I wanted to flee across the border to the New Year as fast as possible. I wanted to slam doors, burn my past. But this is what I know now: I want to enter miraculous time. There is no "new" year without a blessed year before it. How you end one year is how you begin the next.

TAMA KIEVES (journal entry)

Am I looking to create a future that makes up for the lack I've experienced in my past? Maybe I need to heal with my past, so that I'm not seeing a lack. Since I build and attract my future based on what I believe about my past, I'm willing to see a better past.

TAMA KIEVES (journal entry)

Here's the thing about the in-between times. You may want to get going as soon as possible. You're burning a hole in the carpet. But we who are living inspired lives move in conscious, alternative ways. If you really want to spring into action like never before, then do what you've never done before: Take the time to heal. Healing is an action, of epic proportion.

Most of my clients have come to me because they are in transition. Ending a job. Dissolving a marriage. Moving from one phase of their business to the next. I talk to them about the miracle of beginning again, giving ourselves the chance to start over at any time, a million times, because our past does not have to determine our future. Everybody loves this part.

Most want to hop onto the express bus right now, hightail it into the bright lights, big city—perfect new life. They are *so ready*, they say. Translation: *I want to get the hell out of town.* Not so fast, I think. I want you to turn around and appreciate or bless your past. I don't want you to abandon your own life in any way.

It's a law of grace. You won't *really* move on until you move on with love.

Ann was leaving her medical practice. She'd put years into building a community and private practice as an ob-gyn specialist. But she was tired. Cooked. Done. She wanted a new life—within fifteen seconds, not in two months. "I just don't want to be there anymore. Of course, I am going to be responsible, but really, Tama, I just want to run out that door and not look back."

It's hard to have to wait before you move forward. I call this the "ghost phase" of transition. You have already died to this part of your life. Yet you are still in the building. Your spirit has left. You stepped off the cliff. The new life calls you ten times a day, like a seductive new lover with airline tickets to the Greek isle of Santorini, urging you to grab your bags. But you can't get excited or even address your heart palpitations. You must face the projects or people that make you tired, those you are leaving.

"I know part of you feels a million miles away from this office," I said. She groaned in recognition. "But since you're going to be there," I continued, "let's decide how. Don't numb out or count the seconds. I want you to love your way out the door." Thank goodness she was Canadian. She didn't tell me where I could put my love. "Take some of your staff or colleagues out to lunch. Tell them what they've meant to you. Savor a memory. Make a new memory. This is your life. *You will never be here again.* What do you want to do here, while you're still here? How do you want to remember this time?"

> **❝ It's a law of grace. You won't *really* move on until you move on with love. ❞**

Think about the situation you may be putting behind you. How do you want to remember it? Memory is like papier-mâché. You can mold it into a daffodil or a dragon. You can make a better past at any time. A memory is a choice. When Ann did leave her medical practice, she left feeling full of love for her staff, her patients, and herself.

I know you want to step into a life of goodness. I want you to step into a life of goodness *from* a life of goodness. No matter what has or hasn't happened, you can choose to love your past. Now, since I'm going to guess that, like myself, you're not some blissed-out saint, it doesn't mean you have to love the part where your husband cheated on you with the babysitter or the business deal fell through. I suspect we'll all get there. But right now it's okay to feel raw or numb.

Still, there are moments of grace you can remember. Don't lose them. Choose how you tell your story. You are always telling the story. Who are you becoming? What desire, awareness, or power are you awakening through moving through this situation in your life? Make it up.

That story will be a part of your new story.

Collect Only the Good

Okay, it's moving day, darling. Let's do a little conscious creation together. If you were taking a carton into a new time in your life, what would you put in it? What experiences do you want to carry forward? Which scenes do you wish to remember? Are there moments that you would like to experience more of? I think of these as premium seeds to plant in the new life.

It's important to pay attention to the good that is always with us, even in the crazy-town times that drove us to psychic hotlines, dive bars, hair loss and facial tics, or even to writing our own self-help books. Study what worked. These are your jewels. Don't abandon or blacken them because of things you believe didn't work.

Remember to appreciate yourself too. Your courage, or a moment where you grew.

Remember people or resources that showed up, even for an instant. Pack up your box.

You are going to leave everything else behind.

When you leave something behind, treat it like a faded T-shirt. Give it to Goodwill with goodwill. You don't have to blow up the village; this isn't reality TV. Don't obsess over what others did wrong. You're not condoning behavior. You're just not allowing that which was less than loving to influence the quality of the life you're about to create. Leo Buscaglia, the phenomenal motivational speaker known as "Dr. Love," said it like this: "Don't brood. Get on with living and loving. You don't have forever."

If You Don't Forgive, You'll Relive

Where do you feel ashamed or frustrated? Is there something you want to see yourself do differently in this next phase of your life, or right now? I have a friend, Susan, who periodically looks at her "broken promises" to herself and others. One day I talked to her and her voice sounded like music. "I just spent the day catching up on communications or items I owed people," she said. "I feel somewhere near glorious. I'm not leaking energy anymore, feeling crappy about myself. I can concentrate on other goals now."

As you move into a new realm, you will bring forward what you *can't* leave behind. This pain follows you like a stray black dog. It hunts you down and plays the same song over and over on the jukebox, the song you hate. Then some complete yahoo who doesn't even speak the language sidles up to you—and sings that song. You have a problem.

Certain situations, stories we've told ourselves, or relationships from our past demand our understanding and release. Lessons come around until they are healed. They may require tears. Or a truth to be spoken. Or a new realization. Pain won't let us go until we let it go.

Are you free to have a new life? You can't just paint over a crack in the wall. The crack will still show through any color, even Moving-On-in-a-Freaking-Hurry Red or Happy-Dappy Pink. Old beliefs will spoil fresh starts. I hope you set yourself free. Forgiveness is the miracle agent that can release you from every painful story.

Remember, you are not upset about what you failed to experience or do in the past. *You are upset about what you are making that experience mean about your life right now.* You could choose another perspective. You could choose to remember that you are infinitely loved by a complex and purposeful Higher Intelligence, and that what seems like chaos to you is an order so lush with love, your finite mind can't possibly place it in a familiar box.

You have the chance to make it right. You always have the chance to move forward with a new tool, awareness, intention, or resolve in your heart. You can take something "broken" and let it inspire you with new purpose; you can pull a Gandhi and "be the change you wish to see in the world." Only you can wipe the slate clean. You can start by doing any small thing. And anything that moves you into the present is no small thing.

There Are No False Starts. There Are Only False Conclusions.

As you move forward, maybe you feel nervous about trusting yourself, because you've begun strong before, singing songs from the top of the mountain, but then you trailed off and dropped your intention. Maybe you suffered from self-forgetfulness or distraction. You talked yourself out of things. You judged your abilities or how long things seemed to take. You lost faith in your chirping heart. Then you beat yourself up.

Let me whisper something else into your ear: Every time you've ever believed in yourself, you put gold in your veins. The gold is still there. Gold is always gold, even when you forget. You can do it differently this time. Or get closer to doing it differently, until you do.

You're not hopeless until you give up hope.

I know that being a writer, I have had a lot of false starts. I began writing articles and short stories that withered on the vine. Or they disappeared between the pages of a notebook that was stolen by aliens who have now made hit movies on their planets. The writing that got away.

Still, I'm always glad I began, even if I didn't finish. I experienced bursts of transport in the moment. And more important, when I wrote days, months, or years later, my work coalesced. It was all those "false starts," all those episodes of chasing ideas, even with torn butterfly nets, that got me across the finish line. It wasn't as if I sat down one day and built a castle from a vacuum. I used every twig or stone I'd picked up along the way. Everything had helped me.

The fruitful times arise from "useless" ones. There are no false starts. There are only false conclusions.

So right now, begin again. Pick up the magic baton. Decide to lose weight, become a Realtor, write your novel, take some time for solitude, have that spooky honest conversation with your spouse, or dare to fall in love—yes, even at *your* age.

Get real about what you want. These are your years. Dare again. Maybe you'll hit it out of the ballpark right away. Maybe it will take you a thousand swings. It doesn't matter. Take your swing. It's what you're here for.

How You End Is How You Begin

I'm big on training my brain and writing consciously encouraging messages to myself. I've found that if I feed my brain with affirmative perspectives, I leave fewer neuropathways available to my inner critic. It's kind of like feed a fever, starve a fault-finding maniac. Here's an Ending Invocation I wrote to help me honor myself and move on from something that wasn't working. You might find it helpful.

> I bless this segment of my life. I take in all it offered me and all that I received. I thank myself for everything I tried, even if I didn't think it worked. I thank myself for the times I believed in myself, even if I didn't sustain it. I thank myself for the times I know I got it right. That stays with me forever. I thank myself for the times I stretched—and for the times I invested in my truth or hunted for it. I thank myself for it all and for all the good that is yet to be revealed from this time.

You can hit your highest note in this lifetime. But it's not as easy to go into a life of joy if you're still angry or berating yourself. It's just easier to hit a high note from a high note.

Whatever you do, and however you do it, consciously move on with forgiveness, acceptance, and love, as much of it as you can muster. Because how you end one chapter—or one moment—of your life is how you begin the next.

TURNING POINTS:
Move On with Love

If you really want to spring into action like never before,
then do what you've never done before:
Take the time to heal.

Turn around and appreciate or bless your past. I don't want you to abandon your own life in any way.

It's a law of grace. You won't *really* move on until you move on with love.

Memory is like papier-mâché. You can mold it into a daffodil or a dragon. You can make a better past at any time.

Remember, you are not upset about what you failed to experience or do in the past. *You are upset about what you are making that experience mean about your life right now.*

It was all those "false starts," all those episodes of chasing ideas, even with torn butterfly nets, that got me across the finish line. It wasn't as if I sat down one day and built a castle from a vacuum.

There are no false starts. There are only false conclusions.

It's not as easy to go into a life of joy if you're still angry or berating yourself. It's just easier to hit a high note from a high note.

Do Try This at Home: Jump-starts, Inquiries & Exercises

Some of these suggestions are just right for *you*. Others, not your cup of latte, at least at *this* moment. Follow your gut. Feel free to adjust to your liking. Do what's right for you rather than what's written here.

Pick three Turning Points from this chapter. Write them out for yourself. Post them where you will see them. Meditate on them. Journal about them. Do a Freewriting exercise. (See page 252 for more about Freewriting.) Create a piece of art. Pay attention to your thoughts, memories, dreams, and "random" ideas and incidents. Inspired thoughts spark inspired responses. My words begin the conversation, but what do these truths unlock in you?

1. **Dedicate yourself to an inspired practice.** What will you do regularly to regulate and feed your mind-set? Pick a form of meditation, a spiritual discipline, or a journaling practice. Remember, it takes practice to stay inspired. Real life is an opponent that won't quit.

2. **Have a "being party" for one.** Create space for grace. Take a day (or a week, month, or hour) off-line, off-limits, and off your own back. Don't visit with friends, watch TV, or take care of anything. Notice what you feel or desire. *Receive* whatever wants to arise. Make the commitment to practice not judging yourself.

3. **Do one simple thing.** In Alcoholics Anonymous they have the slogan KISS: Keep It Simple, Stupid. Where do you feel overwhelmed or like things are complicated? If you could focus on only one thing, what would it feel great to do? Use this "do one simple thing" method in other areas of your life, too: relationship, health, money. Remember, simplicity encourages mastery.

4. **Accept the unacceptable.** Consider this statement and meditate or journal about what it means to you: "But what you cannot allow yourself to be holds you back from being everything you want to be." What expectations do you put upon yourself that might get in your way?

5. **Pack your carton.** If you were taking a carton into this new time, what would you put in it? What have you experienced

that you'd like more of? Which scenes do you wish to remember? What did you learn? Create a positive statement about your past.

6. **The Forgiveness Challenge:** Let's get free! Whom or what do you need to forgive? What part of yourself do you need to forgive? What beliefs or interpretations do you need to let go of? Do an Inspired Self-Dialogue (see page 248 for instructions) about something or someone you'd like to forgive. All you need is a little willingness to see things differently. Invite a Higher Love to help you. And let this take time.

Do you have a question about this chapter? I'd love to know what's on your mind! *I may just get wildly inspired and answer you immediately.* Send me your thought or question at www.TamaKieves.com/uncertainty-question, and you can also register for a **FREE** Thriving Through Uncertainty Coaching Call designed to shift your mind-set and bring you immediate clarity.

CHAPTER FIVE

IT TAKES A DIFFERENT WAY TO FIND A DIFFERENT ANSWER

YOUR ANSWER IS NEVER WHERE YOU'RE LOOKING

I'm astounded by people who want to "know" the universe when it's hard enough to find your way around Chinatown.

WOODY ALLEN

True knowledge exists in knowing that you know nothing.

SOCRATES

I want to talk to you about finding your way—your electric, true, one-of-a-kind way. *You have a way.* But first you must let go of what you think you know about your situation.

"I have no idea what to do with my life!" I cry.

"You said you like to write," the therapist says in a calm, collected, obviously goading therapist's voice.

"Okay, but what am I going to do with *my life?*" I snort back. The notion of writing is not an idea. It's an idiocy. It's an embarrassment. I've got to make a living and survive, I tell myself. That's a fact. I build a stone wall around my heart.

Back in the days when I was practicing law and craving another life, I could not even consider becoming a writer. Writing was like a haint, a bad spirit wandering in New Orleans, a ghost begging for recognition. I avoided the wayward thoughts. They haunted me anyway.

I don't know when I finally listened to something other than my loud, insistent "rational" mind. But when I did, a writing career became a lone bread crumb on a path, and then *the* path, and then a gong, a festival, a homecoming, and a stratosphere in which I could finally breathe. It changed the facts in my life.

Sometimes you can't find your answers because you don't want to find your answers.

You want different answers. Or you're positive at the get-go what will work and what won't—before you've tried a thing. But an inspired life requires us to move past our "known" identity and into our unknown potential.

This is frightening to only one part of yourself. It is a clarion call to another. If you want to know the truth, you have to be open to *all* possibilities.

Are you willing to realize your way, even if it conflicts with what you *think* the way is? Spoiler alert: Life is more mystical than the tiny brain that seeks to organize it.

I'm a story girl. So here goes. Years ago, I was teaching at Hollyhock, a retreat center on Cortes Island, in the majestic wilds of Canada. Before my program began, I headed to the beach for some solo time. Living in Denver, I do not miss any chance I get to bow before an ocean, offer my dry skin to the Great Moisture Gods, and purify my lungs in salt air.

By the way, I am terrified of getting lost. That's because I get turned around at the drop of a hat. I have no sense of direction.

Sure, I can help anyone find inner direction. But when it comes to external direction, you're better off asking a tourist than me in my own hometown. And don't get me started on tools. Basically, a compass is to me what it is to a zebra. Only the zebra has a *chance*.

I was born and raised in New York City, where pizza parlors and street signs adorn every block. And there are no less than 8 million people to ask, who all have strong opinions and who may not only walk you to your destination, but just may want to feed you pumpernickel bagels, advice, and comedy along the way. Hollyhock is remote.

I tell myself I'll only go for about fifteen minutes, being mindful of the hour, the thinning light of the disappearing day, and the nearing of the time when I need to lead my workshop. I cut down some path to the beach and am swallowed by awe. This is a beast of an ocean. This is a strip of beach at the end of the world, fierce, the kind of place where eagles fly—and they really *do* fly here. There are no knish vendors anywhere. There are no people.

I walk for just a little while before deciding to return. But walking back up the beach, I feel as though I've gone too far. I'm not seeing my exit, so to speak. My heart flutters with its peremptory "We might be lost" theme. It's not quite the *Jaws* music yet, just a tinny mosquito version. It's no big deal, I calmly tell myself, proud to be a Zen girl in the moment as I walk back the other way on the beach. I'm looking for a particular rock that was my landmark.

There are some homes I could climb to, so I remind myself I'm not entirely alone. I see some sort of path near an empty home with a worn yellow frame. That's not it, I know. I would have remembered that. I walk on. I don't see what I'm looking for anywhere. *Okay, calm down. Pace yourself.* I don't have my cell phone with me, moans the worrier. Yeah, like I would have cell reception here at the end of the world.

My workshop starts soon. The light is fading. Crazy girl is starting to rampage: You are on a remote beach in a remote place where you had to take two planes, two ferries, and a cab to get here and they actually told you *with pride* that bears have been sighted, as though this might be a good thing. So I decide, fine, let's just go to one of the houses, hang your head in crybaby I-am-not-Cheryl-Strayed-or-any-kind-of-rugged-individual-who-can-find-her-way-off-a-freaking-beach shame, and beg for help. I scrape myself up to the closest home. I knock on the door. No one comes. I pound on the door, discreetly. Okay, now wildly. All right, then. This is not an option. Now I know I *am* alone. It's getting darker.

I need to find that rock. I didn't walk *that* far. I pass the empty house with the yellowed border. Okay, I know it's not *that* way. I walk down the beach again. Adrenaline thrums through me, which might be helpful if, indeed, it turns out I do need to fight off Big-foot. *Do bears come down to the beach?* This is not a helpful line of thought. Zen girl is gone.

I am lost. I am alone out here. I am supposed to be leading a five-day retreat in less than twenty minutes on finding your way in life. The irony hits me later. *I wonder if they will find my lovely bones.* For what feels like the millionth time now, I go back by the path near that house with the yellowed border. While I know it's not the way, it's obviously a path *somewhere* out of this Canadian Bermuda Triangle, so I take it. I am desperate. I am open to anything. I don't know what else to do.

Just moments after I start walking up this path, my knees buckle with relief. I tremble with gratitude and wonder. I see my rock. I see the goddamn rock. I want to kiss it. No, I want to make out with it. It's the rock I've been looking for this whole time, my landmark, my arrow, the one that completely disappeared from sight. I understand now that I would never have seen it from the beach. I would never have found what I was looking for in the insistent way I was looking for it. I was drop-dead convinced that going up the path by the house with the yellowed border was wrong. And *I* was wrong.

That's when I got the joke. Those who are lost should not insist that they know the way.

I found my way by opening up to the unfamiliar. I found my direction by experimenting, by just going forward in a direction whether it was right or not. I needed to move forward to get more information, not just pace back and forth on the same path, doing the exact same thing I'd done before.

> *You have a way.* But first you must let go of what you think you know about your situation.

According to *A Course in Miracles,* a miracle occurs because you undo what your mind says is true. Because what you assume is true may limit what you could experience. Are you willing to see things differently? This is the question that opens the way for a miracle. It's like Buddha said, "The mind that perceives the limitation is the limitation."

For most of my young adult life, I believed it was true that I would starve if I decided to be a writer. I "knew" that creative people did not make money. I knew I had no connections in the publishing world and that it would be hard to break into a competitive industry.

But my hallelujah-take-me-home shift came by finally asking myself, What if you're wrong? What if you *could* have your dreams come true in this lifetime? *What if you're called for a reason?* What if your life is asking you to go in this direction because you are meant to experience this direction? What if you don't know everything that's possible?

I felt suffocated in my "safe" life. *I had to have another possibility.* And so, I did the "unthinkable." I became humble. I chose to believe that maybe my sense of reality wasn't everything the universe had to offer. Maybe I didn't yet know or realize my own capacity or destiny. Maybe I didn't yet appreciate the radical potential of coming from love—of higher-vibrating atoms singing at the top of their lungs, bright light and the right thoughts. Maybe I hadn't yet experienced a sense of life-altering grace because I'd never embraced what I wanted—and grace would only rush in to support the truth, not the lack of it. Maybe it was time to open myself up to new experiences I just couldn't imagine.

It's now decades later. With four published books and readers spread across the world, I'm standing in the life that my younger self "unrealistically" dreamed of, even though she had no idea how to get here. I am here now because she let go of the limits she assumed she knew to be true. She walked beyond conditioning. And that created new conditions. It seems destiny provided more options than "reality."

You may not be as stuck as you think.

I assure you, you are not limited in the ways you might believe. You are not small or even lost. You are in the place where you can decide to open your mind to new possibilities. Walk down an unfamiliar path, if even for a little way, to get perspective and insight. Wherever you are, the presence of love can find you. Your own inspired intelligence can guide you—unless you insist on being right.

Let me tell you, it can be a glorious thing to be wrong.

It's a wonderful feeling to realize that you have thought such tiny thoughts about yourself and your possibilities in this world and you are wrong, wrong, wrong and the truth of gratification still awaits you. It's a relief to discover there are solutions, strategies, and support you can't foresee—but that exist anyway.

Sometimes, only those of us who are willing to be lost can truly find our way.

TURNING POINTS:
Your Answer Is Never Where You're Looking

You have a way. But first you must let go of what you think you know about your situation.

Sometimes you can't find your answers because you don't want to find your answers.

You're positive at the get-go what will work and what won't—before you've tried a thing. But an inspired life requires us to move past our "known" identity and into our unknown potential.

If you want to know the truth, you have to be open to *all* possibilities.

Those who are lost should not insist that they know the way.

My hallelujah-take-me-home shift came by finally asking myself, What if you're wrong? What if you *could* have your dreams come true in this lifetime? *What if you're called for a reason?*

Wherever you are, the presence of love can find you. Your own inspired intelligence can guide you—unless you insist on being right.

It's a wonderful feeling to realize that you have thought such tiny thoughts about yourself and your possibilities in this world and you are wrong, wrong, wrong and the truth of gratification still awaits you.

STOP FIGURING IT OUT, LET IT OUT

Choose gloriously. Seize your wild-want, not that freeze-dried politically correct mild want . . . only the real dream has the power.

TAMA KIEVES (from *This Time I Dance!*)

Think less, feel more.

OSHO

Maybe you wonder how to discern your true-life direction, but let's be real, you can't even decide what to watch on cable TV sometimes. So, let's have a little talk.

I'm in the business of helping people get resounding answers for their most pressing decisions in life. Now, it's not uncommon for career-coaching clients to call and say something like, "I love gardening, day-trading, playing the oboe, hiking in jungles, Russian love poetry from the nineteenth century, and I'm in commercial real estate. So how do I put that all together?" Then they pause and wait for their magic answer. They will be pausing a long time, I assure you.

I will tell you what I tell them: It's tantalizing to have a thousand ideas, but really, you don't have a thousand different doorways with your name emblazoned on every one of them. The mind is a big, goofy flirt and just loves ideas and promises. But in any given moment, your powerful heart has committed itself to only one clarity, maybe two.

You don't even have a decision to make. It's already been made and encrypted within you, like the rhythm of your toes softly padding on the floorboards and the delicate, determined map of your fingerprint. It's just there, strange as the moon, and yet familiar as your breath.

And even if you do have many interests and directions, you polyamorous lover of life, you still have only one thing you wish to do right now. That's all that matters. Let's get concrete. You don't want to do *everything* in *this* moment. This moment has its own decree. And each moment will guide you to where you belong, unless, of course, you argue with yourself and resist.

Remember, the mind likes to window-shop. It fancies the life in this country charm boutique, then wants to try on the red leather boots in another. But the soul invests all of itself. It's not shopping for mild distraction. It's not enthralled by possibility. It's tracking the scent, the scent of destiny.

You can't talk yourself into sticking with one thing when it doesn't stick; a ribbon isn't Velcro. You crave transformation. You're not answered through rationalization, though you can talk about it all night. Something within you knows your power and cannot rest in less.

> **Of course you feel unclear. You're scrabbling around for clues, arrows, reasons, statistics. . . . You're looking with the mind for answers of the heart.**

So how do you get to the answers of your heart, gut, soul, or inner weather forecaster?

Well, I have to tell you a story.

Some years ago, I was presenting several workshops on a cruise ship. At the port in Cozumel, Mexico, I decided to snorkel. On the empty scenic beach, the resort blasted Mexican and country music from huge speakers just in case we Americans, straight from a noisy cruise ship, got instantaneously bored or agitated and ran riot because we were left alone with our minds for half a second without distraction. Admittedly, some of the vacationers did look bewildered with no "hoot and holler" win-big-bingo game in progress.

Of course, I, one of the peaceful, loving "gurus" on board, immediately hated the music, resenting the carnival-fake-forced-fun loudness of it all. I could feel the vinegar in my blood. I ached for quiet. Plus, I had a headache, which, let me tell you, does not play well at all with cheerful accordions and guitar twangs. Then, of course, feeling like the five-headed alien (all of them with headaches) who obviously doesn't know how to have a good time, I was also annoyed with myself for being irritated at all, *in Cozumel*, on a weekday, on a Gratitude Cruise, I kid you not.

I waded into the ocean with my snorkel gear. The surface of the water was choppy and no matter which way I turned, the color and texture looked the same. Like that churning water, my mind felt jangled and overstimulated, muttering to itself in one continuous argument, like a street person I once saw in New York City having a screaming match with someone from long ago or not of this world.

Then I dove below the surface. And my experience changed dramatically.

I entered this new dimension of extreme silence, swaying blue neon fish, lilac-colored coral, undulating movement, and expansiveness. It was magic. A whole new realm engulfed me. Any sense that it was Monday or that I was Tama disappeared. I was jolted into wonder. In this dimension, I could see things I would never have seen from the surface. Beauty erased all conditioning and inner cross talk. I felt a sense of wholeness. And of love.

It's a great metaphor for how we will discover our truth. Beyond the noise and below the surface of the choppy water, another world awaits, a living world of color, texture, and distinction. It's always there. Yet it's invisible to your ordinary surface mind. The whole ocean looks the same until you dive deeper. It's the same thing with our minds. Ideas all look the same at the level of the mind.

Of course you feel unclear. You're scrabbling around for clues, arrows, reasons, statistics, and even a brochure with a money-back guarantee. Maybe a little insurance policy attached. *Now we're talking.* But you're unclear because you're trying to find a neon blue fish on dry land, where it will never be. You're looking with the mind for answers of the heart.

Your true answers are below the surface of the choppy daily mind.

They await you in inspired time. They exist in another state of consciousness. You won't dive deeper by being reasonable. It's love that changes everything. It's play. It's peace. It's not trying to figure things out, but letting them out instead.

I have endless things to say about this, which is why I do what I do for a living. But let me offer you three nonlinear ways to beckon the deepest answers of your knowing heart.

Find Peace, Then Answers

Most of us are desperate for clarity or direction, because we believe it will bring us peace of mind. Ah, grasshopper, it works the other way around. It's peace of mind that frees answers.

Agitation stirs confusion, like a madman running through the crowd screaming, "Fire, gunmen, aliens, bad hair, the apocalypse, and people are coming over and you haven't cleaned the house!" And then asking, "Oh, what do you want to do with your life?"

Settle down. Give up your need for an answer. I know that's hard. It's the secret of life and it works. The master sage Lao-tzu says in the *Tao Te Ching,* "No desire is serenity. And the world settles of itself." I take that to mean we stop trying, grasping, and climbing the walls. And then the big-sky Buddha mind envelops us or we slip into surrender, the feeling of inner quiet that sometimes comes after a long hike or good cry. From this ground of being, we don't require answers to feel okay. And with this self-love and acceptance, we can do anything. That's when we start to know what we really want to do.

Where do you find stillness? Or feel your most intimate feelings? Is it in a run along the river bank, on a blue meditation cushion, journaling, or talking to a friend or mentor? Look to connect with your spirit more than you look for answers. Peace is the gateway to intimacy, insight, conviction, and self-knowledge. When you stop pushing yourself for answers (or pushing away the truths you know), you will see what is already there.

Forget Answers, Uncover Desires

Here's a suggestion you may have already heard me offer before. But it's a Zen-type truth that will iron out your wrinkles. Ditch the notion that you need to figure out what you will do with the rest of your life. Here's a better focus: What do you want to do in this moment?

Oh, and let's leave your idea of realism at the door. I don't care if you don't know how you could do the thing you desire. I just want to know your raw desire—because desire, before you talk yourself into "practicality," packs heat, joy, and rocket fuel.

If you could do absolutely anything, what would you want in this moment? Start there. You may want to curl up into a ball and cry, or you may desire an uncluttered studio or office space. You may want to paint the portraits of the birds at your bird feeder or hike in the kingdom of Bhutan. Listen to what arises for you, even when it seems audacious, random, or unfocused. Take one tiny movement toward this possibility. Love feels good. Acting on your instincts will strengthen you. You will learn more about yourself. Your desires are not frivolous. Your desires are doorways.

You may also discover that you know what you want but you have a limiting belief in the way. And here's what I will tell you: If you follow what you desire, you will grow your desire. When you grow your desire, it can fuel you past any limiting ideas.

Trust the Process

You might be wired to want results overnighted, which gets in the way of real results. I've seen people patch together answers just so they could leave the wilderness of not knowing. These answers fall apart with the first challenge. Fake direction doesn't last. The real power comes from the real journey. Your authentic life will emerge from the courage and integrity to not know while continuing to explore.

How long will this take? Clients and workshop attendees often ask. It depends, I think to myself. How long have you ignored your heart or choked the life out of your instincts in the past? How long will you pelt rocks at anything that moves in a direction you don't understand? When will you love yourself enough to trust your way?

Are you rushing to get "there"? A Course in Miracles teaches that "infinite patience brings immediate results." The lack of patience brings wasps that sting you in the head, but, again, maybe that's just me.

Finding your real answers is an adventure in honesty and growth. One bread crumb leads you to the next and then the next. Where you start off is not where you will end up. And if you're anything like me, you may even find it comical, in a twisted, you've-got-to-be-kidding kind of way. For example, when you end up sitting cross-legged and teaching A Course in Miracles for a living when earlier in your life you specifically chose not to get an MFA degree because that was too airy-fairy or bohemian.

Your clarity is not out of reach. It's only the mind that wants to label and file things away like a testy librarian, aggravated at an order she does not recognize. An authentic quest is more of a journey for a snorkeler, a shaman, or a mountain climber. Your answers will draw you into new territory. And more important, they will demand you learn a new language, the language of your spirit.

You don't have to know your answers all at once. Some answers take years to evolve in full. You will know what you need to know when you need it. Meanwhile, get out of your head and into your feelings. Trusting yourself will not be an idle journey. Your brain may see all of this as fruity. Yet it will not be unfruitful. The heart may seem silly to the mind, yet it's the mind that's ineffectual on the path of heart.

TURNING POINTS:
Stop Figuring It Out, Let It Out

You don't even have a decision to make. It's already been made and encrypted within you, like the . . . delicate, determined map of your fingerprint.

Even if you do have many interests and directions, you polyamorous lover of life, you still have only one thing you wish to do right now.

The whole ocean looks the same until you dive deeper. It's the same thing with our minds. Ideas all look the same at the level of the mind.

Of course you feel unclear. You're scrabbling around for clues, arrows, reasons, statistics. . . . You're looking with the mind for answers of the heart.

Your true answers are below the surface of the choppy daily mind.

You won't dive deeper by being reasonable. It's love that changes everything. It's play. It's peace. It's not trying to figure things out, but letting them out instead.

Most of us are desperate for clarity . . . because we believe it will bring us peace of mind. Ah, grasshopper, it works the other way around. It's peace of mind that frees answers.

Look to connect with your spirit more than you look for answers.

Your desires are not frivolous.
Your desires are doorways.

HOW TO LISTEN LIKE A LOVER OF THE TRUTH

We all possess a mainline of personal genius. We all have direction. It's just a matter of learning how to coax the genie out of the bottle and to shut up and listen instead of argue with the electric unknown.

TAMA KIEVES (journal entry)

I am always taken by what others desire—the choreography behind it all—because when you really get to see what someone wants, it's often the ultimate healing for whatever they have walked through in life. It's like the master plan unfolds, the chess game is revealed, the chemistry makes sense, and the algebra adds up. I always want to slap my knees like a hillbilly and marvel, "Well, would you look at that!"

TAMA KIEVES (journal entry)

I meet many people blocked to their own desires and I want to wring my hands in sadness, because I know the joy and awe of living one's dreams in one's lifetime. And sometimes I feel like I'm like the crazy host at the party who says, "You have to try the ginger chicken . . . the sesame tofu . . . the cobbler . . . the brownies." I want everyone to swallow bliss. I want everyone to feel as though they're standing on the mountaintop, having their own personal picnic with God and God just says, "Can you pass the Wheat Thins, please?" and you do, but you can't help giggling because it's just ridiculous to be this alive. Some days I am living proof that this is possible—only some days, but those are the days that are worth everything. And I want to picnic with you.

So, how come you are born with talents and infinite resources, but you don't know what you want or how to find your right next steps? Or how can you feel so restless, *so ready* to get somewhere, and yet so muddy or paralyzed at the same time? I think it's because we don't know how to listen to ourselves. We have too much personal history or identity interrupting the conversation. Or a rushing need to make things immediately make sense.

I've been coaching others for almost three decades and I'm going to tell you about the most powerful mechanism I know for getting answers. (Drumroll, please.)

I call it creating a safe and sacred space—and you can do this at home, boys and girls. It's a time of dedicated nonjudgment, fascination, and attention.

Another way to say this is practicing unconditional acceptance of what you think or feel. Unconditional acceptance is the holy grail of listening. It's a form of mindfulness. It's something you practice like learning how to ride a bicycle, unless, of course, you are a unicorn—a *Swiss* unicorn, the rare creature that doesn't take sides. That means you don't immediately attack a new idea that threatens a desired self-image. Or interrogate yourself within an inch of your life as to how to execute the hair ball your unconscious mind just coughed up. Listening is not evaluating, fixing, or planning. It's listening. It's a verb all by itself.

> **Unconditional acceptance is the holy grail of listening. It's a form of mindfulness.**

Because when you lay aside self-judgment, you can hear intuition and inspiration. Sweet mother of all that is possible, this is better than *cheesecake*, because hearing your truth is sweetness not of this world. Again: *You cannot listen to self-judgment and guidance at the same time.*

Here are two words to start your practice: *sacred neutrality.* Maybe you were hoping for one word: *abracadubra.* Or some morsel from the Kabbalah or even some fresh catch of the day from Dr. Phil. Well, let me tell you, sacred neutrality is the door. It's the portal. It's the way into the belly of the Universe. It's the corridor to truth, and the truth is the answer to hunger. Now, a bossy part of you thinks it knows the truth. But the truth is often what you *don't* know.

The wisdom path of *A Course in Miracles* teaches, "When a situation is dedicated wholly to truth, peace is inevitable." Now, interestingly enough, it does not say when a situation is dedicated to winning the Powerball or some other solution you think you want. Because your big truth is what you really want. But don't worry. Your big truth doesn't mean you will just run off to the hills or join an ashram. Your big truth doesn't mean you won't get it all: the white dove of your soul answer *and* a way to feed your kids. In fact, it's the only chance in hell you will.

When I'm practicing sacred neutrality, I'm just looking for a pinpoint or gleam of someone's real desire. I'm not secretly hoping it's one direction or another. I'm not on any team. I'm as neutral as a scrap of cardboard. I've got my mental lab coat on; I'm just an observing scientist gathering data (though I do tend to giggle). The data will speak for itself.

To me, nothing is silly or dangerous or too far off the beaten path, though, trust me, I have been tested on this one. It's all communication. It's all energy. I'm interested without the need for immediate gratification. I'm not jumping on the first stalk that shoots through the ground and deciding whether it's a cash crop. I'm not buying a domain name on GoDaddy or building the church. I'm not making any idea mean anything, until it does. I'm just listening. I know the truth will repeat itself. The truth outlives every other idea.

It's easier for me to stay clear, of course. I don't have the same background story. I'm not influenced by the same pesky inner narrators, the ones who talk too loud, like your aunt from Brooklyn, who picks at her teeth, wipes her hands on a flowered apron, and says, "So, what, now you think you're a Rockefeller?" loud enough for even the dead Rockefellers to hear. I don't hear her or any of your "consultants."

Someone can leave a current doctor's treatment plan, or ditch a donor, or family member and I won't lose a wink of sleep. I don't have to make up for a botched marriage or a botched batch of marriages or a decade of cocaine abuse. I have nothing to prove. I have nothing to gain. I just pay attention.

You might find it hard to discover true answers because you're not asking true questions, *neutral* questions, unconditional questions, the best questions. Here's a common example, for those of you who might be looking for that great white whale—your "life purpose" or right work. (Oh, go right ahead and modify this for your issue.) I'd want you to ask, "What do I love?" You might say, But I've asked that. And here's what I think you've asked: *What do*

I love to do that makes money, better yet, buckets of money? What do I love to do that won't make me go back to school? What do I love to do that I won't drop a year from now, that I don't need the car for, or that my husband/parents/kids/coworkers won't roll their eyes at? Once you have your truth, you can work backward and answer the conditions that are important to you—later. First, you're just looking for an honest truth or desire.

Let go of those questions with a hundred fishhooks. They yield fishy answers. They keep you in your head. I don't want you listening to a discourse on music theory. I want you pulsing to a drum beat. "What do I love?" is a simple question.

Let go of controlling the answer to make it one you think you want to hear. Nothing big and alive and sloppy and true can get through a controlling inquiry. The truth is not here to fit into your apartment. The truth might just be a house.

As a sacred witness to each client's journey, I often ask, "What do you want to do right now?" I don't traffic with trying to figure out all of life at once. The more ease I create, the more we will bump into epiphanies and action steps. Everyone has an inner directive to live an authentic life. I know that what wants to be revealed will surface. This cream always rises to the top. It's just a matter of time and trust.

Besides, every thought or even detour gives me information. I'm not just stalking your right romantic partner, parenting solution, or best source of funding. I'm stalking your consciousness. I'm trying to discover *why* you choose what you choose. I want to know what you believe about everything. Beliefs command your choices. And it's always a warped belief that warps your sense of direction.

Hinduism reveres the different aspects of the divine; one of them is Shiva, the destroyer. Sacred neutrality will destroy your old stories about who you are and what you can have in this lifetime. In the presence of undiluted love, everything falls away but the truth.

I like to think that a good listener is like a nice version of Shiva who maybe carries a lightweight pink diamond pickax to decimate hollow identities.

Life asks us to grow into our real identity, to let go of one expression and give birth to another. When we don't listen, life gets louder. You know the deal: First it's the heart's whisper, then the nudge, and then the two-by-four. Lately, I've seen too many who ignored the two-by-four. That's when the thousand-year-old sequoia falls, and let me tell you, while it may be silent in the forest when no one is around, it's a death-metal concert in a canyon when it falls on your life.

Maybe you've gotten fired. Or surprised by a lump. Or you can't figure out how to get more clients in the way that you have gotten them in the past. I see these challenges as unorthodox support, with the crazy fingerprints of the infinite all over it. You are so loved, you are not allowed to settle for an almost life. You are not being allowed to go on as always. You are meeting the mystery head-on, being invited to awaken in a new way. Healing isn't about restoring yourself to how you used to be. Real healing is about becoming *more* than who you used to be.

What should you listen for when you're listening for the truth? I hunt for heat or energy. I don't have fancy barometers in my bag of tricks. I long ago ripped up assessment tests and diagnostics because as much as I want to help define someone, I'm more interested in expanding him and setting him free. Besides, the soul will often lead us off the grid, out of the box, and into a clarity beyond labels. Sometimes we are discovering what hasn't yet been defined or validated by society.

Sacred listening is like being a cosmic optometrist who simply puts a new lens over your eyes. "Can you see more clearly like this?" I ask. "Does this float your boat?" "Does this make you giggle?" "Are you seeing God yet?" I don't care what you choose. I know that something has already chosen you.

I hope you will become your own sacred witness. Be neutral. Be kind. Be *available* to yourself. The secrets are all there. They are as plain as day in the right time and the right light. Approach yourself with the brand of patience that could wait until the end of time because you are that worth it. And cultivate an exquisite interest in everything you think and feel.

Listen with sacred neutrality, the way a butterfly would look at you—no opinion, no history, no agenda, just a sense of *being*, a respect for another living entity. Be with yourself with presence. Dig deeper when you sense a disruption, a discomfort, or a feeling without a name.

Remember, it's such a deep and precious intimacy to know what you want, to allow it and express it. It's such a prayer, a sense of forgiveness, of being unabashed and shining with freedom. It is a union to finally speak the name of your beloved, or to allow yourself simply to care about what you care about and to value and claim it, and devote any part of your life to it.

Our true desires don't need to make sense. And we don't need to know how we will get there. We're not looking for strategy. First, we're looking for honesty.

TURNING POINTS:
How to Listen like a Lover of the Truth

Unconditional acceptance is the holy grail of listening. It's a form of mindfulness.

Listening is not evaluating, fixing, or planning. It's listening. It's a verb all by itself.

You cannot listen to self-judgment and guidance at the same time.

Let go of those questions with a hundred fishhooks. They yield fishy answers. They keep you in your head.

Let go of controlling the answer to make it one you think you want to hear. Nothing big and alive . . . can get through a controlling inquiry. The truth is not here to fit into your apartment. The truth might just be a house.

Healing isn't about restoring yourself to how you used to be. Real healing is about becoming *more* than who you used to be.

As much as I want to help define someone, I'm more interested in expanding him and setting him free. Besides, the soul will often lead us off the grid, out of the box, and into a clarity beyond labels.

Be *available* to yourself. . . . Approach yourself with the brand of patience that could wait until the end of time because you are that worth it.

FOLLOW THE BREAD CRUMBS TO THE BANQUET

I've often used the metaphor from Hansel and Gretel about following the bread crumbs home. I have this feeling that my soul has left these bread crumbs in every stage of my life. They're always there. But now try explaining to a bank that you don't have a business plan—you have a hunch. Or tell your doctor that your latest "treatment plan" is a bread crumb. An inspired life may never translate into a linear plan. It's a luminous plan.

TAMA KIEVES (journal entry)

If you insist on having a destination when you come into a library, you're shortchanging yourself.

ANNE LAMOTT

Sometimes you can't find your answers, because you are playing chess with your life. In chess, you calculate all the moves. But living an audaciously inspired life is a different game. You start in checkmate. Admit you're clueless, then open your heart to the four winds, the eight noble paths, or just any one speck that stirs your curiosity. You don't find answers. You find moments—experiences that somehow create you. And you follow these bread crumbs to the gingerbread house —or the Grammys or wherever you're trying to go.

Your brain hates bread crumbs. *You're just going to follow a path because there's a crumb on it? That's your research? That's how you're going to invent your life?* Hell yes, it is. That crumb is a messiah. It's a message from God. It's an arrow. It's a promissory note. And it will take you all the way, but not a way you know.

My good friend Lisa is a Juilliard-trained pianist who has awed audiences with her performances and who owned her own music school in Half Moon Bay, California. Several years ago, she started talking to me about her love of dogs, beyond Sanchez, her own mischievous yellow Lab. "I'm going to these dog agility trials and I just *love* it. What the heck do I do with this?" she asks.

"I don't know. Follow the love," I say, as though there would ever be anything else to say.

"Tama, I'm a classical pianist. I don't want to be a dog trainer or a veterinarian. How can this be something? I just love the dogs." She giggled. Yes, giggled. A telltale sign of a bread crumb.

One day Lisa attended a talk by a longtime sound researcher who was using the power of music to heal people. *I want to play music to heal dogs,* she suddenly realized. She'd received another bread crumb. Daring to set up a meeting with the sound specialist, she suggested playing classical piano compositions to calm dogs down from separation anxiety, loud noises, and other stresses. He did the research, measured conclusive results, and they began collaborating.

To date, they have eighteen albums on the market, including their number one bestseller, *Through a Dog's Ear*, published by Sounds True, a leading holistic learning audio company. She's been on CBS's *The Early Show* and her music plays in shelters worldwide. No one in their right mind could have put these two exciting concepts together. But Lisa had followed the bread crumbs, the language of the intuitive mind.

Oftentimes, a bread crumb won't make sense in terms of your "identity." It may change the story of who you think you are. That's because it's guiding you to more of yourself, perhaps the secret parts you have not yet met, realized, or sanctioned.

When I was in college, I met Ben at a dance club in the Upper West side of Manhattan. He was a playful, sensual, wild curly-haired man. And as we talked, we realized in a city of 8 million people, we lived just houses away from one another, in another borough. Shazam! The woo-woo choo-choo pulled out of the station. That "something else is going on here" feeling wasn't just physical chemistry. It was the fun chemistry, an electricity, a playfulness, and an anything-could-happen-now feeling, a thoroughfare of green lights.

I don't remember if we kissed in the club or in his car. I do remember his kindness and forthrightness. "I'm only going to be here until the end of summer," he whispered. He was moving to the desolate far ends of the universe after that. I think they call it Utah.

"You might not want to date me since I'm leaving," he said. It wasn't a "safe" plan. It wasn't leading anywhere, except to guaranteed loss. Besides, to my kosher-keeping Orthodox Jewish parents, dating Ben would be as unkosher as eating shrimp and pork, *together*. I was supposed to find and marry a nice podiatrist, a mensch who would buy the four-bedroom home on Long Island with the oval-shaped swimming pool.

There was no way my mother and father would approve of me bringing home a guy in ripped jeans who was moving to Utah to hug red rocks and camp under the stars. *Better you should pick daisies, if this is how you're preparing for your future.* Dating Ben was jumping off the *Good Ship Lollipop* onto the *Titanic.* This romance held no promise of future gain. But I didn't need future gain. I knew I was gaining something right now. It was magic.

Ben healed my wounded self-esteem. I blossomed. And, as it turned out, he did *not* leave at the end of the summer. His plans changed. But it didn't even matter. The relationship ran its course and ended when it ended for other reasons. And I am so grateful I did not miss the experience of being with that wild, expansive dreamer who beckoned the genie out of me. He gave me something far more valuable than diamond stud earrings from Tiffany; he gave me a significant piece of my identity to take with me into the rest of my life. Priceless.

The fearful part of you insists on guarantees and a straight shot. But not everything is meant to last forever or line up in a way you can see right now.

Some events or circumstances are catalysts or stepping-stones. That's what a bread crumb is. It's something that is right for the moment.

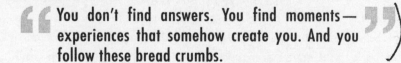

You don't find answers. You find moments— experiences that somehow create you. And you follow these bread crumbs.

Years later, living under the bright blue skies of Denver, where everyone can always find a parking space, so you know this *has* to be heaven, I flashed on the memory of Ben, that golden curly-haired man, electric, full of the possible. He was so alive. "You have to see the skies out west. It's like nothing you've ever seen," he bubbled.

"You *have* to go out west." He'd said it like a man who had discovered chocolate for the first time. I have no idea if that's why I applied for legal jobs in Denver on a lark years later. But I believe now that it's possible that Ben had been a messenger, an ally of my destiny in tight ripped jeans.

Here's the thing. Something that seems random or out of the blue at one point in your life can seem like the linchpin of the whole infrastructure later. It's like when you look back, you see that things just couldn't have been otherwise. Moving to Denver seems like that to me now. I thought I was moving out here as a fun experiment and because I'd been offered an exciting job with a high-powered law firm. I didn't consciously choose Denver, thinking, Now, *that* would be an excellent place to fall apart, leave a law practice, and journal like a madwoman. But I'm thinking my unconscious mind, servant of the soul, understood the higher plan.

Really, would I have left law, waited tables, given myself permission to "find myself" and explore writing if I had still been living in New York City? I don't know. Living in Denver has perks. Can you say rent? I cannot say enough about the ecstasy of a lower cost of living. Also, Denver isn't as—how shall I say this—*rabid* about ambition and status climbing. People here care more about mountain climbing.

A social gathering doesn't immediately launch into an interrogation: Who are you? Who do you know? Where is your work showing? Of course, Denver might paint its streets orange in honor of its football team, but I can live with that. Overall, to me, Denver, graced by the Rocky Mountains, seems gentle, which is a very big plus if you're planning on having a meltdown. Maybe it's the sunshine—320 days of it a year. No matter what you're going through, it's clear that even *you* will have a sunny future.

When I teach my workshops on unleashing your calling, I instruct students to stop asking, "Is this what I want to do for the rest of my life?" A better question is "What feels right to me in this moment?" Likewise, whatever you're going through, I want you to simply follow a bread crumb. You're not choosing what you will do forever. You're choosing what you will do for now.

Your whole life is a meteor shower within a mosaic, laid down tile by tile. It's not just a straight line to a goal or a race of expedience. A butterfly net might be a better tool than a map.

Think about it. Dorothy in *The Wizard of Oz* had to take the whole giddy journey through poppy fields with crazy monkeys and a witch and everything, just to get to a place she could have gotten to with a mere click of her heels. The click would have taken her there, but she would not have *arrived*. She needed to follow the yellow brick road, or the bread crumbs. A meaningful life is not a straight line. It's a hurricane that picks up a house and lands on you and sends you on a journey into Technicolor.

"What do I want to do with my life?" is way too big a question. The mind does not have those big-picture answers. But the soul does. And in its infinite wisdom, it doles out illumination in increments.

Spirit speaks in the now. It doesn't speak about the future.

When I first left law, I felt the desire to write poems. "Oh, now we're talking," hissed my critical inner voice. "This is what we busted butt for in antitrust law, so that you could write about the geese?" But you don't get to choose what you love. It chooses you. And it's often just what comes before a comma, not a period.

For example, writing poetry led me to writing deeper essays about the journey of career transition, which turned into my first book, *This Time I Dance!* And as I wrote, I followed the intuition to start a support group, which led to teaching, which led to coaching, which led to putting on national retreats, which led to global programs online and more. And diving into writing, however it started, led me to write and publish four books with my dream publisher, an imprint of the largest publishing house in the world. One thing led to another and another. This is the radical path of following bread crumbs to everything you want.

Speaking at a commencement speech at Stanford, Apple founder Steve Jobs stole my strategy and made it public, for which I forgive and bless him. "You can't connect the dots looking forward; you can only connect them looking backwards. So you have to trust that the dots will somehow connect in your future," he said. "You have to trust in something—your gut, destiny, life, karma, whatever. This approach has never let me down, and it has made all the difference in my life."

Give yourself permission to be led by your light. We live in a world that asks you for a five-year plan. But when you're in transition, which is always, I suggest a five-minute plan. Follow the bread crumbs. Follow love. Always follow love. Love takes you places you wouldn't believe. And it's often sunny.

TURNING POINTS:
Follow the Bread Crumbs to the Banquet

You don't find answers. You find moments—experiences that somehow create you. And you follow these bread crumbs.

A bread crumb won't make sense in terms of your "identity." It may change the story of who you think you are.

The fearful part of you insists on guarantees and a straight shot. But not everything is meant to last forever or line up in a way you can see right now.

Some events or circumstances are catalysts or stepping-stones. That's what a bread crumb is. It's something that is right for the moment.

Something that seems random or out of the blue at one point in your life can seem like the linchpin of the whole infrastructure later.

> Simply follow a bread crumb. You're not choosing
> what you will do forever. You're choosing what you
> will do for now.
>
> Spirit speaks in the now.
> It doesn't speak about the future.
>
> You don't get to choose what you love. It chooses you.
> And it's often just what comes before a comma,
> not a period.

CLARITY IS IN YOUR FEET, NOT YOUR BRAIN

We keep moving forward, opening new doors, and doing new things, because we're curious and curiosity keeps leading us down new paths.

WALT DISNEY

You don't have to go bungee jumping or slinking into a Kama Sutra class. I'm just saying that doing new things is a way to discover new information about yourself. You have to leave the couch—or your office, or the life you know—behind. Just buy a purple toothbrush. Do something different.

TAMA KIEVES (e-mail to a client)

Lauren was an alternative coach in Boulder, Colorado, who was half power pixie and half rocket scientist. She had a gift for turning driven, broken, tired people into open-hearted, functioning, actualized citizens of the world. The woman had earned a black belt in kung fu "just for fun." I guess listening to everyone's problems all day may have made her need to attack something at night. But weekly she encouraged me to "play," to try new things in order to discover more about myself. Play, as in not immediately marry, incorporate, scale it, or win a medal. Visit the cult, don't join it. Just *try* something.

I sat there clenching the tissue box, not wanting to tell Ms. Kung Fu how strained I felt just finding socks that matched in the morning. I couldn't imagine ever wanting to voluntarily add something new—and not a sure thing—into my life. I was doing everything in my feeble power to avoid uncertainty. I'm sure that zealous woman babbled on about the joy of challenge and I looked at her with my bleary, pleading eyes and said, "English, please." But all these years later, I remember the light in her eyes on a Wednesday afternoon. I remember the ease of her skin. That woman was having fun.

These days I coach others who feel stuck in the story of themselves. I help them dive into new realms of potential. I know that when you feel stuck or like you've plateaued in your success, you're craving experimentation, action, and magic—and not, my darling head cases, more analysis. It's time to wake up different hot zones in your brain or unleash a new part of your identity, a sapphire in your buried treasure chest. It's there waiting for you.

Sometimes you don't know what you want anymore, because you don't want what you know. *You want what you don't know.* You yearn to wake up. It's time to take an adult education class, meet a new acquaintance, visit another neighborhood in your city, or do something unusual, whether or not you're in the mood. Because, really, you won't be in the mood. You're bored, stuck, and timid, and you feel like that clump of muck stuck in the drain of the kitchen sink, until you do something new.

A mood is not a fact.

There's this whimsical notion that inspiration arrives as a clap of lighting. Or maybe a prophetic dream in which a dusty scroll unfolds, which would be rather lovely, though cruel, really, if you have a menopausal memory problem. Fortunately, there's a more reliable way to unlock your enthusiasm: Sample something new. Anything. Lots of things. Pay attention. Chase a glint. And repeat.

I remember when I first bought a house. I had no idea what I was looking for. Zilch. It was like the Sahara in my head. Some people have elaborate, exacting ideas of their needs and desires. I knew I didn't want to live in my apartment anymore. That's what I had.

"What do you have in mind?" the real estate agent asked. I looked at him numbly, and maybe even provocatively, as though with a little encouragement he might tell me the *right* answer. So we started with some of the things I knew I didn't want. I did not want to live next door to a brothel or a toxic waste dump. I did not want a tree stump. I did not want green eggs and ham. I did not want neighbors on the lam. And lime green siding was out. Mr. Realtor smiled weakly. I have a feeling that wasn't one of the days he loved his job.

Then the Realtor showed me different neighborhoods and styles of homes. Over time, as we looked at different places, clarity began to emerge. I realized I loved older homes, but I wanted extra closet space. I loved the idea of having a private backyard and garden, while being close to a coffeehouse and trendy restaurants. Then came skylights and hardwood floors—*cherry* hardwood floors—and vaulted ceilings where possible. Pretty soon, I was rattling off features as though dictating an old family recipe.

I would never have figured it out or gotten that clear in my mind. I got clear in Bob's Toyota Camry, driving around and viewing properties. I recognized desires as I looked at kitchens, sunrooms, decks, bathrooms with white claw-foot tubs, and porches. I couldn't name my preferences in the beginning. I had to prime the pump. I needed to see options. When I saw examples, my desires kicked in and ran wild.

I've seen this same dynamic when I teach writing classes. If I tell my writing students to write "anything," many will stare at me blankly, frozen in the paralysis of too much choice. I tell them to write about the blue box, and *bam*, they're off to the races with memories and scenes. Psychologist Rollo May explains in *The Courage to Create* that creativity often requires an "encounter." Most artists don't create from thin air. They encounter a landscape, an object, a person, or a bad date. From this brush with reality, they meet themselves. Their expression is a response to something as much as it's a creation of something radically new.

Want to discover who you are now and what your guidance is asking you to do? Your inspiration is often waiting for you in the wild country of doing new things, not *thinking about* doing them.

Oh, wait. You might be afraid to make a mistake.

You may be afraid to try things because you don't want to "waste time." The voice in your head that says this rolls its eyes and speaks as drily as the vodka martini you are about to suck down instead of an experience in your life. You don't want to make a mistake, or "another" mistake, some of you say, as though you're keeping tabs, which of course you are, and according to the vicious calculations of the tab Nazi, you're losing.

But life is a series of trying new things, fizzling, faltering, seemingly going nowhere, and then awakening. It's the system. It's not going to change. I have wanted to hide in my bed and magically sprout into a superstar. It hasn't worked. Hiding is withering, because risk is a vitamin and without it you die.

I once taught a class of young artists to explore their gifts in the world. Most of them, like most of us, wanted to avoid making mistakes. But holding back is not how we thrive. In my book *Inspired & Unstoppable: Wildly Succeeding in Your Life's Work!*, I talk about this and since I can't say it much better now, I'll quote what I wrote: "I wanted them to take risks, consume risks, billions of them, as though they were hungry baby birds opening their beaks for worms. I wanted them to know that everything was safe because everything would teach them and eventually activate their bionic strength and fire. I wanted them to know that openness would strengthen them more than caution and protection. I didn't say this to them, so I'll say it to you: It doesn't matter where you enter the stream. It doesn't matter how you begin. Just jump in. Get moving."

> " Your inspiration is often waiting for you in the wild country of doing new things, not *thinking about* doing them. "

Please jump in. Stop dismissing your ideas. Any inspiration is an invitation to new abundance. It's not just the opportunity to write a song or a software program, or enroll in a grief support group. It's the invitation to create yourself. The creator is changed by the created. Yet if you refuse to listen to your own new ideas, you hold back the boundless within you. You may think you're just being conservative. But how could it ever be wise to deny your greatest powers?

Why would you tell yourself that you could only achieve what you've already experienced? You're still developing, aren't you? It's just not realistic to deny the miraculous. It's self-annihilating. The reality is you are a miracle. You are a growing, conscious spark of the infinite and alive. You are being called to awaken new strengths.

You won't learn how to fly in the nest. You have to dare. It's nerve-racking sometimes. Get over it. Because you were born to fly, not hide.

Excitement doesn't come from the things we can control. It will come from the things we *don't* control.

Recently I put on a new program as a speaker. I've led workshops for years, so you'd think I'm an old hand, good to go. Yes, well. The inner child in me whined, "I won't know what participants will ask. I'll have clunky answers with two left feet. What if I ramble? What if I'm boring?" Oh, the places you don't want to go. I hate this part of trying new material. I want to be perfect. I want to dazzle. I don't want to be uncomfortable. But one of my yoga teachers—a rather hot one, I might add—encourages us to fall out of a new pose but at least try it. He commands: "Perfection doesn't grow. Only imperfection grows." So I gave the new workshop. I gave myself permission to ramble rather than rot.

Here's what I find *fun* about growing: I'm not in control. I am guided by an inspired power. I am not limited to the crude strengths I've experienced thus far. I did that beta make-everyone-guinea-pigs-just-for-me brand-new workshop and I gained what I could never gain alone in my room. I walked in with wobbling knees and bees in my chest. I strolled out a lion. I became more of myself by using more of myself, discovering unknown power as I walked into the unknown.

The participants shared breakthroughs, insights, and stories I never could have predicted or manufactured. There was an energy in the room. This was a co-creation. It was humbling. It was moving. And I would have missed it—if I hadn't dared it.

Russell Simmons, the hip-hop mogul with fashion and record labels and multiple HBO reality shows, says he created his empire by following his inner voice and taking risks. In his book *Do You!*, he says, "Time and time again I watch as the people who listen to their higher selves move on to bigger and better things, while the people who listen to the low notes end up stuck in one place or fade away altogether. They never realized that in ignoring their higher selves, they're blocking their ability to be blessed."

Where might you be holding back on opportunities for growth? Fear keeps you small, and smallness keeps you fearful. It's a pitiful system and it ages you like toxins, years of cigarette smoke, and gorging daily on Häagen-Dazs coffee ice cream—which, it turns out, is not a food group.

Keep listening to what you know you need to do. Your truth is never an instinct that diminishes you. Remember, you have a presence within you that can do anything. You are not limited to what you know from the past. You are not limited to what others have experienced either. Real life is always evolving.

You're hungry for the new because you hunger for yourself. You know there are still unexpressed reserves within you.

It's safe to go beyond what you have experienced before. It's necessary. Expose yourself to growth.

TURNING POINTS:
Clarity Is in Your Feet, Not Your Brain

You won't be in the mood. You're bored, stuck, and timid . . . until you do something new. A mood is not a fact.

Hiding is withering, because risk is a vitamin and without it you die.

Your inspiration is often waiting for you in the wild country of doing new things, not *thinking about* doing them.

You won't learn how to fly in the nest. You have to dare . . . Because you were born to fly, not hide.

Excitement doesn't come from the things we can control. It will come from the things we *don't* control.

Where might you be holding back on opportunities for growth? Fear keeps you small, and smallness keeps you fearful.

Remember, you have a presence within you that can do anything. You are not limited to what you know from the past.

You're hungry for the new because you hunger for yourself. You know there are still unexpressed reserves within you.

Do Try This at Home: Jump-starts, Inquiries & Exercises

Some of these suggestions are just right for *you*. Others, not your cup of latte, or at least at *this* moment. Follow your gut. Feel free to adjust to your liking. Do what's right for you rather than what's written here.

Pick three Turning Points from this chapter. Write them out for yourself. Post them where you will see them. Meditate on them. Journal about them. Do a Freewriting exercise. (See page 252 for more about Freewriting.) Create a piece of art. Pay attention to your thoughts, memories, dreams, and "random" ideas and incidents. Inspired thoughts spark inspired responses. My words begin the conversation, but what do these truths unlock in you?

1. **Snorkel past the surface.** Meditate with a mantra like "I am loved." Or set an intention or inquiry, then do something that engages your attention in a different way. Doodle in a coloring book. Knit. Ski in silence. Walk in the park. Focusing on something else, especially if it doesn't engage your left brain, will often allow you to relax and connect. These are mini-pilgrimages.

2. **Become a witness.** Try listening to your feelings or desires without attempting to explain or justify them. When you uncover desires, do not ask *how* to make them happen. Observe. Be fascinated. Pay attention as a form of mindfulness. Be like an anthropologist, without judgment or assumptions. Be encouraging.

3. **Ask the right question.** Give up trying to figure out what you will do with your whole life. Ask: What do I want to do in this moment? Or journal, "If money/time/social values weren't

an issue, I would . . ." Or imagine and describe your ideal day. Take one tiny movement toward one of your desires.

4. **Follow a bread crumb.** Do it right now. Remember, a bread crumb might hold no promise of "future gain." What is speaking to you in this moment? What inkling comes to mind? Is there a bread crumb you're resisting because you think it's silly or doesn't make sense?

5. **Do something new.** Shake it up, baby. Create a list of five to ten new things you can do, just for taste testing, experimentation, or a creative encounter. You can do this in different areas of your life as well: five new things in your relationship; five new things at work; five new books, movies, museums, or concerts to experience.

6. **Do a fun cluster mind map.** First do a "cluster" mind-mapping exercise. Write the word FUN in the center. Then free-associate all your thoughts about fun, both positive and negative, memories, experiences, concepts. Keep free-associating. Then do a Freewriting exercise (see page 252 for directions) on whatever you discovered in your cluster.

Do you have a question about this chapter? I'd love to know what's on your mind! *I may just get wildly inspired and answer you immediately.* Send me your thought or question at www.TamaKieves.com/uncertainty-question, and you can also register for a **FREE** Thriving Through Uncertainty Coaching Call designed to shift your mind-set and bring you immediate clarity.

CHAPTER SIX

TRADE IN YOUR
COMFORT ZONE FOR THE
STELLAR ZONE

WAIT FOR THE OTHER
SHOE TO . . . FLY

*And the sun and the moon sometimes argue over who gets to
tuck me in at night.*

HAFIZ

*It's a service to feel good and receive this good. When you feel
good, you can and will further the good of others.*

TAMA KIEVES (journal entry)

One of the most courageous things you can do in this lifetime
is to allow your life to become great. Yes, you may think, I
should have *that* problem. But you do have that problem. It's
a bit of neuroscience, baby. You are hardwired to overlook joy.

Neuropsychologist Rick Hanson writes about what brain science has called the "negativity bias" of the hardwiring of the brain. The bias is thought to be a residual survival instinct, as in it was more important to pay attention to the saber-toothed tiger that might take a run at you than it was to notice the tiny blue flowers the color of your loved one's eyes. Says Hanson, "The result: a brain that is tilted against peace and fulfillment."

I think it's time to adapt and evolve. I don't know about you, but I'm going to tilt my brain toward joy. Science has also begun to tilt toward joy, documenting how people who feel more positive emotions have greater access to their cognitive and physical resources. *Booyah!*

Sure, we need to pay attention to threats. But we don't need to disregard our good in the name of being realistic. It's time to stop calling negativity "realism." I have an idea. Let's just call it negativity. Because miracles are as real as crises. They happen every day. They're just not on the news. There *are* moments in life of searing pain. There are also moments in life of excitement and the transcendence of pain. I'm fine with calling a spade a spade. But I'm also fine with calling a diamond a diamond.

I'm not talking about just hoping for more good in your life. I'm suggesting that you begin to practice not blocking the good that is already here—as well as the good en route.

We're afraid of good.

It's a power. It's a hypnotism. It's new territory. It feels out of control, like pulling you out into the sea. Something in us wants to stay on the shore—keep things a bit lumpy, the devil we know, the comfort of the uncomfortable familiar.

Have you ever sabotaged yourself when something was beginning to work out? Or put the brakes on your breaks?

Oy, I have.

I was leading my favorite retreat and I was thrilled because my numbers were great, more students than ever before. At the exact same time, a professional magazine contacted me about doing an article that would reach my ideal audience. So I was answering interview questions over the Internet in my private hotel room, feeling like Little Ms. Rock Star. And at the same time, I'd been running an online special for one of my e-courses, and the orders were streaming in. I'd always experienced trickles. This was happy madness. I felt like there was a festival in my brain and three bands were playing at once. I was delirious, grateful, and, frankly, astounded.

Then I started to realize that there were even more orders than I'd thought. And then, while I was online, *more* orders started to come in. And then I heard it. I swear to God I heard it. A harsh inner voice. It said, "That's enough now," as though it were scolding a child that had been singing loudly and banging pots and pans.

That was enough out-of-control-ness, enough good, it said without saying. I had begun to feel overwhelmed. I'd gone from feeling exuberant to feeling cold tingles, the fingerprint of fear. It all happened so fast. And just like that, the orders tapered off. I swear I put a hex on my own success.

Psychologist Gay Hendricks, author of *The Big Leap*, coined this dynamic the "upper limits problem," which he describes as an unconscious desire we all have to keep ourselves smaller and out of our "zone of genius." We all freak out for different reasons, then bounce ourselves out of heaven. The work is to build the musculature to encourage the influx of grace. It takes grit to allow a force of good to work through you and for you.

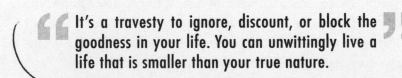

> **It's a travesty to ignore, discount, or block the goodness in your life. You can unwittingly live a life that is smaller than your true nature.**

For me, I think it was a challenge to the story I had been telling myself. I was used to feeling vaguely disappointed that I hadn't reached higher levels of success. It was my cosmic shtick, if you will.

I knew this limitation like my own right hand. It was unsettling to be in a different identity, in the mansion of amplified reality.

But life gives us the chance to get realized, instead of "realistic"—as in to let go of the small stories we tell ourselves about what is possible. We have the chance to reinvent ourselves. We have the chance to be vessels of greater powers.

And this is the life path of the inspired ninja, the one who chooses to open to a greater life.

It's a travesty to ignore, discount, or block the goodness in your life. You can unwittingly live a life that is smaller than your true nature. You won't consciously mean to do it. But you will do it. You will create the life you fear by paying attention only to the stories that reinforce what you do not really want.

A new life demands new choices. And one of the greatest choices you will ever make is to take your joy seriously, at least as seriously as your pain.

I know firsthand the cost of brushing off happiness. Years ago, to support the release of my first book, *This Time I Dance!*, I put myself on the road. It was a daring, heroic move, investing money in myself, speaking to practically any group that had a bunch of chairs; water was optional, crackers a luxury. At the first event of my hodgepodge "tour," I spoke to a creative business networking group. They loved my talk on "Discovering Your Creative Edge," and I loved them loving it. I felt like I was belting out a melody that had lived inside me my whole life. And they were singing the harmony that had lived inside them. Time disappeared. The small meeting room in the moderately appointed hotel became the Taj Mahal. At last my dreams had become real. I had a "national audience" for my message, or at the very least, an audience that didn't lick its own leg and yowl for Friskies. I was on my way. Cue the cartwheels.

That afternoon, still cartwheeling in the secret realms of inner joy, I walked into a Cost Plus World Market, one of those stores that sell ethnic home accessories, fun art, and things you really don't need but suddenly have to have. I sashayed down the aisles, boogie author, she who had just nailed her first real talk on this national adventure.

I picked up a piggy bank, a leather olive green pig with red and purple wings. "When pigs fly," I thought to myself and grinned. My journey of writing a book without a publisher or agent in sight and getting it nationally published and now speaking to people who wanted to hear me, in a state where I didn't live, seemed way more miraculous to me than a flapping sow. I was living what had been impossible *to me*.

I held the crafted object. "I should get this," I thought, to symbolize shattering discouragement and conventional limitations, rising above the mud of doubt. I continued to hold it in my hands, soaring with gratitude, suddenly in love with the artisans who had crafted such a thing, all of those who create in this lifetime, the presence of beauty all around us, and all of life. I was inspired. I noted its carved flowers.

"Yeah, but you know how things go," another inner voice, the most familiar one to me, piped up. It's my careful voice taking things down a notch, the one that guards against pain, hunts for risk of being hurt, believes pain has more gravitas than joy. This "smart" voice always has me living in what could go wrong. This voice tells me that it's safer to buy the wilting sale flowers at the supermarket when I am in love with the long-stemmed white roses.

The voice continued, "It's just the beginning of your trip. You don't know how the rest of the events will turn out. You could be disappointed and then you'll feel dumb about your fanciful totem. You could be overestimating your success." *Yes, as though, God forbid, I rewarded a moment that represented everything I'd ever wanted. This would be the calamity?* Then the voice threw me a bone: "Let's just wait and see how things turn out." And on that sad advice, I left the store. I never bought that pig.

That night I did a book signing at a bookstore. I'm not sure if the

Universe could have possibly done a better job at creating a shadow experience. So few people came. I swallowed hard as I realized it was time to begin and no one else was coming, no matter how long I stalled. Then a man with long stringy gray hair abruptly and repeatedly interrupted my reading with wandering political rampages and very private jokes, every author's nightmare rite of passage. The crowd, or more accurately, the wretched handful, stared at me helplessly.

I surveyed the empty chairs, and thought about the cost of the plane fare, hotel, and other "investments of faith" of this trip. I felt like a piñata, clubbed until the sweetness emptied out of me. "Good thing you didn't get that silly pig," said the voice inside. I cringed at the thought of having believed that everything would turn out just right, believing I was now finally on that roll I'd always dreamed about.

Today, years later, I know I should have bought the pig. I should have bought my celebration totem, because in that moment I felt fully alive—I knew love and achievement and the reality of my vision. It would have been wise to anchor that pivotal moment, to mark and memorialize that experience with more than a fleeting reverie.

The following disappointment didn't change the truth of the original life-changing moment—*until I let it.*

When I said, "Let's wait and see," I turned my power over to outside circumstances. That "wait and see" was an admission that I could change my mind about myself, about what had already transpired, and about the faith I held in the Higher Intelligence that whispered to me daily. That "wait and see" was an insider's bet on the dark horse of difficulty I'd trained myself to expect. But more than that, it was a vote to make moments of pain carry more consequence than moments of joy.

"I'm having more fun than I've ever had in my life," Anna, a wellness coach and trainer, said to me recently, giddiness in her voice. We'd been working together for a while and her business was gaining momentum. "I keep waiting for the other shoe to drop," she said. I was struck by how we douse ourselves consistently with limitation, tell ourselves, before we even *take in* our joy, that all good has to come to an end. What goes up must come down.

"We are meant to grow and expand. It's natural," I told her. We have the drive to develop our capacities, just like the pianist who commits herself to practice. It doesn't mean that every day is a banner day. But with practice, we develop, and everything gets better. "The better it gets, the better it gets," I said, quoting Esther and Jerry Hicks, some of my favorite teachers in learning how to consciously feel good.

This is the work for all of us courageous ones committed to living our best lives. We're not ignoring threats. But we're not minimizing love, astonishment, or the time of our lives either. We are taking in the nutrients in our lives so that we can grow stronger. We will not be harmed by taking in our good. We are designed to thrive.

When good things happen to you, don't wait for the other shoe to drop. You're just getting started. You are tapping into who you really are, which is why it feels so good. You are connecting to the Great Love, which is available to all of us. And you can do even greater things with greater love. You're just revving up. So, I wouldn't say the shoe in the air is about to drop. I'd say the shoe on the ground is about to fly.

TURNING POINTS:
Wait for the Other Shoe to . . . Fly

It's time to stop calling negativity "realism." I have an idea. Let's just call it negativity.

It takes grit to allow a force of good to work through you and for you.

Life gives us the chance to get realized, instead of
"realistic"—as in to let go of the small stories we tell
ourselves about what is possible.

It's a travesty to ignore, discount, or block the goodness in
your life. You can unwittingly live a life that is smaller than
your true nature.

You will create the life you fear by
paying attention only to the stories that reinforce
what you do not really want.

One of the greatest choices you will ever make is to take
your joy seriously, at least as seriously as your pain.

The following disappointment didn't change the truth of the
original life-changing moment—*until I let it.*

When good things happen to you, don't wait for
the other shoe to drop. You're just getting started.
You are tapping into who you really are,
which is why it feels so good.

SOMETIMES, YOU HAVE TO FEEL THE PAIN

*A spiritual perspective does not deny your pain or any aspect of
your human experience. It simply denies its power over you. It
gives you the strength when the tears are falling, and the power
to invoke miracles that lie beyond.*

MARIANNE WILLIAMSON

Acceptance is the key word here. If we resist pain, it will tighten its hold and strengthen its intensity; but the moment we fully accept it, we may overcome its stern dictatorship.

PIERO FERRUCCI

Life is the art of facing what you don't want, on the way to creating what you do want. The moment you chase the blue butterfly of desire, it's likely that you will move through the wastelands of disappointment, rage, and self-criticism. It's just the nature of transition. You are always passing through uncomfortable territory on the way to expansion.

I've also noticed that the more conscious I've become, the more sensitive I am to pain. In the past, I might have been numb or unaware. But now, no such luck. I'm involved in my own life. It's like when your foot falls asleep. As you wake up, you suffer the pins and needles of becoming more alive.

So, let me tell you this, my precious, conscious chickadee. How you deal with pain will determine your success and joy in this life.

Years ago, I discovered a courageous and profound way to deal with myself when I'm in pain. It does not involve tequila, Percocet, or binge-ordering cubic zirconia jewelry from the Home Shopping Network. Nor does it rule anything out.

This happened some years ago, but it's not like I've never dealt with pain again. I'd been "triggered" again by a nasty bout of self-comparison. My insecurities were raging. "It's not fair!" some part of me cried over and over. I slid into a funk of deprivation and frustration.

Let's just say I've been here before. It's the same sorry broken record of "I will never get to where I want to be." I don't want this agony to return. It has come to my house so many times and broken the dishes and kicked in the walls. But when it comes I feel as though I have little say. All my years of therapy, spiritual practice, and even teaching do not protect me from this vulnerability—which really, *really* makes me want my money back.

I know some spiritual leaders say that this pain is "optional." Well, let them walk on water in stilettos; I'm drowning. My pain is the only dish on the menu—the only menu in the only diner. Basically, it's what's for dinner. You may find yourself here sometimes. You're hurting. Yes, you know you're making yourself miserable by what you're thinking. But you are so far beyond finding that helpful right now. You just want a helicopter out of your despair.

Ironically, I was at a beautiful retreat center when this experience happened. Yes, life *does* have a sense of humor. There were ongoing workshops on meditation, yoga, and healing taking place. I paused by a still pond blossoming with water lilies. Barefoot and bald meditators walked by me, smiling with serenity. I wanted to trip them as they passed. I am not well, I tell you.

Heal my mind, I pray to any God who will listen. *Take these thoughts away*. I say the words, pleading and demanding. I stomp my foot, a princess calling upon the powers of the heavens as though they are disobedient maidservants. Nothing happens. Evidently, in this pain I cannot even pray right.

"Try focusing on something positive," I demand of myself. It's almost embarrassing how much good there is in my life, and how I choose to lie down on a bed of rusted nails instead. Realizing this makes me feel worse. "There are children starving in Africa, and they're probably *singing*," says my suddenly "spiritual" inner critic.

I'm sure I'm messing up my "vibration." I can see the quantum physicists shaking their heads now, whispering, "And it's not like she didn't see *The Secret*." I bet I'm creating a force field of negativity, which is like a calling card attracting—no, *begging* the lowlife energy of the universe to find me, because, obviously, *I'm* simpatico. Now I'm in even more pain, because I'm feeling bad about myself for being in pain.

That night, I talk to Nancy, a woman I have just met. Nancy is a healer by trade. But more than that, she is a healer by the way she looks at me. Her face is as open as a window in springtime and her eyes have seen it all, yet they look at me with burning interest. I feel the air slow down around her. I swear she is charming the molecules into sacred space. I start telling her about my situation, strategically inserting only the details that validate my cause and make me look pretty good, and not as much like the ragged, spiritually inept character at her table. I ask her how to deal with the pain of the situation.

I am hoping she will give me some Sanskrit mantra or insight to make it instantly disappear. I am hoping she has some kind of talisman tucked up her sleeve. I am hoping she will say something to prop up my wounded, terrified ego, maybe something like, *You're obviously a rock star who deserves better treatment.* Or better yet, *Here let me wave my magic wand, and don't worry, just for you, I'll waive my fee.* Or worst-case scenario, but still fine with me, I expect her to say, *I know a woman who can tell you which mother in which past life did this to you. I know a guru, a lobotomy specialist, a smack dealer; I'll get you connected.*

But she says none of those things. She says something I am not expecting. When I ask her, "What should I do?" she says quietly, "I guess there is nothing to do—but feel the pain."

I guess there is nothing to do but feel the pain. These words slow down time.

Part of me wants to say, "Come again?"

But the wise part of me, the one that instantaneously recognizes truth, wants to giggle and toss jelly beans at her feet. That part understands and claps its hands.

"Feel the pain," she says, and she says it with the kindness of a thousand years, like water that has loved a jagged rock and smoothed it into shining. Her healer's voice surrounds me with spaciousness, as though she can wait forever for me to take in this message.

I feel her recognize my sorrow and suddenly I recognize it— and I recognize that *it's okay* to feel sorrow.

I don't need to deny it or make it wrong or try to sweep it off my doorstep and scrub away its shadow. The moment she says, "Feel the pain," I feel as though the broken sorrows of the whole world are laid before me, the raw hearts of everyone, everywhere, who has ever felt pain. The hungry. The sick. The frightened. Somehow, we're all in this together, we've all been hurting at times, suffering in our own way, and I would not make these others wrong for anything—and finally, I do not make myself wrong either. I feel compassion.

This is what whispers to me in her words: Stop running and come in out of the rain. Wrap your little girl in a warm woolen blanket. Let's put on a pot of barley soup. Forgive your ego, your frightened one, for its tirade, for demanding the moon as proof of being loved, for needing things to be otherwise, for taking offense because the wind blew a certain way—not your way. Take those tight shoes off. Why, you've been running away from your truth for so long, you must be tired. Here, let's soak those feet in lavender oil.

The moment Nancy says, "Feel the pain," I don't feel lonely or separate from my life anymore. I feel as though I can be in this exact moment, in this exact state of mind. I feel as though she is asking me to allow Divine Genius, the eternal lover of the present moment, back into my heart. I feel as though she is reminding me of my real nature, a presence so beautiful and vast, it could sit with pain of any sort, frustration, anger, and betrayal, and welcome every wasp, spider, and aphid into the garden. Love isn't asking me to change or improve. I'm being asked to allow myself to experience the medicine and message of the moment.

Suddenly I realize I don't need Spirit to take away the pain. I only want Spirit to sit with me while I feel the pain. I need to sit with this part of myself. I need to hear her story, not fix it, agree with it, push it away, or try to change the circumstances that have caused it. I need to sit with this frightened part of myself. She needs to be heard. This is mercy. This is *maitri*, a Buddhist practice of loving-kindness. With acceptance and love, the poison will move through. This frightened part of myself will know how to move forward from here.

In the past, I have envisioned the Presence of Love sitting down by my side. It's the Holy Spirit, Jesus, Buddha, Allah, the Shekinah, or the spirit of the trees, sea, and grasses. Strong Love sits beside me. Strong Love sits behind me. Strong Love sits before me and above and below me. Strong Love can witness and contain anything. Strong Love can absorb the sting. Strong Love doesn't want to be anywhere else.

In the end, pain opened my heart to myself. It's always that way. I feel the love of the Infinite when I feel my own love. I feel that love when I stop running away from any part of myself or any experience I am having. I am willing to feel my pain. I am willing to feel my love. I am willing to feel my life.

An inspired life is not a life of avoiding pain. It's not negative to feel pain. No feeling is ever wrong. I am not weak or limited for feeling pain. This life is one of impermanence and change and demands a great deal from all of us. My spirit remains invulnerable. Which means it's safe for me to feel vulnerable. It's not pain that makes me feel isolated and frightened. It's my resistance to pain that closes my heart to myself and my experience.

> **" I feel the love of the Infinite when I feel my own love. I feel that love when I stop running away from any part of myself or any experience I am having. "**

I invite you to sit with yourself in the middle of a feeling that is uncomfortable—and bring in self-compassion. You deserve this grace. Feel the pain. I hope you can hear me whisper this to you, with the wisdom of the ages in my voice, a fierceness and gentleness that wraps around you.

I have faith in your ability to heal yourself.

I have faith in your ability to allow and absorb and find comfort with the truth of exactly where you find yourself in this moment.

I have faith in all of us.

TURNING POINTS:
Sometimes, You Have to Feel the Pain

You are always passing through uncomfortable territory on the way to expansion.

I guess there is nothing to do but feel the pain. These words slow down time.

I need to sit with this part of myself. I need to hear her story, not fix it, agree with it, push it away. . . . She needs to be heard. This is mercy.

With acceptance and love,
the poison will move through.

Strong Love sits beside me. Strong Love sits behind me. Strong Love sits before me and above and below me. Strong Love can witness and contain anything.

I feel the love of the Infinite when I feel my own love. I feel that love when I stop running away from any part of myself or any experience I am having.

An inspired life is not a life of avoiding pain. It's not negative to feel pain. No feeling is ever wrong.

My spirit remains invulnerable. Which means it's safe for me to feel vulnerable.

BECOME YOUR OWN COMFORT ZONE

We are meant to walk forward no matter what. As warriors for authenticity, we choose from love, the juice of being awake and on fire. Or maybe just awake and crawling. Or sometimes, just moving forward any freaking way we can.
                                        TAMA KIEVES (journal entry)

Don't listen to the crows. There is one within you who knows.
                                        TAMA KIEVES (journal entry)

If you want to live a self-actualized life—and trust me, you do—you will face fear. Now, I don't know about you, but my limiting ideas about myself can get as loud as crows. It can get damn uncomfortable. Maybe you think that emotional pain is the sign to turn around. But sometimes pain is the index that you're moving in the right direction. Sometimes, the only right direction is the direction of your pain.

I'm not talking about the kind of pain that signals to you that you're doing something wrong for you, like staying in an abusive relationship because of vows or continuing to ski, beating your chest like a silverback gorilla, when, really, you've broken a femur and should be screaming for morphine.

I'm talking about the fears that come up when we decide to grow. You may hold back from what you want, and you might call it lack of time, money, or inner strength. But I will tell you, you may be choosing from unconsciousness. I'd hate to have that happen on my watch.

The habitual self is motivated to keep us the same. It's wired to attack or flee any circumstance that rocks the boat. Yet going through life on autopilot is a suicide mission, because our soul's desires require us to break through this conditioning. Your True Self has the mandate not only to stay alive, but to *feel* alive.

It takes an act of mutiny to step into your destiny. That's what birth is.

But how do you get past that immediate impulse to fight, flee, or eat massive amounts of Danish butter cookies? These beautiful options are brought to you by the amygdala, the primitive, reptilian brain that doesn't know a thing about your inner spiritual warrior, or daring to date again or to direct a documentary. I don't know about you, but I don't want a lizard in charge of my evolution. I want an eagle. I want an archangel. I want Steve Jobs in his black turtleneck, or some other inner rock star CEO with monster vision and the cojones to fall down and dare again.

I want to choose from my soul's needs—what I passionately want—more than from the involuntary fears and pride that cheapen my potential. This is hairy, soul-splitting work at times. But the prize is sweet and outstanding and I can't seem to settle anymore for a life that offers anything else. Like an entire wave of people on this planet, I'm staying committed to making choices from my evolving self rather than my defended self.

It's not easy to go up against the herculean force of the familiar. As for me, I'm not into fanaticism. I'm no Navy SEAL. I won't be boot-camping my way through life's transformations. Go all the way, all at once—no exceptions, no excuses, no buttered popcorn.

I need to find my own pace. And I will make my boldest moves by listening to the kindest voice of guidance rather than being ridiculed and shamed into making the "right" decision.

That said, I do believe in supervising myself. Some of my unsupervised impulses are teenagers. They would eat bags of Doritos, joyride in residential neighborhoods, and smoke dope and crumpled packs of Marlboros if I let them. They would chase dark beautiful men into dark mysterious places that turn sad in the light. I've found that following my bliss is not a path of hedonism. It's a spiritual path, which means I am growing my devotion to the highest part of myself. That means I make choices that lead to bliss but don't always feel blissful.

Balancing these considerations, here's my bottom line: Face the uncomfortable things you need to face. But face them with kindness for yourself and a love that doesn't quit. I want you to win the marathon. I don't want you to have a fleeting week of discipline. This isn't an affair. It's a powerhouse marriage. I want you to open a door inside yourself that never closes again. I want to help you to keep walking forward, no matter what. Your destiny calls to you. You ache for it. And you deserve to go past your comfort zone into the stellar zone.

I'll break this down for you, because I've seen motivational speakers onstage and felt uplifted, but then I still couldn't face *my* fears. I always wanted to know exactly how "the expert" navigated his or her fear, like a blow-by-blow demonstration. Of course, I suspected he or she didn't *have* any real fear, because he had burly, salty Viking genes, or she grew up on Park Avenue, or someone else actually *believed* that things were "easy as pie." I needed my people, people who panted and procrastinated.

I want to give you hope—or as they say in evangelical churches, I want to give a testimony. I've struggled with panic, borderline phobias, Jewish relatives (need I say more and *What, you don't want the brisket I just made for you? And what do you know from evangelical churches while we're here?*), and the usual bottlenecks of low self-esteem and trust issues. Yet I have cajoled myself into moving forward consistently—and crafting a mission, career, and life I adore while doing it.

Here's my usual MO. When I dare something that stretches me, I walk forward both as spiritual warrior and as whimpering inner child. I make nurturing deals with myself. For example, I give myself permission to back out of things. The deal is I am required to step forward. But if I'm too uncomfortable, I can step back. And then begin again. This commitment to myself makes me feel safe. In safety, I am willing to dare things that make me feel unsafe.

I'll give you an example of facing one of my fears. It's not exactly a Gandhi or Mandela moment. But it's what I've got. And it works.

I am part claustrophobic, part control freak, and the owner of one finely tuned overactive mind. One summer, I was in New York City on a day that was probably 140 degrees Fahrenheit, but it only felt like 200, and I was riding the subway, which had turned into a trip to the rain forest or, in my guidebook, the ovens of hell. Packed into the uptown 3 train, in which the air conditioner had quit working, I felt walled in by the heat. Naturally, it crossed my mind, compulsively I might add, that I was in a tunnel under a city of more than 8 million people. Normal people read the newspaper, diddled with their phones, or grooved to tunes. This is where "intelligence" is way overrated. My insanity is quick, expressive, and plausible, though missing the big-time obvious point of being self-destructive.

Here's how I worked with myself. I did not say, "Buck up, for Christ's sake—no one else here needs a paper bag to breathe into and a therapist, now do they?" And I also didn't say, "Okay, break the window, hurl yourself out, get to freedom, now, now, now."

I chose a loving voice within, a sane voice that simply asked gently, "Can you be with this discomfort right now?" It continued with rationality and compassion. "You can get off at the next stop if you need. You can take a cab. I'll do anything you need, even if it's expensive. But can you go a little further? Can we try it? Would that be okay?"

The crazy part of me settled down, knowing she was loved and that, unlike times in the past—say, when she had to graduate Harvard Law School—she could have a definitive say. "Yes, I can ride a little longer," she said with ragged breath. And so it went. I kept that dialogue running for the next six stops, until my station.

I walked off of that train like an Olympic athlete who had taken home the gold. I had turned a knee-jerk situation into a series of mountaintop shamanic awakening experiences. I had stepped beyond the savage pull of stasis and familiar identity. I had moved beyond black-and-white, either-or. I had stepped into the realm of nuance, conscious volition, and new emotional muscles. I had discovered the wonders of staying honest, present, and kind. It's astounding to experience your own comfort in an uncomfortable situation. You can expand your comfort zone, your world, and your options.

> **I want to choose from my soul's needs — what I passionately want — more than from the involuntary fears and pride that cheapen my potential.**

I have learned to "ride the train" of many of my discomforts. I have stayed with writing when I wanted to burn everything and run to the hills (or at least the mall) because sometimes the more you face something that matters to you, the more you want to run. I have shown up at speaking engagements when some part of me would rather have shown up for brain surgery, *as a recipient*, with at least the guarantee of some nice high-grade anesthesia. I've shown up for "my bliss," again and again, paused before the terror alerts, and then walked into larger possibilities. Part of me died every time. Part of me was born every time.

When I work with clients I tell them, "We're not here to prove anything. We're not here to force growth or commitment. We're here to stay honest about what is possible in any given moment. So, sit down and write that memoir or begin that conversation with your boss or teenager or get back to lifting weights." Resistance will kick in; it's what keeps people from their best lives. "I'm bored. I'm hungry. I suck at this. This isn't fun. This won't ever go anywhere," the complainer will prattle. Steven Pressfield, the author of *The War of*

Art, reminds us, "The more important an activity is to your soul's evolution, the more resistance you will feel."

Just as with my clients, I'll ask you to turn this into a holy encounter with yourself, a meditation or conscious practice. Stay with the activity the wiser part of you wants to do. Stay a little longer. Go a little further. One day you will hear that complaining prattle as some familiar songbird in the yard. It will be in the background. For now, it still grips you.

When you feel resistance, can you stay honest with yourself? Ask yourself, not with derision but with playfulness and presence, "Can I stay with this activity a little longer? Will this boredom kill me? Will hunger really waste my bones if I don't get up to eat that bagel? Can I experiment with this, even if I don't have a guaranteed outcome? Or is this too much for me right now?"

Go beyond, just a little, where you have gone before. Walk past that demon of automatic reaction. It's worth staying present. You can discover an untapped well, a spring of freedom, your atman, a second wind. Ask yourself, will it hurt more to stay with this action, or will it hurt more to not stay with this? Slow down, breathe, and make a conscious choice.

Buddhist nun Pema Chödrön says in her book *The Wisdom of No Escape*, "Once you know that the purpose of life is to walk forward and continuously use your life to wake up rather than to put you to sleep, then there's that sense of wholeheartedness about inconvenience."

I'd love for you to have a life in which you do not shut down to growth and opportunity. Let love guide you more than fear. Meet your Whole Self, the one who can breathe through anything and walk you through any circumstance.

Keep daring. I want you to get where you're meant to go. I want this for all of us.

Ride your train, no matter how hot—or beautiful—it gets.

TURNING POINTS:
Become Your Own Comfort Zone

Maybe you think that pain is the sign to turn around. But sometimes pain is the index that you're moving in the right direction.

Your True Self has the mandate not only to stay alive, but to *feel* alive.

It takes an act of mutiny to step into your destiny. That's what birth is.

I want to choose from my soul's needs—what I passionately want—more than from the involuntary fears and pride that cheapen my potential.

Open a door inside yourself that never closes again. . . . Keep walking forward, no matter what. Your destiny calls to you. You ache for it. And you deserve to go past your comfort zone into the stellar zone.

We're not here to prove anything. We're not here to force growth or commitment. We're here to stay honest about what is possible in any given moment.

It's astounding to experience your own comfort in an uncomfortable situation. You can expand your comfort zone, your world, and your options.

Ask yourself, will it hurt more to stay with this action, or will it hurt more to not stay with this? Slow down, breathe, and make a conscious choice.

YOU OWE IT TO YOURSELF TO MAKE BRAVER CHOICES

And the time came when the risk to remain tight in a bud was more painful than the risk it took to blossom.

ANAÏS NIN

There's that horrible analogy about how a frog would never jump into boiling water. But if you heat the water gradually, it tolerates it. It doesn't register the danger. The frog boils to death in increments. Well, if that's true, I bet I could save my life in increments. Moment by moment I can make a braver choice.

TAMA KIEVES (journal entry)

In a particularly hard pose in yoga the other day, the kind that has me counting minutes until class is over, and maybe until my life is over, the teacher said something that I swear felt like throwing a diamond at my head: "Stay with this pose for just five more breaths and you'll have the satisfaction and accomplishment forever." He continued, "You can have a breakthrough if you go past what you always do. Something new may open up in your life. You will have this result for the rest of your life. You will have it for all your lifetimes."

I had been just about to crawl into flat-dead-middle-aged woman pose, which I happen to have down cold. For most of the class, I'd been listening to complacency, that muzzy-mouthed companion, and cozying up to being less than I could be.

I'd been making "easy" choices that did not give me ease. I was playing small.

But now, holy Shiva, I was in. I wanted to show up, take the uncomfortable high road for just a few more breaths, and have a new experience, some forward movement in my life, a new result I would have for the rest of this lifetime. Who could resist an offer like that? Then I realized I always have that offer on the table. I can always reach for greatness instead of familiarity. I can always choose comfort in this lifetime over comfort in this moment.

People ask me how I spent twelve years writing *This Time I Dance!*, how I stayed dedicated for that long, particularly without an agent or publisher or at least a trust fund or savior spouse sheltering me from the financial burdens of real life. I tell them, good strides happen minute by minute. It's the tiny choices that determine your life. Moments add up to months and years.

When I was writing, I wasn't thinking of years. I was just doing the best thing in the moment. It felt wrong *not* to write. I just kept asking myself, "What do I really want?" or "If I were listening to my Highest Self, what would it ask me to believe or to do?" I don't think I could have consciously made a commitment to years of my life, and, definitely, not to twelve years without a single guarantee. Yet I could commit in each moment.

I just had to listen. There was already a desire there, an instinct or pull to reach for my greatest love and growth, as there is in all of us. Those moments became a direction. That direction reflected a destiny. That destiny has become a growing national organization that inspires others, a bit of a worldwide community, a thousand bubbles that landed on the head of a silver pin. And most meaningful of all, I found a connection to a divine strength that I rely on in every aspect of my life. Those small, conscious choices led to incomprehensible fulfillment and abundance. They still do.

I have often shared in writing workshops that even if *This Time I Dance!* had never been discovered by my "fairy godmother" (a former publicist for Random House casually trolling Amazon) and then picked up by a major New York publishing house, I still would have enjoyed the result of my choice for the rest of my life. I had given myself a chance. I had acted with formidable self-love and respect. I had written the whole book, and even took a year to self-publish it. I had followed the iridescent butterfly all the way—and would never, ever have to wonder what might have been.

I had trusted my own inner guidance more than the storm warnings of fearful people who battened down their lives and still lived in fear. I had gone beyond my own narrow, "practical" ideas of what I could be or have in this lifetime. I put a toe in the water I wanted to swim in—and it gave me the ultimate leg up on life. It changed the way I slept at night. It took away my fear of death, and my fear of life. It changed the way I stood in a room full of people and it changed the way I sat with myself. It changed the way I say my name, and what I teach the children just by my existence. It has changed every other choice I will make in this lifetime. I know that consequence will last all of my lifetimes.

And if I had not taken the chance and written my book, that would have changed my identity as well. That act of self-denial would have been my ground of being. The truest part of me would have died. Though I may have dressed every day and brushed my teeth at night, I would have wandered the internal gray halls of pointlessness. I would have looked in other windows for joy, with eyes that had already been sealed.

I don't want to know what that self-betrayal would have cost me. I don't want you to know it either. *You can always choose again.* You can choose right now to make a choice that will honor your magnificence. Once you make the choices that honor you, you call upon the higher powers within you. You activate your root strength and raw magic. If you knew the significance of this choice, really there would be no choice.

Believe me, you want to know the experience of being alive in your soul. It doesn't come from doing what you've always done. It doesn't come from ignoring your potential or deepest desires.

Being radically alive doesn't come from going along with mass consciousness when you have maverick instruction within you—which you do. It doesn't come from choosing comfort in the moment over comfort in your lifetime.

A *Course in Miracles* teaches that in a spiritual life walk, we choose between littleness and magnitude. It says, "Littleness and glory are the choices open to your striving and your vigilance. You will always choose one at the expense of the other." It continues, "There is a deep responsibility you owe yourself, and one you must learn to remember all the time. The lesson may seem hard at first, but you will learn to love it when you realize that it is true and is but a tribute to your power. . . . Every decision you make stems from what you think you are, and represents the value that you put upon yourself."

Sometimes it doesn't *feel* glorious to let go of our littleness. It may require that we make a painful choice now, which pries us out of the habit of choosing less for ourselves. For me, the honorable choice is always the one that increases how much I love and respect myself.

> **❝ I can always reach for greatness instead of familiarity. I can always choose comfort in this lifetime over comfort in this moment. ❞**

I'll dredge up this example from my past. In my twenties, I was briefly crazy about a man named Scott. I was a young lawyer and he was, too. Scott had faraway eyes that hinted of secret sadness and spacious landscapes of emotions. Oh, but let's get real. He was intermittently emotionally unavailable—that holy grail, the king caviar of aphrodisiacs. This blue-eyed sorcerer was intensely present and loving in a moment, then gone in every way. I was in his tractor beam, miserable, and signing up for every minute of it.

One night he invited me to a party and I leapt at the chance. I hung around him, or in his orbit, for most of the evening while he socialized with every single other person in the room. I waited, knowing that when the crowd finally cleared, I could share the night with him. I had actually thought this scheme was *masterful*, instead of sad. Then I noticed there was another woman lingering in the shadows, orbiting Scott, too, the same plans smoking in her hooded eyes. I determined to wait it out. So did she. The party thinned as the night turned into morning, but stragglers remained, and so did we.

Finally, I made a choice I am forever proud of and will carry into all of my lifetimes. I walked out the door. I made one fragile, heart-wrenching gesture of self-respect. I sobbed the entire way home. I had not wanted to leave. I did not want to go back to my apartment alone and scared. I did not want to give up on the dream of Scott, though clearly it was already threadbare, a scrap of a nightmare, and nothing more than that.

I have so much gratitude for the bravery of my younger self in that moment. Her painful choice led to easier and more loving relationships in the future. The familiar and "easier" choice would have led to yet more nights of craving joy instead of moving toward it. I've often thought of that other desperate woman. She won the "prize" that night. The result of that choice extended past that evening, maybe into future neglect, competition, therapy sessions, and even future lifetimes.

There is a Tibetan proverb that says, "If you want to know your future, look at what you're doing in this moment." I don't know about you, but when I read that, I felt like somebody had thrown a bucket of seawater in my face. It's so easy to get caught up in the momentum of not choosing our boldest behaviors or vital aspirations in each moment. It's easy to settle for what we think we can have, no matter how inferior or flea ridden it is. I'm not talking about momentary spiritual acceptance of what is, which beckons freedom and forward movement. I'm talking about resignation and aligning with fear.

Do you find yourself going through the motions? I invite you to experience the golden blood of devotion moving through you instead. Choose your glory. Don't let the voice of weakness tell you what's possible. You are stronger than you know. You are not as tired as you think. Dignity will energize you. Accomplishment will excite you. Go past resistance. Walk through imaginary walls. Give your highest potential the highest potential of success. Always be gentle with yourself—and be fierce.

Glorious choices come from conscious choices. Remember, that autopilot is a kamikaze pilot. When it sees the possibility of moving into new territory or greater love, it dives into the paralysis of the docile. It protects the status quo. It is the guardian of habit. Autopilot will never elevate you. Autopilot can never help you soar.

I want you to have every good thing in this lifetime. Why be less than you can be? Give everything to your everything. I'm not advocating perfectionism. That comes from feeling inadequate or never good enough. Excellence comes from your divinity, from turning to the infinite resources within you.

You have a spiritual mountain lion within you that can rip through every limitation and change the way you walk in the world—and the world you walk in. You always have another chance to dedicate yourself to your magnitude. You always have another chance to dare again, reach higher, go further, and express more of your eternal True Self. Respect your precious time here. Please don't play small with your moments, yourself, or your life.

And if you forget, I'm happy to throw a diamond at your head.

TURNING POINTS:
You Owe It to Yourself to Make Braver Choices

I can always reach for greatness instead of familiarity.
I can always choose comfort in this lifetime over comfort
in this moment.

I had given myself a chance. I had acted with formidable
self-love and respect. . . . I had followed the iridescent
butterfly all the way—and would never, ever have to
wonder what might have been.

Once you make the choices that honor you, you call upon
the higher powers within you. You activate your root
strength and raw magic. If you knew the significance of this
choice, really there would be no choice.

Being radically alive doesn't come from going along with
mass consciousness when you have maverick instruction
within you—which you do.

Sometimes it doesn't *feel* glorious to
let go of our littleness.

Choose your glory. Don't let the voice of weakness tell you
what's possible. You are stronger than you know.

You have a spiritual mountain lion within you that can rip
through every limitation and change the way you walk in
the world—and the world you walk in. You always have
another chance to dedicate yourself to your magnitude.

Respect your precious time here. Please don't play small
with your moments, yourself, or your life.

Do Try This at Home: Jump-starts, Inquiries & Exercises

Some of these suggestions are just right for *you*. Others, not your cup of latte, or at least at *this* moment. Follow your gut. Feel free to adjust to your liking. Do what's right for you rather than what's written here.

Pick three Turning Points from this chapter. Write them out for yourself. Post them where you will see them. Meditate on them. Journal about them. Do a Freewriting exercise. (See page 252 for more about Freewriting.) Create a piece of art. Pay attention to your thoughts, memories, dreams, and "random" ideas and incidents. Inspired thoughts spark inspired responses. My words begin the conversation, but what do these truths unlock in you?

1. **Raise your "upper limits."** Keep a specific and detailed appreciation or gratitude list. Build your joy muscles. Do not dismiss compliments. Pay attention to specific things in your life or environment that "raise your vibration." What you focus on grows.

2. **Receive your good.** Notice: Where do you feel guilt or discomfort about having good things happen or increased abundance? And why? Thoughts around this? Find positive role models of abundance and ease. Meditate or journal on this: "It is my responsibility to allow myself to receive. I am connecting to the Great Love in all of us. I can do greater things with greater love."

3. **Anchor a great moment with a celebration totem.** Have you experienced a moment recently or in the past in which you felt fully alive or felt in your bones things were working out? Mark or memorialize your experience. Can you create or buy a symbol for this?

4. **Feel the pain.** Where have you been avoiding a painful feeling? Fear? Anger? Humiliation? Brokenness? Grief? Invite this part of yourself to share its story. Feel the feelings. Get out of your head. Can you sit with yourself in compassion and acceptance? Breathe. Listen to music. Feel. Let go. Comfort yourself. Connect to your compassion for others.

5. **Risk with strength and sweetness.** Make a commitment to stretch and to be your own comfort zone. Dare something important to you. For example, I will begin that uncomfortable conversation with my husband (strength) and if it gets too scary for me, I'll give myself permission to get off the phone (sweetness). And begin again.

6. **Go for the glory!** Create a "Littleness and Glory" list: Make a list of choices that make you feel little. And ones that help you access dignity, grandeur, or glory. Become conscious of your choices. Go for the glory this week. Go past complacency or comfort. Where can you stick with something you value a little longer? Focus on making braver choices.

Do you have a question about this chapter? I'd love to know what's on your mind! *I may just get wildly inspired and answer you immediately.* Send me your thought or question at www.TamaKieves.com/uncertainty-question, and you can also register for a **FREE** Thriving Through Uncertainty Coaching Call designed to shift your mind-set and bring you immediate clarity.

CHAPTER SEVEN

MAKE PROGRESS, NOT WAR (WITH YOURSELF)

MAKING IT SIMPLE TO MOVE FORWARD

In stages, the impossible becomes possible.

T. K. V. DESIKACHAR

Be not afraid of growing slowly. Be afraid only of standing still.

CHINESE PROVERB

I am going to tell you about cleaning up my clutter, baby.

I'm really telling you the secret of finding your niche in the work you love. I'm telling you how to learn Spanish or end world hunger. Or figure out who you are, now that you no longer even have a shot of fitting into your old skin. I'm even telling you how to move on from the one whose name must never be mentioned, though you mention it way too much.

This is about making progress in every way.

My home office resembled a bit of a junkyard for years, accented with tasteful teal walls. I'd answer the phone acrobatically (thank God for yoga). I knew exactly where the slip of paper with the red dash was, though to others my desk looked like the remains of a parade after a windstorm, a tornado, and the apocalypse. I am a lover of potential. Others say a clutter freak. But we're splitting hairs.

For years, I swore I'd sift, sort, and jump into current time. One Friday night, armed with meditation and gospel music, I finally decided to tackle a fat pile and the contents of all my desk drawers. I dumped everything on the floor. It looked like a whale or planet had thrown up. The debris was CD covers, half-started articles, a ring I meant to fix, scraps of images for art projects, bank statements, unknown bits of unknown things, and disintegrated "important" phone numbers. I was doing fine until I had the thought, "This is going to take so much longer than I thought."

Then I was sorry I had started. I felt bad that I'd believed I could do it. I immediately felt overwhelmed, zapped, depressed. And now I felt stuck in this mess I'd created.

It was too much. It was like a doctor had given me all the medicine at once instead of in doses. The body needs to heal in stages. Apparently, so does everything else.

But I had tried to zip through a decade's accumulation of unconscious choices in microwave-cooking time. I thought I could just whip it out.

Later, I cried to a friend with organizational chops. (She's a certified something and can find her car keys in under an hour.) She said, "Oh yeah, you never do it that way. Just take one corner. And set a time limit. Do it for twenty minutes."

Incremental change had not occurred to me. I wanted to power through years of inattention. I wanted this discomfort out of my life. I wanted to make progress and change my sorry, sloppy self into a minimalist—right this very second.

It was then I realized my "ambition" had another name: self-condemnation.

It wasn't love that said, "Fine, let's get this done, you freak." It was fury. It was oppression. It was self-hatred parading as enthusiasm.

But change that sticks requires diligence and patience, and I just have no patience for that. Yet the smart CEO within, who values real progress over flash-in-the-pan efforts any day, says, "There is no rush. There is no need to go faster. Take the time you need." This intelligence runs circles around the maniac of fits and spurts. Real power operates as serenely as a Quaker sewing circle. Quiet stamina crunches miles, heals illnesses, builds businesses, and opens the heart to greater love.

And there's scientific street cred to back this up, because God forbid we could be nice to ourselves without a reason or research.

Robert Maurer, PhD, in his book *One Small Step Can Change Your Life*, advises practicing the "kaizen way," a Japanese system of small goals and small steps. He documents how when we approach any big change or departure from our usual behavior, we trigger the amygdala's fight-or-flight response. The brain shorts out higher thinking in favor of basic survival. We experience this as being completely paralyzed or blocked. I experienced it as a sudden desire to consume an entire bag of blue corn tortilla chips and then judge my thighs.

But kaizen teaches that tiny actions slip past the radar. Non-threatening actions or inquiries help us move forward without fear. These small steps are the backbone of progress. When your fear isn't triggered, you have access to your rational and inspired mind. Creating a sense of ease for yourself encourages breakthroughs and accomplishment.

In any life change, especially when you are going after a deeper dream, you will want to learn how to move forward in small, consistent ways. You can't willpower your way through a wall. And there will be walls and chain-link fences. As you move toward your truth and potential, you will flush up your own opposition or any insecurity that has ever been in the way.

There is a reason you didn't make a conscious choice or didn't "listen to your gut" the first time. And that same fear will now show up wearing chain mail and chugging Red Bull. You will have jiggled the hornet's nest. And the hornets will not have studied the Bible or Buddhism. They will not turn the other cheek or count their breath. They want to sting your ass.

I've seen my coaching clients resolve to write their memoir or dare to raise their rates in their business. It starts off gloriously, but then the old foe in the alley meets them. "You're not that good. You've always been inferior. There's so much better talent out there. You should have made it by now, anyway," grouses the voice of the anti-calling.

"You're making progress," I tell them. "You're hitting the fear or pain that held you back. This is your do-over moment. Now you have the opportunity to move past that voice and choose something new. Take a tiny step. Make it super easy. Don't go proving something right now. I want this to be so easy, there's no resistance."

The same goes for you. I don't care if you militantly follow through on a goal. I care that you love yourself enough to pace yourself. I'd rather you take small steps or stop in the moment than drill into the hornet's nest of fears all at once and then stop for all time. I want you to learn how to become unstoppable. I'm after a bigger outcome than just the immediate results in front of you. I want you to set yourself free. However, you won't find freedom in one fell swoop. You will find it in continuous, small, life-affirming steps.

No one likes to hear this, but it's true. An inspired life requires tolerating incompleteness and uncertainty. This is a life that will always ask you to go beyond what you think you can do. Because that's how you meet your secret shaman, the part of you that surprises yourself with will, willingness, and the mental mojo to keep showing up. You're not here to "finish" things. You're here to *work through them*. Self-discovery is a process that never ends—if you're lucky.

It's not like you can eat enough so that you never have to eat again. It's better to have trail mix with you on the trail. You're just never going to be done with hunger. And you're never going to be done with change. So, give up the idea that you can do a massive push through it.

I remember talking to a website designer. "It takes forever to do a website," I whined, hoping for some chummy professional agreement. She smiled one of those thirtysomething smiles and said, "Oh, you'll never get it done." I smiled a thin, please-let-this-not-be-true smile. Endless work on a website? That sounded as good as endless gum surgery to me. I felt the need for an express exorcism. Demons snarled and pawed within.

Ms. Chirpy Designer continued, "Just when you get it done you'll have changed your mind and you'll want to do it differently. You'll always be growing." This from a technical person, no less. And there you have it. You'll always be growing.

> **" You're not here to "finish" things. You're here *to* work through them. "**

So, here's my new focus. I'm in this forever. I am in this for the joy of doing it.

I am not just getting things "done." I am making it simple to move forward. Maybe even fun. I am deciding to throw away one pen that doesn't have ink, or file one piece of paper. Or I am editing one paragraph of a script for a video. Or I am finding one thing I love about my partner, when I have gone down the warpath of thinking everything needs to change this instant because my life depends on it, or more accurately, *his* does.

A client of mine said, "I don't have to change my whole diet today. I'll start by drinking more water." Another reported in, "I'm not going to find my calling this week. I'm going to go to a meet-up group on alternative dispute resolution. Or I'm doing yoga for six minutes a day. Then from there, I'll take my next kaizen actions." I beamed, Jewish mother turning Japanese.

It gets better. Taking tiny steps will also put *magic* into your outcomes. "My need to finish things—kind of in a short-tempered way—blocks me," I confessed to a friend who paints every day. "Ya think?" she said. Then wisely shared, "When I've tried to 'do' a painting, or 'finish' a painting, I get stuck and the result looks over-worked. And then sometimes I'm frozen and can't move forward. But when I step back and say what's one tiny little thing I can do on the painting just to paint, just for the fun of it, that's when I get back into simply loving the process of painting. And wow, I love the surprises I experience then!"

I am in love with these tiny, pragmatic, significant steps. I know that really we are all practicing something so much bigger than the tasks at hand. We are deepening our secret powers, finding ways to slip out of the cage of overwhelm and frustration and into the territory of knowing what to do—one simple action at a time.

This isn't about getting it done. This is about knowing you can consistently handle facing uncertainty or challenge, and that's good news, because life is big and broken and wild and wily and not like anything on television.

I've come to realize that how I clean a desk drawer is also how I'll show up for a friend's prolonged fight with cancer or another's gradual healing of chronic fatigue. It's how I will deal with the loss of a job or a child, or any other monolithic change. I will lean into small, simple things I can do and the overwhelm will lessen.

Taking one tiny step in the right direction—recycling the

newspapers if you want to save the environment; writing for seven minutes if you want to pen your dissertation—this is the frontier of progress. This is sexy, meteoric stuff, though your ego will accuse you of being ridiculous. But with every small action, you bypass the foe, slip past the guards, skip off into the land of Showing Up before the ancient lizard brain realizes something massive has just occurred.

Going tiny is the new big. It's the only way to take on life-size goals. I am learning to access incredible bravery through the power of bite-size actions and composure. The crazy one within me screams, "It's never enough, it's never enough, you're too slow, you're doomed!" But I am going past my frightened ego, past this disbelieving one, and making continual progress.

With each small step, I am owning my integrity. I am doing what I can. I am carrying forth the light within me. I am moving past my shame. I am crossing the finish line every single time, in each momentary action.

This is not a small step. This is serving my potential and humanity. This is self-realization. This is never-ending achievement. This is no drop in the bucket. This is what's on my bucket list.

TURNING POINTS:
Making It Simple to Move Forward

When you are going after a deeper dream, you will want to learn how to move forward in small, consistent ways. You can't willpower your way through a wall.

Love yourself enough to pace yourself. I'd rather you take small steps . . . than drill into the hornet's nest of fears all at once and then stop for all time.

You're not here to "finish" things. You're here *to work through them.*

Here's my new focus. I'm in this forever. I am in this for the joy of doing it. I am not just getting things "done."

Taking one tiny step in the right direction . . . this is the frontier of progress. This is sexy, meteoric stuff, though your ego will accuse you of being ridiculous.

With every small action, you bypass the foe, slip past the guards, skip off into the land of Showing Up before the ancient lizard brain realizes something massive has just occurred.

With each small step, I am owning my integrity. . . . I am carrying forth the light within me. I am moving past my shame. I am crossing the finish line every single time.

This is not a small step. . . . This is self-realization. This is never-ending achievement. This is no drop in the bucket. This is what's on my bucket list.

IT'S ONE STEP THAT LEADS YOU EVERYWHERE

Go ahead and "look stupid." But don't be stupid. Do it anyway. Do the thing that matters. I'd rather be an idiot for my dreams than a measured colluder, an accomplice in the defeat of them.

TAMA KIEVES (journal entry)

I hear about people who "fell into things" just like that. Sure,
they tripped and fell into a bucket of money or a happy mar-
riage. Why doesn't that happen for me? When I stumble, I
fall into a briar patch. Then it starts hailing. Then my thera-
pist has a migraine, an aneurysm, or a hair appointment and
can't meet. Maybe ever.

TAMA KIEVES (journal entry)

You may think that happy, successful people shot up like beanstalks, knowing exactly what they wanted to do. They drew up the perfect plan on crisp white paper, not a grape jelly or red wine splotch in sight. They got it done, then sailed right along into instant manifestation land. They're lying on a white beach in Bora Bora beside turquoise water right now—near a bonfire of self-help books.

But people who are living fulfilled lives aren't lucky. There is a common denominator, a simple technology at play. I call it the genius code. It's moronically simple and sometimes diabolically hard to do. It's this: No matter what, they took one step in the direction of their hunch or desire. *They kept taking steps.*

It's one step that leads you everywhere. There is always a next step. You may want a guarantee before you take it. But the step *is* your guarantee.

I'm not a fan of quantum leaps that involve actual leaping. As far as I can see, it's the daily nuances that matter more than one big push. It's the willingness to consistently follow the iota of guidance when it prompts you. The smallest suggestions matter, just like over time, raindrops carve canyons and ideas transform nations.

Besides, there are no small steps when it comes to listening to your truth. You are either following what you know or following your doubt. It's practically the meaning of life, and you get to practice it in every single instant.

Will you listen to the small nudges of intuition or will you choose small-mindedness? Over time, choices compound just like the interest on savings or debt. Good choices lead to more good choices. Sad choices lead to more sad choices. Momentum builds momentum.

> **It's one step that leads you everywhere. There is always a next step. You may want a guarantee before you take it. But the step *is* your guarantee.**

I'll give you an example. I wanted to be a paid speaker at this one conference that, well, let's just say in layman's terms, hadn't given me the time of day, though I did get a spiffy form rejection letter—complete with a sales pitch to attend the conference at full price. A friend of mine got invited to go camping with some of the organizers and he invited me and my partner, Paul, to join him. I want to meet the organizers on that trip, I thought immediately. It felt like a ray of clarity. Then came the cold feet: It would be a long drive, time away from actual income-producing work, and days spent with individuals who obviously saw me as chopped liver instead of prime rib—or prime time.

"Have you no self-respect?" whined my ego. "Why would you want to go with people who didn't invite you to their conference?" I started waffling. These are the moments of truth that will make all the difference. This is where your life gets created. It all comes down to which internal voice you listen to. I don't know about you, but for me, resistance, the force that overrides my instincts, often barges in like the secret service, doing damage control for my ailing self-esteem. But this kind of "damage control" does damage.

Now, to clarify, I want to avoid humiliation at all costs. I'd say that it is practically one of my prime directives in life. But then there's this other me, I'll call her Yoda-Tama, all emotionally healthy and farseeing, who cannot bear even the *thought* of regret.

She—and I—just can't stand the idea that maybe I had a chance and I didn't love myself enough to take it. Yoda-Tama quotes the comedienne Lucille Ball, who said, "I'd rather regret the things I've

done than regret the things I haven't done." So, to stay true to myself, I am willing to go beyond my own self-consciousness—and act
conscientiously on behalf of my instincts and desires instead.

Thank goodness on that day the sun was shining or maybe
some passerby had smiled at me or I'd watched a great movie the
night before—who knows?—because I had a clear thought, a good
thought about going on this camping trip. *I do have self-respect*, I
thought to myself. *I respect my instincts more than my inhibition.* I just
felt like my friend inviting me on this camping trip was like the
Inspired Master of Ceremonies throwing me a line. I took the cue
and packed.

On the trip, I met Carol, one of the organizers, and told her
how much I wanted to present a workshop at the conference. "I'm
sorry, Tama, the speakers have already been selected," she said de-
finitively. Then she smiled. Now, this may just have been a smart
move on her part—you know, be nice to the desperate person in
front of you and all, since you're going to be stuck in the wilderness
with her for a few more days. But I took it as the dead bolt being
released.

"Stay in the conversation." I remember hearing that phrase from
a sales coach years ago. It meant never just fold when someone says
no. Go deeper. Go wider. Find out what the no is really about. Find
 out if you can meet the person's hesitation with information or a
resolution that works out even better.

Now, normally, I love this kind of junk about as much as I'd love
having an MRI or colonoscopy. It feels pushy to me, like when a
telemarketer calls and "stays in the conversation" until you find
yourself lying to him ever so slightly about having a fire in the
house—or screaming profanities about his company, his children,
his *dog*, just so you can hang up and get back to your Nonviolent
Communication or knitting with a Jesus group.

But then again, we're talking about your life here, everything that
matters to you. It's worth just having a little more communication

when you can. Your life deserves the extra poke at possibility. You don't know what ideas can arise. Maybe it goes nowhere. But your life is worth a conversation. It's not about being pushy. It's about being purposeful. I'm asking you to stay true to what you want and find out what's available.

"I'm happy to speak for free," I volunteered. I knew I really wanted to be at that conference. I had this white-hot feeling that I belonged there. "Well, at this point," she said, "I'm sorry, but there's not even any meeting rooms left for workshops, since they're all in use." She went back to eating some baked beans off her paper plate, poor woman, assuming I'd let her chew.

But my inspiration, knowing sense, messiah complex, or whatever it was just wouldn't quit. I spoke from the place in my core that loved the work I do. "Maybe I could offer an optional workshop during lunch, maybe outside, allowing people who wanted to drop in." A butterfly flitted nearby and Carol looked at me in a way that let me know she was done with me, but not done in the I'm-annoyed-and-never-want-to-see-you-again way. "Let me see what I can do," she said.

So get this. She called the next week. A conference room at the hotel had opened up. I don't know how and I didn't ask. Then Carol said that while they still couldn't pay me, they had decided to cover my travel expenses. I was thrilled.

At the conference, the video team picked my workshop to film, which gave me more exposure and also professional footage I could use in my business to promote my speaking.

After the conference, Carol surprised me. "I didn't feel right not paying you," she wrote. "So please accept this check for your wonderful workshop. I've gotten such great feedback." But that wasn't the end. It was only the beginning.

Some other conference organizers saw me speak at this conference and invited me to speak at their coveted event in San Francisco. At that event, I met a woman who invited me to lead an all-day workshop at her organization in New York City. Someone saw me speak at that event and invited me to speak to a large audience in Seattle. I'm not even telling you about the clients I got from these experiences or the individuals who then showed up at retreats. Or the national reporter who called me after a Seattle bookstore clerk (who'd seen me speak) had recommended my book to her. I am not making this up. It's years later. And that bright coin is still rolling down the hallway. And that's just the connections I know about.

And I think to myself: What if I hadn't listened to that first hummingbird hunch to go on that camping trip? What if I'd ignored the desire to talk to Carol? Or what if I had stopped, understandably and politely, when Carol said they had already chosen their speakers? I would have missed so much. And as one of my clients has reminded me, "*I* would never have met you and found *my* dreams." This adds another layer to the intricacy. By following our intuition, we play a part in a larger plan that involves the good of others too. That can throw a curve ball of guilt at you. And I'll use anything that works.

The literature of success is filled with people who just kept taking steps toward what they wanted. The creative genius Walt Disney was famous for his sense of perseverance. For example, he wanted to make the book *Mary Poppins* into a film. But Pamela Travers, the Australian-born British author, refused. I've read that Walt Disney visited Travers at her home in England for the next *sixteen years*. That is staying in the conversation. Most of us would be lucky to remember there *was* a conversation. You know the end of this story. And generations of viewers get to see what Walt Disney had seen all along.

And let me tell you about Ray Bradbury, the famous science fiction writer. He shares his story in a great book called *Zen in the Art of Writing*. One day the young Bradbury, at the time living in a thirty-dollar-a-month apartment, felt moved to take a walk on the beach. Strolling, he glimpsed some debris that he creatively imagined as the skeleton of a dinosaur. That night, he got out of bed and wrote a short story about a hulking beast. He ended up selling that story to *The Saturday Evening Post*. The film director John Huston read the story and asked Bradbury to write the screenplay for his film *Moby Dick*. Because of working on *Moby Dick*, Bradbury wrote an essay that got read by the 1964 New York World's Fair people, who he says "put me in charge of conceptualizing the entire upper floor of the Federal Pavilion." Because of that pavilion, the Disney people hired him to write the script for Spaceship Earth, the attraction featured in Epcot's iconic sphere. You see where this is going.

What if Bradbury had decided to turn on his equivalent of Netflix instead of walk on the beach that first day? Or what if he hadn't gotten up to write that short story? What if he'd thought, I need my sleep, I've got CrossFit in the morning?

When you hear stories like these, it's so easy to see how each step is needful and clicks like a domino. Bradbury walked on the beach when the impulse struck. He ignored the sale on men's leather belts at Macy's. He got out of a warm bed and wrote the words that became the story. He didn't say, "Maybe tomorrow." Or "Once I get the kids through college, organize the toolshed, handle my fear of success, finish this sudoku and this unopened bottle of scotch, and consult with my financial adviser and life coach." He didn't ask, "Where's *that* going to go? He followed the tingle of invitation, or in his case the moan of a dinosaur. He took the step.

When it comes to your next steps, follow your intuition. Keep the ball rolling. Move the chess piece forward and stay in your game. You'll see things differently. You'll unleash new brain chemistry. And you'll experience a spike of integrity, no matter what.

Every step is an answer to a prayer. Every step is a devotion. Every step is a pledge: I will serve. I will listen. I will honor. I allow life to reveal itself to me in masterful increments. I allow the Creative Mystery to instruct me in a step-by-step strategy I could never foresee. I will not waste the guidance. I obey my guidance instead of my resistance. I will not squander chances.

This is a practice. This is a dedication. This is real progress. This will make all the difference.

TURNING POINTS:
It's One Step That Leads You Everywhere

It's one step that leads you everywhere. There is always a next step. You may want a guarantee before you take it. But the step *is* your guarantee.

There are no small steps when it comes to listening to your truth. You are either following what you know or following your doubt.

Over time, choices compound just like the interest on savings or debt. Good choices lead to more good choices. Sad choices lead to more sad choices.

To stay true to myself, I am willing to go beyond my own self-consciousness—and act conscientiously on behalf of my instincts and desires instead.

Stay in the conversation. . . . It's not about being pushy. It's about being purposeful. I'm asking you to stay true to what you want and find out what's available.

By following our intuition, we play a part in a larger plan that involves the good of others too.

Every step is an answer to a prayer. Every step is
a devotion. Every step is a pledge: I will serve.
I will listen. I will honor.

I obey my guidance instead of my resistance.
I will not squander chances.

REMEMBER WHEN YOU GOT IT RIGHT

We are conditioned to let go of the inspiration, to say it wasn't real. But the practice is to let go of the negation, to say that wasn't real.

TAMA KIEVES (journal entry)

It is better to believe than to disbelieve; in so doing you bring everything to the realm of possibility.

ALBERT EINSTEIN

Do you ever feel like you're not making enough progress? (I'm just so psychic, aren't I?) Well, you might have this crazy idea that success is a static condition, like a solid redbrick house. But I believe progress is a series of moments, individual holy stars beaming in a black moonless sky. I'd love you to claim your shining moments.

Every day, I work with coaching clients involved with different stages of creating their own empires, healing from the inside out, finding their true note in their organization, or just climbing out of a paper bag. And this much I can tell you: No one is *always* doing great. No one ever feels as though she is selling every doughnut in her doughnut shop. But everyone has had at least one inspired moment when life just works. And that's the gold I hunt for—the moments when the truth prevails.

An inspired moment is the Universe's way of introducing you to yourself. It claims you. It authorizes you. An inspired moment teaches you who you really are. You've had them. It's a moment when you knew you were born under a red star and meant to do something outrageous or purposeful and significant. It's the moment when you knew you had to have a child or move across the world. It's a moment when you knew everything would be okay, even though you had no clue how you knew.

Inspired moments are the times when you connected with your true blueprint—a quiet wisdom or boundless love. These were the moments you felt improbably free and complete. These are the moments you felt as solid as a redwood, even when you were teetering on a dusty footpath at the edge of the world. These inspired moments are real. But if you do not feed them, they cannot feed you.

To live an extraordinary life is to trust your inspired moments more than you trust in anything else. I don't care if you have felt as though since that time nothing came of it. Or that you botched up your chance. *I want to know what you knew when you knew.* That's your soul's knowing. That's your true story—not so much the form of what was going on but the feeling. Yes, this practice flies in the face of a culture gone mad with warnings and intellectual hesitation. Most of us are reminded to heed our limitations more than our inclinations. But you don't have limitations. You have limiting beliefs.

Let me offer you an example. To become a professional speaker, I had to get past my limiting beliefs. I'd had a lot of fear. For years, I'd be panting at the thought of certain kinds of speaking—not in excitement, mind you, but more like your average house cat jimmied into a carrier flying down the highway.

"You see this speck," said my friend Paula, as she pointed to some pockmark in the wooden table. "That's your fear about speaking." I wanted to interrupt her and tell her that no, really, my fear was Godzilla with a toothache, marching through Midtown Manhattan, roaring and crushing skyscrapers into origami. She pointed to the speck again. "That tiny, tiny nothingness is all it is."

Then, like magic, I suddenly had the image of a canker sore, a tiny white dot in your mouth that feels like a rock concert in a phone booth, intense and overwhelming. I got it. The speck wasn't my identity. It wasn't the full-time me. It wasn't me! And it wasn't the truth about what I could have in life. It was a loud and angry dot. It *felt* like all of me at the time. But it wasn't.

There *is* another me who speaks. She is clear and natural and connects with the audience, as though she's reaching across the kitchen table passing the biscuits. She is in her element. She is goddamn sunlight.

I flashed on one of *those* moments. Years ago, I spoke at a high-end women's leadership event. I was on fire. It was unspeakable what happened in that room—but you know me, I'll speak of it. I'd tell you I got a standing ovation, which is true. But really I think I got an infusion.

Still, I'm embarrassed to share that I'd allowed the angry dot to make my speaking career decisions for years. I held shabbier visions for myself. I sided with the frightened me. I didn't see this as fear. I saw this image as my true, albeit diseased, identity, the one I secretly spoon-fed and soothed in the basement while people mistakenly praised my abilities.

Psychology experts have coined the term "impostor syndrome," in which high-achieving individuals do not believe in their achievements, and rather feel as though they are scamming the world. If you've ever felt this way, I've got news for you. Fear has been scamming you. It's the fraud. It's the one in the shiny cheap suit hustling you to believe in its sad portrayal of your possibilities. It's selling discouragement by the truckload on every street corner in the world.

This is what I want you to know: Only your strength is real. Everything else is practice.

The wisdom of A Course in Miracles teaches that "only the love is real." Everything else is fear—a temporary disconnection from the powerhouse that you are—a powerhouse that is not mealy-mouthed and has never once had the belief that you shouldn't have sung at the top of your lungs when that cute guy called or that your idea for a business was dumb. Fear is fog obscuring the mountain, but it's not the mountain. It's mud coating the golden Buddha, hiding but never destroying the gleam. Real love is real. Your excitement is real. The times you got it right, that's what's real. That's why they felt so right.

> **Remember what you knew when you were on fire, not when you were tired. Stay faithful to what you knew when you were most alive. Those are your diamonds.**

When you're not inspired, you're not in your right mind. The power is off. You're not plugged into your true capacities. But just because the plug isn't in the socket doesn't mean electricity doesn't exist. Of course, you will experience times of disconnection. Still, disconnection doesn't mean the power has disappeared from the building or that there never *was* a building. It just means that you've allowed a circumstance to become your identity instead of remembering your identity—and shifting your circumstances.

Sure, I know that doubting ourselves is the "human condition." But it's not the transcendent one that is also true about you. When you're connected, the exact circumstances of your present life don't matter as much as what you know inside. You know unwavering love. You're not worried about transitory appearances—because you know another truth. It's not about being delusional. You don't negate your circumstances or current abilities. You just don't let them define you.

Still, it's status quo to be suspicious of excitement and dreams. Some see inspiration as just a sugar high of the mind—unsustainable, a wafting pipe dream. They quietly suggest you shouldn't operate heavy equipment—or your life—while under its influence. You are encouraged to doubt this wild, pure strength and trust more in the times when you lose it than in the times when you felt more like yourself than you ever had.

Now, pessimism we put stock in. We trust our cynicism as though it's wisdom, the voice of experience instead of embitterment, the way the world works, no questions asked. We think negativity is getting down to brass tacks, instead of moments when we *lapsed*. We don't see fear and anxiety as flights of imagination. We see *those* as probabilities.

But your dreams can take off at any minute. You can write a screenplay that Sundance produces, even if they've rejected your work before. You can quit drinking this time. You can still buy a farm home on the hilltop in France, though you're struggling to pay rent in Boise right now. You can change the face of education or ineffective legislation, even if you've never had a website or a Facebook page. This happens. But only when we feed the light within us.

Don launched his new digital photography business after coming to one of my retreats. He wrote me an e-mail: "This is the best Christmas morning I've had in years. And it's only Nov 18th." A client said he heard Broadway show tunes playing in his head as he prepared for a media appearance. A friend found the man of her dreams and saw dominoes falling into place, click, click, click. "I finally realized how much I am born to love," she said.

These moments of *becoming* are real for all time.

These are the times when life just made sense, and you felt like you'd landed in your own skin at last. Like you finally smelled the musk of a lake or forest you had searched for all your life and you knew you had arrived. This was vital information.

Even if the moment passed. Even if conditions changed. *It was still true*. And it's time to pick up where you left off. It's time to take the gift of knowing everything you knew was possible in a given instance, and study it as though it was your own Rosetta Stone or a tablet that God—on one of her infinite mercy days—chucked at your head, along with those endorphins, coincidences, and lightning bolts to *maybe* get your attention. Because you're not supposed to base your life on the moments when you stumbled. You are the moments when you rose.

I discovered the poet Jack Gilbert, a beautiful spirit, in *The Sun* magazine. And I love how he explored an inspired moment, the myth of Icarus, said to have "fallen" because he flew too close to the sun. The myth suggests we might not want to trust our instincts or grand desires. But Gilbert says, "Everyone forgets that Icarus also flew" and "I believe Icarus was not failing as he fell, but just coming to the end of his triumph." I love that reminder. And, sure, you may be tempted to point out, because you're picky like that, that Icarus fell to his death. Yet some of us are dying from lack of flight and lack of genuine connection to who we really are. And I can only imagine the feeling of legitimacy Icarus felt, soaring at last, thinking to himself, *I knew it. I knew it. I knew I was meant to do this.* I'm reminded of a Cuban saying my friend Teo taught me, that translates, "You can't take from me the dances that I've danced."

When things change, it doesn't mean you failed. "Following your bliss" or "guidance" isn't an immunization from life, a Get Out of Jail Free card, or a guarantee of a neat, straight line. You can meet the love of your life and still divorce and face some horrible little abandonment issue you saved for a rainy day. You can finally leave your corporate job to enroll in an executive coaching program, only to have a loved one have a stroke and require your care. Life is messy. Thriving is not an unwavering condition, as much as it's an unconditional response to life.

Only you get to define your progress or your real identity.

How will you measure your life? Do the latest bank statements negate the moments you waltzed in the yellow moonlight in the square in Vienna, forgave your drunken father or yourself, campaigned for animal rights, did a handstand in a yoga class, read your poem at open mic night, or fell in love? Will you turn on yourself in this way? What about *who you became* by walking in the direction in which you were called? Are you still walking forward? You have no idea what's still available. Because what's in front of you doesn't define what's inside you. And it doesn't define where you're headed.

Please remember what you knew when you were on fire, not when you were tired. Stay faithful to what you knew when you were most alive. Those are your diamonds. Everything else is an angry or fearful dot. A moment of disillusionment about who you are is not a moment of clarity.

I don't know about you, but when I leave this planet, I'm taking the diamonds. I'm taking the love. I'm taking the truth. I'm not taking the moments when I didn't hit my note. I'm taking the moments when I did.

TURNING POINTS:
Remember When You Got It Right

An inspired moment is the Universe's way of introducing you to yourself. It claims you. It authorizes you . . . teaches you who you really are. You've had them.

Inspired moments are the times when you connected with your true blueprint. . . . These inspired moments are real. But if you do not feed them, they cannot feed you.

I want to know what you knew when you knew. That's your soul's knowing.

Only your strength is real.
Everything else is practice.

The times you got it right, that's what's real. That's why they felt so right.

Thriving is not an unwavering condition, as much as it's an unconditional response to life.

You have no idea what's still available. Because what's in front of you doesn't define what's inside you. And it doesn't define where you're headed.

Remember what you knew when you were on fire, not when you were tired. Stay faithful to what you knew when you were most alive. Those are your diamonds.

HOW COME IT TAKES SO LONG TO SUCCEED? (AND HOW COME YOU'RE ASKING THAT QUESTION?)

We want a medicine man or a New York Times–endorsed expert to tell us what to do or to confirm we're on the right

path. And while we search for this information, we miss vital
information, the information that arises from our souls.

TAMA KIEVES (journal entry)

Secretly, I believe there's a divine appointment—a time when
you finally stop searching for reasons for your supposed failure
and start cherishing your own becoming instead. A life-
changing experience only comes from a life-changing relation-
ship with yourself.

TAMA KIEVES (journal entry)

I've met many individuals who are working on long-term dreams or
goals. I watch them worry like grandmothers, patting down an
imaginary apron, or get all frantic like some butterfly in a bag, as
they talk about their perceived lack of progress. It's the question
that plagues so many daring to live unconventional, inspired lives:
Why does it take so long for things to turn around? Why does it
take so long to succeed?

If you've been consciously looking at your life for any amount
of time, you will no doubt fall into the tar pit of the blame game.
I've slipped into this abyss without even knowing there was one.
Like Lot's wife in the Bible, I kept looking back. Unlike her, I wasn't
afraid of what I was leaving. I was more afraid that I *wasn't* leaving.

I kept thinking I *must* be doing something wrong. It was obvious
everyone else had it altogether. I saw it on TV (though I managed to
ignore the drug commercials for depression, high blood pressure,
fatigue and anxiety, which should have been a clue). I kept looking
for a fly in the ointment, my core issue, my pattern, an ancestor's
pattern, *something* to blame for still being in a life in process.

Well, I'm poetic, moody, and emotionally apocalyptic, and I
journal more than I move, so there was that.

Or maybe I just didn't go to the right astrologer, business coach,
or witch doctor. Maybe I should have seen John of God or at least

Tony Robbins, or spent a tiny bit less time plundering Nordstrom and thrift stores. Maybe I should have shoveled out my subconscious mind, gotten a chiropractic adjustment for my karma, taken an Internet marketing course, or moved to the Bay Area. And don't get me started on family. Don't even.

I often imagined others bungee jumping their way into outstanding results and making Silicon Valley salaries, leaving legacies instead of apologies, or having the inner peace of Jesus, a home life of baked bread and Scrabble, and steamy love affairs in Ibiza.

Why weren't great things happening to me? I knew I had some decent potential stock. I knew I belonged in a life of goodness. I knew I had gifts to give. I knew we all deserve love and opportunity. I kept trying to figure this out, solve my life's dilemmas like an algorithm or the ultimate Rubik's cube. I kept trying to learn what others knew and how they pulled it off.

I can't tell you when it happened, but I finally realized the most important thing: *There was nothing to figure out*. The reason I couldn't find the "something" I needed to change was because I'd been wrong thinking that there was something I needed to change. I'd thought that if I could just track down the one defect, then I could make life perfect. Everything would all come together in a Hollywood flourish and stay that way forever.

But there was nothing wrong. There never is.

Yes, I know, my fellow savvy eye roller, it's a harps and patchouli "spiritual" thing to say, but it *is* a spiritual thing. It's a jug of water in the desert, a jug of *holy* water, if you ask me. It's the absolute turning point. It's the threshold. It's surrender and acceptance and the freedom of an emotional Mardi Gras all rolled into one. It's the ground of being for a different way of life.

In *A Course in Miracles*, it says the ego's main teaching is "If this were different, I would be saved." Essentially, it's a way of making sure that you never land in your life right here and now. Instead you look for a rescue, a fix, a guarantee, a finale. You make yourself wrong. You push away the life before you, the circumstances that are here to serve you, convinced you know what is true. You deny your own love—separate from what is—and guarantee an inability to thrive.

Yet in life, *there will always be uncertainty*. There will always be a gap, a space between where you are and where you want to be. This isn't failure. This is life, especially for someone who continues to grow.

You have every right to desire progress. But it's disabling to condemn where you are. Thriving comes from loving, not from withholding love. This is a miraculous adventure. And nonjudgment is the only way you will discover your True Life, a life you cannot imagine, one that you want with all your heart, the one that is already here and available to you.

> ❝ **You have every right to desire progress. But it's disabling to condemn where you are. Thriving comes from loving, not from withholding love.** ❞

If you want to grow, turn your focus toward the sun. Begin to ask yourself: What am I doing well? How have I progressed? What feels good to me? What's been moving in the right direction? How can I be self-affirming right now? This isn't *Sesame Street* for the slow crowd. This is open sesame—the unlocking of more than you knew you could have.

You're always moving forward. You may have a narrow definition of what success would look like. You may feel as though the rug has been pulled out from under you. I'd say you're on a magic carpet ride. You're no longer in the life you planned. This is a life that is bigger than your plan. This is inspired jurisdiction.

Sorry, Dorothy, you're not at the big box stores at the mall anymore, where everything is as usual and you have the illusion of order, control, and manageability. Because when you're growing, opening to your own signature soul adventure, nothing is going to be predictable.

This is not a path of thriving through manipulation and control. You are learning to fly—to lose ground and find grounding *wherever you are*. Thriving means trusting your own experience to lead you where the deepest part of you longs to be, instead of fighting your life and yourself at every turn. There's leeway. Fluidity. Trust, love, and energy. This is real success.

Rhonda was in my Inspired & Unstoppable Life Tribe and for months she'd been struggling with trying to force the ending of her dissertation, and a move to another state. Finally, she decided to stop beating herself up and pushing. "I'm feeling more free. I don't know exactly what I'm doing, but for the first time I'm really excited by that." She added, "I'm letting life be life on life's terms. I kept thinking I needed to figure it all out. Now I see there's something bigger going on. It's not up to me to make it all happen."

It's not up to you to make it all happen, either. There is a mystical confluence, a divine backstory and stage construction coming together—or let's just say things happen when they are ready to happen. In Zen, they say, "Spring comes and the grass grows all by itself." Likewise, it takes nine months for an embryo to grow into a fetus, and no mother wants to rush this gestation and deny her child every possibility of development (unless she's fully pregnant in August and it's hot as hell—then she could be tempted to pry the thing out with a crowbar). And the fetus doesn't need to say affirmations or learn the six steps to better toe development to save time. Things in nature aren't about saving time. They're about taking time, as in utilizing *where they are* to grow into their fullest expression. Nature is all about the right timing.

I know it's scary to let go of "control"—as though you have it. We live in a world of intellectualism, where we're taught that if we just learn enough or do it right, we can take charge. We will never have to face our wobbling selves, our badgering fears, and trust that things are working out. But this is such a small way to live.

I see this in my programs. Students want the three steps, the eight steps to success. Hell, they'll do the 180 steps, and even a few tap dances, jumping jacks and Hail Marys, if that's what it takes. They just don't want to hear about the only step that makes all the difference, the one step that feels like a free fall—that feels, perhaps, like giving up, yet is the fast track to everything you could ever want. Trust yourself. Love yourself. Bless your journey, for you are surely on one. The mystic Andrew Harvey says, "You have to leap into the fire. Nobody will do it for you. Nobody *can* do it for you."

Of course, "official" steps make our pointy-headed egos feel like they're accomplishing things. Our egos love shiny binders packed with impressive worksheets with good graphics and wonderful logos. They can tell you what they learned. But who cares what you learn? I care about how alive you feel. Are you tingling with presence? Are you dancing in the moonlight, even when it's just you alone in your kitchen, underneath an environmentally sensible halogen bulb? Do you know something inside yourself that can't be taken away, even if circumstances change? Let me tell you, love is so much bigger than control.

It's always been *love* that has moved me forward. All the data or strategy in the world couldn't give me the solidity of one inspired moment. I've had times when I felt this sweet, crazy, freaking divine connection and I'll tell you right up front that it didn't happen when I was judging myself or my life. It didn't happen from planning my life and following through like an automaton either.

I needed uncertainty to stay open. I needed to stay open to receive more than just an answer, but a true way of getting all my answers. This connection rings all the bells. It is the one true thing that has made me feel alive and made everything worth it. This startling power didn't add on knowledge. It peeled away my limited "knowledge," revealing the *knowing* that is always there. My progress wasn't provable. But it was irrefutable to me. Love reveals conviction, not of the mind.

I've finally taken in how successful I am, too. I've started appreciating what I have accomplished, inside and out. This is a deliberate focus and it works. Otherwise, whatever I achieve, my ego will dismiss. It will point to some new castle in the distance, as though being there will make me so much happier, and as though I wouldn't bring that same longing mind over there.

I no longer need to "fix" something or find a "perfect" answer or repair for a life that will always be in process—and in grace. I am less concerned with what the deluge of information on the Internet or in the media suggests. I want to hear the still, deep, dark, electric truth within me. I want to follow what only I can know.

Of course, I've learned incredible information from others along the way, and will continue to do so. But that's not where my fulfillment has come from. My outstanding success is not clever. My satisfaction comes from the power of self-alignment. I am not rushing to be somewhere else so that I can finally accept myself.

I am not blaming anything for why I am held back. *I am never held back.* I am standing on holy ground—because wherever I am standing, I am standing wholly. I am no longer measuring my progress by my circumstances; I am measuring it by *my experience of and response to* my circumstances.

Finally, I trust uncertainty more, because I am never uncertain as to how much I will choose to love myself and every fiber of this fluctuating, emerging life.

To me, this is success. I want you to have it.

TURNING POINTS:
Why Does It Take So Long to Succeed? (And How Come You're Asking That Question?)

There will always be a gap, a space between where you are and where you want to be. This isn't failure.
This is life, especially for someone who continues to grow.

You have every right to desire progress. But it's disabling to condemn where you are. Thriving comes from loving, not from withholding love.

You may feel as though the rug has been pulled out from under you. I'd say you're on a magic carpet ride. You're no longer in the life you planned. This is a life that is bigger than your plan.

Thriving means trusting your own experience to lead you where the deepest part of you longs to be, instead of fighting your life and yourself at every turn.

It's always been *love* that has moved me forward. All the data or strategy in the world couldn't give me the solidity of one inspired moment.

I no longer need to "fix" something or find a "perfect" answer or repair for a life that will always be in process—and in grace.

I am standing on holy ground—because wherever I am standing, I am standing wholly. I am no longer measuring my progress by my circumstances; I am measuring it by *my experience of and response to* my circumstances.

Finally, I trust uncertainty more, because I am never uncertain as to how much I will choose to love myself and every fiber of this fluctuating, emerging life.

IT'S COMING: MORE GOOD THAN YOU CAN IMAGINE

When one door of happiness closes, another opens; but often we look so long at the closed door that we do not see the one which has been opened for us.

HELEN KELLER

If you haven't gotten "there," it's because there's something for you here. You're not missing out on anything in life, unless you're missing out on this moment.

TAMA KIEVES (journal entry)

They say the older you get the faster time seems to move, or maybe that's the more you read Facebook, I don't know. What I do know is that most of us are always wishing we were "there," that we had done the "right" things, secretly carrying our shame suitcases stuffed with regrets, imagining the life we cost ourselves with our own negligence. God, but we're cruel to ourselves—and misguided.

I have a story to tell you about a ritual of release I did. I'm hoping it will open you to the abundance that is heading your way right now.

When my second book, *Inspired & Unstoppable*, was first released in hardcover, I was feeling anxious and fearful about how much I "hadn't gotten done" to prepare for the launch, the precious days when a book first comes out and you're golden and have chances to promote it that you will not have again, or so says every single publicist.

I hadn't finished designing the website. Well, I'd never actually finished designing *me*, as in who I was going to be—so *that* was a problem. I hadn't come up with some sexy launch strategy, like how

I would let everyone know about this book, why it was better than sliced bread, and why they needed to have it because otherwise they would surely go insane and eat their young. I didn't have bonus products, like downloads or cars to give away. And with each day, I became more anxious and couldn't sleep at night.

I felt like I was running out of chances to finally go all the way, and at the same time, I was running out of steam. I had such a limited time to become "the bomb," to make up for my whole life and all, and I was just a tiny bit ragged around the edges. If I'd met you at a party, my name badge would have said, "Hello, I'm Freaked Out and Twitching," which is ever so reassuring in a self-help author. You may have looked at me and suddenly remembered you had an appointment in another part of the world, or at least on the other side of the room. And you surely would have felt better about your own life no matter what, even if you were going in for a hip replacement the next morning.

Finally, one day, I drove to the mountains to see some nature-type long-haired woman, an intention coach a friend had recommended. This is what you do when you're desperate. You pay complete strangers to talk you down from the ledge. This nice woman I'll call Mary talked to me in her backyard yurt, listening carefully as I piled on the desires I wanted to have fulfilled in my life. The poor woman probably hadn't imagined the hurricane she'd invited into her nice, safe, nature-harmonious sanctuary. No amount of burning sage was going to clear this air.

After some time, I tried to study what Mary was thinking—because I was trying to decide if I needed to manage my image or if Mary might need to manage her medication. She'd been silent for long spaces of time, which made me babble more. I couldn't tell if she was captivated or horrified or deciding upon which sex toy to use tonight when her acrobatic younger Italian lover arrived. But I digress.

"Okay," she said. "Come on, we're taking off." I'd been warned that she was prone to spontaneous inventions of healing rituals, so

I followed dutifully like a baby chick. We hiked to a sun-drenched field where a raging stream ran.

Mary told me to step into the stream. The water was ice-cold and the current ferocious, but she found a place in the middle where I could easily stand. My ankles stung from the cold, then turned numb. My first lesson: Shocking discomfort wouldn't kill or stop me; instead, my "comfort zone" would expand. Actually, that was my second lesson. My first lesson was: Get more information about who I'm hiring.

The generous Colorado sun beat down upon me in full summer radiance. The water was as frisky as kittens playing with a sock, splashing my legs heedlessly as though they were rocks.

We prayed out loud. Yes, this is what some of us intelligent, creative types do here in Colorado, in the beauty of the wilderness. Then she turned up the high-priestess-shaman-rabbi sassy factor. She commanded that I release all that I'd been worrying about, all I should have, would have, and could have done.

She pointed to the water rushing behind me, and pretended it was carrying away everything I'd intended to do but didn't accomplish.

"Whoops, there goes the e-mail campaign you could have done for the book," she hooted. "Whoa, there's a great idea for a book launch that just rushed by you. Oh my, someone else downstream just got it, loves it; it will become a *New York Times* bestseller now." I watched a leaf fly by on the current of the water, just as she said those words. There was no fishing it back.

"Oh, look, there go the phone calls you didn't make. There go the e-mails you didn't answer." I yanked my head back in that direction, watching the current sweep twigs, leaves, and debris with it. It was all happening so fast. I felt helpless. I wanted to dive in after them. I wanted to rescue every single one of my chances. I wanted a slow motion do-over. I wanted to do my whole life over. I wanted a pass. But the current was moving too fast.

I kept looking behind me, missing anything new that might be coming my way. She kept speaking faster. I couldn't keep up. I couldn't make it right. "What are you feeling about this?" she asked. And after a few intellectual, self-conscious stabs at it, I finally croaked the magic words. "Everything is out of control," I said. "I can't keep up." This shaman-priestess–Midwestern woman prodded me on. "Yes," she said, her voice booming like thunder. "What else?"

"I can't control it. I'm not in control." The words tumbled from my lips, as slippery as the water itself.

And then I laughed, the laugh of those who have gone too far and know they are never coming back the same. I laughed at the age-old joke of trying to control my life as though this time I just might. I laughed as I remembered every other time I had surrendered and come to realize that there was something bigger than my own will, that it wasn't my laziness or stupidity, it was my alignment with something essential, majestic, and mysterious, something that felt like True Life.

I just stood there and experienced what it would feel like to really let go. I felt giddy. I felt naked. It felt dangerous and pure at the same time. She asked me if I could forgive myself, because maybe, just maybe, I couldn't have done anything differently than I'd done it, and maybe, just maybe, it didn't matter. It didn't matter a fig, or a battered leaf or a broken twig.

> **I didn't have to do all those other things. *I had to do what I could do.* I was meant to follow the flow of my being over the force of my intellect.**

For just a split second, I dropped my anger, ache, and weight. I dropped my failures and self-comparisons. I felt like jelly. I let go of thudding disappointments, so many of them, a sack of potatoes, heavy as hell, black rot fermenting in the bottom of this bag I'd carried with me all the time.

I let go of my inadequacy, the part of me that felt immobilized when it came to doing all the things I imagine more ambitious people do. I realized it was gone, done. I couldn't get back the time. And later, much later—maybe years or seconds, I don't know—I was in the goop of shamanic time, off the clock and off the grid and maybe off my rocker, or on it for the first time, I realized that I didn't even want to get back the time that had passed, that I didn't want to do it differently. That in fact, I'd moved in some kind of weird perfection infused with its own acumen. I didn't have to do all those other things. *I had to do what I could do.* I was meant to follow the flow of my being over the force of my intellect.

Then she had me look in front of me. "What do you see?" she asked.

"A forceful current," I said.

"Tell me more about it."

"It's strong. It's relentless," I replied.

"Do you think it's going to stop bringing new energy?" she cackled.

"Not anytime soon, that's for sure."

She didn't have to say the rest. I got where she was going. I started to cry with sloppy, juicy, silent gratitude. I beheld the energy of that current. I felt like a weary disciple seeing the anointing eyes of a Christ who had never ever stopped believing in me, even when I heckled him and groused—and I'm a card-carrying, bagel-eating Jew by the way. I saw Krishna, Allah, my hatha yoga teacher, golden retrievers everywhere, inventors, poets, philanthropists, civil rights activists, a deep green lake where my soul resides, and mothers rocking and feeding their children. That stream became love and life itself.

I saw this loving current of life, how it would always give and give and give.

The water surged forward, filling in gaps, renewing itself with spontaneous, impossible abundance, and I realized life is always rushing at us—with new chances and opportunities to usher us into wholeness and expression.

"I've been so busy looking at all I haven't done or don't have that I haven't been aware or available to what's coming my way," I said.

Now I saw nothing but endless, fierce abundance. I remembered a lesson from *A Course in Miracles* that says, "Let miracles replace all grievances." I got it. It was all a matter of consciously applying my focus. Grievances came from looking backward. But miracles come from focusing on the life in front of me, and the promise of the current.

Love isn't linear. It's infinite, honeycombed, holographic, and pervasive. Likewise, the life you are meant to live doesn't depend on what you have or haven't experienced in the past. It doesn't matter what you think you've bungled or broken. It doesn't even matter if you've thought you're forever broken. It's not about your opinions. It's all about *presence*.

I started recalibrating internally. The wisdom of all the sages became crystal clear to me. The past doesn't create the future. The present does. I could step into a shift at any time, no matter what. I don't understand this with my brain, but I don't understand spiritual liberation, how the gentleness of dusk by the ocean wipes away my sorrow, or falling in love either. I can't even imagine how Skype works. All I know is that if I free myself of grievances and stories about my past, even the past of a minute ago, and all that I assume I know, I awaken to new capacities, brain cells, frequencies, and experience. I become available to everything that's available.

We live in an unstinting Universe. Every second is a feast of giving in a life-affirming reality, and we are connected to this crazy creative substance.

There is an unseen stream that's here for you.

There are breakthroughs and radically new opportunities with your sweet, singular name on them flying your way with more behind them. It's always your time. You've never missed out. Love brought you to the brink of this moment and love will carry you all the way. Receive your life. It's all here for you now.

TURNING POINTS:
It's Coming: More Good Than You Can Imagine

She asked me if I could forgive myself, because maybe, just maybe, I couldn't have done anything differently than I'd done it, and maybe, just maybe, it didn't matter.

I didn't have to do all those other things. *I had to do what I could do.* I was meant to follow the flow of my being over the force of my intellect.

The life you are meant to live doesn't depend on what you have or haven't experienced in the past.

The past doesn't create the future. The present does. I could step into a shift at any time, no matter what.

We live in an unstinting Universe. Every second is a feast of giving in a life-affirming reality, and we are connected to this crazy creative substance.

There is an unseen stream
that's here for you.

There are breakthroughs and radically new opportunities with your sweet, singular name on them flying your way with more behind them.

It's always your time.
You've never missed out.

Do Try This at Home: Jump-starts, Inquiries & Exercises

Some of these suggestions are just right for *you*. Others, not your cup of latte, or at least at *this* moment. Follow your gut. Feel free to adjust to your liking. Do what's right for you rather than what's written here.

Pick three Turning Points from this chapter. Write them out for yourself. Post them where you will see them. Meditate on them. Journal about them. Do a Freewriting exercise. (See page 252 for more about Freewriting.) Create a piece of art. Pay attention to your thoughts, memories, dreams, and "random" ideas and incidents. Inspired thoughts spark inspired responses. My words begin the conversation, but what do these truths unlock in you?

1. **Take kaizen steps.** Take one goal, desire, or project and come up with five tiny steps you can take toward achieving it. Take one tiny step. And repeat. Make it intentionally easy to succeed in your goals. For example, if you want to write every day this week, set the goal to write once this week.

2. **Reclaim three inspired times.** The more you tell these stories, the more they expand. Do a Freewriting exercise on "Three Inspired Times"—times or experiences when you *knew* something or life was clicking for you. *What did you know when you knew?* Make these your fairy tales, your Bible stories. What lessons did these times teach you? What did they make you feel? Is there a way to take some of that knowing into your life now?

3. **Stay in the conversation.** Where do you need to reach out or follow up on something? Where are you being polite instead of purposeful? Stop being self-conscious. You never know. Be spontaneous. Connect wildly. Give someone new alternatives. Don't back down.

4. **Stalk your losing story.** Do you have a favorite story you tell about why you're not where you want to be? Fill in this blank: "If ____ were different, I would be saved." This isn't a reason. It's an attack on yourself. What does it feel like to know there is nothing wrong with where you are?

5. **Determine your "open sesame" success formula.** Begin to ask yourself: What am I doing well? How have I progressed? What feels good to me? What's been moving in the right direction? How can I be self-affirming right now? Go deeper. Consider sharing your answers with someone else.

6. **Step into the stream.** Go to a stream or river, draw one, journal about one, or bring it into a meditation. Stand in the middle of the current. Look behind you. What grievances do you hold? What things do you think should have happened? What are your disappointments? Let them go. Now face the current, the rush of life. What is present on the horizon? What are things that could come? Things you can imagine? Things that excite you?

Do you have a question about this chapter? I'd love to know what's on your mind! *I may just get wildly inspired and answer you immediately.* Send me your thought or question at www.TamaKieves.com/uncertainty-question, and you can also register for a **FREE** Thriving Through Uncertainty Coaching Call designed to shift your mind-set and bring you immediate clarity.

NOW WHAT?
CONTINUING TO THRIVE

THRIVE IS A VERB

I know you want an extraordinary life. And that means you will need to make extraordinary choices.

More than that, you will need to make these choices again and again.

Thrive is a verb. It's not a noun. It is not a state that happens and then that's it, you're done. It's not like you close on the cottage by the lake, you snag the movie deal, you beat the cancer, your daughter kicks the grungy monosyllabic boyfriend to the curb and then *poof* you are forever free of uncertainty, discomfort, and the need to find your way back to the garden of trust, meeting your True Self, and listening to your own internal compass.

Thriving is a practice. It's a way of living. It's the cultivation of a mind-set that allows you to engage with every minute of your life and make inspired, imperative choices. You have an infinite presence within you that requires expression.

We are called to grow or to die. To love our children, significant others, friends, basset hounds, and the stranger on the train more honestly. To sing jazz vocals, heal sadness, teach, launch new products, industries, and technologies, and serve others and the trees. To radically grow in communion with ourselves and banish every dark inner dialogue. Staying true to ourselves is a moving target. And we relax more, only by stretching ourselves more.

That means we take risks and face old stories of limitations every single day: fear of rejection, lack of security, vulnerability, and shame. We choose strength instead of weakness again and again as though for the very first time. And when we need practice, life sends in a tutor or henchman.

Author Carlos Castaneda, writing about his training in shamanism, said a spiritual warrior needs "a worthy opponent" to help liberate his powers. It seems to me that every day of your life is a worthy opponent. This worthy opponent keeps you on your toes or near your meditation seat. It throws ice water in your face when you're about to turn lukewarm. For example, it lets you know your secret flame has just married well or a friend has early-onset Alzheimer's. Life won't let you painlessly fall asleep on the couch with fuzzy hopes, atrophying muscles, lint in your belly button, and unused potential. Sometimes, a worthy opponent is just the trickster you need to help you turn casual engagement into a blast of brilliance.

Every day will propel you to your edge. There will always be uncertainty. You won't tuck this thing into bed. You can't hide under your bed. Uncertainty will continue to drive you toward your spirit's indispensable clarity.

"I thought I was unstoppable," said Pete after we'd done a session. "Then *whomp*, I'm triggered. I'm frustrated. I feel defeated. Why do I keep going backwards?" he asked. He sounded as though all his recent progress communicating with his business partner had disappeared off the books.

"What makes you think you're going backward?" I asked.

"Well, I'm stopped again." Pete had hung up on his partner in a heated conversation.

"Oh, honey," I told him. "This is the work. This is integration. You're going from knowing these things intellectually to knowing them in your blood and your involuntary responses. You're moving into embodiment. You're practicing your swing until you are an instrument of wild grace. Okay, so maybe, right now you're more wild than wild grace. But that's where we're headed." Peter laughed and concluded, "Yeah, and when I master this, then I'll try it with my ex-wife."

Maybe you developed some mastery. You got an A. But then you graduated. Which means you get to go back into the gnarly woods. You're triggered again with self-abandonment, self-comparison, a sense of lack of fairness or financial insecurity—your weapon of choice—whatever you need to tweak you into practicing your swing.

You are being trained to be everything you can be in your lifetime, or as *A Course in Miracles* says, to embody the Presence of the Alternative. To know an unwavering peace of mind. And to never forget your connection. In every single situation, you're being asked: Can you use your tools here? Can you trust that you're led? Can you let go of judgment? We learn by application and repetition. We own our personal power by letting go of every belief that we don't have it.

No one would play an easy game for long. You'd hunt for more challenge and intrigue.

But life is like a brilliant video game. It's a monster. It's a beast. It's a thing of beauty. Just when you get to one level, the rules of the playing field change. The foes move faster. The blessings and allies are so disguised, they are harder to find, believe, or organize.

Now the "bad guys" reject your novel. They give you a lazy coworker, a boss with a personality disorder, a politician that cuts the funding for your program. You're not at the mall anymore. You're off the map again, learning how to trust the mystery and discover your destiny. You must use your practice. Obey your heart's communication and direction. And, of course, you will. Then the bells will ring. Everything will flutter into place and you will emerge with new mastery and a brighter light. *Your spirit just loves this game.*

This is the magic of practice. It gets better. We become more fluid with each limit we surpass. When I'm in pain or tempted to believe that I'm beaten, I remind myself that no fear can withstand my devotion, patience, and focus. I can always see things in a new way. I will become who I am meant to become. I am not defined by the circumstance. I am the storyteller. I am the shape-shifter. I am the beloved. Anything you give me, I will throw into the blender. This process will yield even sweeter freedom. I will not beat myself up for being in pain or stuck. I will practice for as long as it takes to be free. I will thrive. And like the great teacher Paramahansa Yogananda says, "Persistence guarantees that results are inevitable."

How will you practice? How will you devote yourself to thriving? I suggest you commit to believing in yourself and your life, unconditionally. And to undertaking the most formidably loving relationship with yourself that you have ever known. The quality of your inner life *is* your life. Besides, my thriving friend, you have gifts to give our world.

A *Course in Miracles* teaches that "who you think you are is a belief to be undone." You think you can be stopped. You think you can be diminished. You think you can fail. But that's the game. You can never lose. You already have everything you need. You have this crazy alchemical love within you and it's yours to give in any situation, which changes every situation and even *changes you* as you give it. You do not walk alone. Will you choose to listen to the disconnected, smallest version of yourself? Or the highest allegiance of your spirit? You have a choice.

Choose love. Choose again. Choose now. Ding, ding, ding! We have a winner.

THREE PRACTICES
I RECOMMEND

If I had to tell you just one thing about thriving through uncertainty, I'd tell you this: Do whatever it takes to discover, connect, and deepen your relationship to your Inspired Self.

Actually, this "one thing" really has two parts. First, it's the willingness to get to know yourself—your hopes, dreams, fears, and who you *really* are beyond your conditioning, or who you think you "should" be. This is an active practice, so even if you think you know yourself, stay current because you're always shifting and growing. And if you're not honest with yourself, you can't have a real relationship with the Divine Creative Current, with Infinite Love, with the Higher Mind, or whatever you call this greater intelligence.

The second part is to experiment and stick with a spiritual path. Find your way to whatever belief system and experience expands and comforts you. If you are not consistently immersing yourself in a larger truth, I promise you, the world of limitations will insidiously and inevitably have its way with you.

There are so many helpful techniques and practices available. We're all wired differently. I suggest you experiment and explore. It doesn't matter if something is the sun and the moon for someone else—find the ideas and practices that set you free.

In general, meditation or prayer and exercise are the best anxiety killers I know. I'd suggest incorporating them into your life. They will change your brain chemistry and your entire outlook. It's self-destructive to be in a period of uncertainty and not utilize activities or practices that ground and free you. There are so many varieties of meditation or spiritual practice, and just as many ways to move, exercise, and shake your beauty. As for me, I've studied and taught the spiritual psychotherapy program *A Course in Miracles* continually for years. And lately, I'm a vinyasa yoga girl as well.

But since I'm talking about practice and devotion, I want to clarify that the number one thing I did and continue to do is: *I do what I love*. That's my ultimate meditation in this life. It's a compass and a game changer. Working with my own creativity has connected me to something larger. It's how I started knowing I'm not alone. It opened a portal. Doing what I love has healed me.

Oh, but I bet you wanted something specific. So, I'll dish. In addition to my study of A *Course in Miracles* and practice of yoga, and devotion to writing, speaking, teaching, and coaching, I've used the following three practices most to help stay centered on my path. These three practices have helped me know myself and move beyond fear, confusion, and the corrosive belief that I'm not making any progress.

1. Inspired Self-Dialogues

This is my name for a life-saving journaling technique I use to get past fear and listen to my "inspired guidance." I find it exceptionally helpful because if my mind is scattered or agitated, (should that ever happen!) giving voice to my fears helps me focus. It's also a startling reminder that no matter what kind of mood I'm in, I always have access to a brilliant, calming wisdom. This has helped me believe that I'm always loved and guided, even though sometimes I'm feeling disconnected. Very disconnected.

Here's how it works. First, write your fears or concerns about whatever is troubling you or keeping you from moving forward. Then invite your Inspired Self to write back to you and answer you. Imagine this voice as your advocate. It's the most strength-filled, loving voice you could ever imagine. I sometimes imagine it as a success coach extraordinaire. Some of you may be religious and you might imagine the voice of God or Jesus or a guiding angelic presence writing back to you. Some of you might think of this voice as your Wise Spirit, the Beloved, the Inspired Self, or your Higher

Mind. And some of you might write to a fictional character or someone in history. For others, this voice may be the voice of a nurturing relative, teacher, friend, or lover.

When I give this exercise in classes, I see that many students find it helpful to think in terms of what they would say to their best friend or their child—someone they want the absolute best for in life. If that's helpful to you, then think along those lines, and shine that positive light and intelligence on yourself.

You might feel as though you're just making this up. Or that the voice is too nice to you. It may feel awkward. Do it anyway. The more you do this practice, the more this voice and presence will become real to you. The more you develop a relationship with this voice, the more you will experience it in other ways, too. I have dialogued with it on paper so often that sometimes I can even do it in my mind, without writing.

I wrote more about the Inspired Self-Dialogue in *Inspired & Unstoppable*. I'm borrowing a section from that book to offer you an example of this technique from one of my journals:

(Note: For years, I called my voice Inner Teacher, then shortened it to Teacher.)

M. (me): I'm afraid I am writing a book that won't sell that much.

T. (Inner Teacher, Teacher for short): Dear one, you have always doubted your own path, and you have always walked it with grace. I am with you. I am not guiding you into dangerous or useless territory. I am calling you to where you will thrive. You desire what you deserve. You desire what you are. You know this inside, which is why you have come this far.

(I could have stopped there, but if I didn't feel peace or didn't trust the advice, I'd continue the conversation until I did.) Like so . . .

M. How do I know that I'm not just telling myself what I want to hear?

T. You know by how it feels. You know what feels like truth and what feels like wishful thinking. One feels solid. The other does not. You also know because you have the energy to go forward. That means something is calling you forward. Also, you may think that you are telling yourself positive things because that's what you want to hear. But I ask you to consider that you may tell yourself scary and dark things, because they are what you want to hear. It is not always comfortable to hear positive things. I ask you to go forward, precious one, because you can never lose by following your truth. You will always benefit by experiencing the fruits of your truth. You can never benefit by deciding to put your truth aside. It will always haunt you. You will always wonder. Follow your truth and you will know the truth.

M. Thank you.

For the best use of this technique, write your ugliest fears or "argue" with your Inspired Self. This isn't a place to be polite or "stay positive." This is a place to acknowledge your anger, frustration, confusion, or sadness and let your Inspired Self provide the loving insight and perspective you require. It's meant to be a radically honest and healing conversation. Believe me, I've gotten down and dirty with my Inspired Self and those conversations have been amazing.

2. The Win List

I find this technique to be very helpful when you feel like you're not making progress or getting anywhere. I work with many artists, entrepreneurs, and visionaries, people who have big dreams or desires and often feel as though they're not doing enough or that things are not moving ahead quickly enough. And when you're in the middle of a transition, a Win List practice can be especially helpful as it validates the steps you are taking that you might not recognize otherwise.

Doing a Win List is a great exercise in focusing your mind on what you want to see. It trains your mind to pay attention to how, what, and where things are moving in the right direction. You will also start to see more "wins" when you're looking for them. This teaches you that you always see what you're looking for, which is why you want to consciously choose an empowering focus daily.

Here's how it works. You might want to keep a Win List every day. I suggest you write at least five, but closer to ten items on your list. This isn't a to-do list or a checklist of all you accomplished. For your Win List, I want you to write actions you took in the right direction. I also want you to write and acknowledge what I call inner actions, as in emotional or mind-set shifts. Also, include any times you noticed support, abundance, a coincidence or synchronicity, or anything that helped you feel a sense of life communicating with you, being on your side, and showing up on your behalf.

Make sure to include your tiniest inner shifts, as these life-altering victories are often neglected. For example, you might put on your Win List: "usually I'm depressed and stay in bed for thirty minutes extra, but today I only stayed in bed for twenty-nine minutes extra." Or "I said no when someone asked me to do something." Maybe you caved in two minutes later in that situation. But I want you to acknowledge the time you got it right. Or maybe you started a painting. And while later you may have decided the work was terrible, I want you to note only the win on your Win List: "Today, I dedicated myself to a new painting."

Every step in the right direction counts. And don't forget the subtle shifts that you might never remember if you didn't write them down. For example, you were thinking you should trust yourself more, and just at the instant you had that thought, the sun broke through the clouds and you just giggled, sighed, or cried. Note these kinds of connections and communications.

Finally, don't be afraid to note multiple wins from one thing. For example, "I connected with a lead at a networking group that might bring me in to do some consulting." And "I introduced myself to that lead, following my intuition." And "I loved the energy of our conversation and the upbeat feeling I carried afterward."

3. Freewriting

This is a writing or journaling practice designed to bypass your conscious mind. It's a well-loved technique of writers. But I find it's also a wonderful way to unlock your secrets, things you didn't know you knew or felt or desired. It's a great way to explore your beliefs, stories, imagery, and memories. For years, I've thought of freewriting as a form of meditation, because as I write, I train my mind to focus in one direction and ignore the distracting voice of self-judgment.

Here's how it works. Pick a word, memory, image, question, or topic (I suggest you use some of the Turning Points in this book). Write for fifteen minutes (or ten or whatever you set) and *do not think.* Do not stop, pause, or edit. Keep your pen moving (or keystrokes clicking on the laptop). Say anything. Repeat yourself. Free-associate. Feel free to ignore the topic at hand. Come back to it if it helps. Follow the energy. Don't be afraid to bump into something else you really want to write about and detour into that. Follow what wants to be written. Dare to stay with the heat, even if it leads you to an uncomfortable truth or expression. Do not judge. Do not edit or perfect. Just spew. Brew. Blow. Flow. Write it raw. Write so fast that a truth or knowing gets by the gatekeeper and slips into the light of consciousness.

You might try this technique multiple times on the same subject. You will get new insight or lines every single time.

And if you're fascinated with freewriting, you might enjoy Natalie Goldberg's classic book, *Writing Down the Bones*.

With any kind of practice, it's practice. You will deepen and discover what works best for you. Give it time. Give it love. Let go of any preconceived notions of what needs to happen. Let yourself be guided. You're likely to be thrilled at the results you experience, especially over time. Be patient, dear one. Be persistent. Be free.

RESOURCES TO KEEP YOU THRIVING THROUGH UNCERTAINTY

Thrive is a verb. It takes practice to stay inspired. I cannot say that enough. You're bombarded with limiting messages daily. Please actively dedicate yourself to the practices, conversations, and people that strengthen you.

I would love for you to be part of my worldwide inspired community dedicated to living and working from inspiration instead of fear. And I'd love to hear from you! (E-mail is best.) I'm also on social media daily. And here's how we can connect:

Tama Kieves
P.O. Box 9040
Denver, CO 80209
(800) 334-8114

www.TamaKieves.com (Make sure to sign up for
my FREE e-newsletter, for inspired articles, discounts,
coaching tips, program and retreat announcements,
and more!) And check out my blog.
Facebook.com/TamaKieves
Twitter.com/TamaKieves

MORE FREE SUPPORT YOU CAN ENJOY RIGHT NOW

Meet Your Inner Teacher Audio Meditation and Home Practice Guide. I've designed a special audio meditation set to luminous music to help you connect with your Inspired Self or Inner Teacher. Please take this journey as my GIFT TO YOU. A connection with your Inner Self is worth everything. I'll include some of my best instructions and practices for strengthening the most important relationship of your life. **www.TamaKieves.com/uncertainty-gift**

Thriving Through Uncertainty Coaching Call (They're always recorded, so even if you can't join me live, make sure you receive the recording of this interactive experience.) Your purchase of this book lets you sign up FREE for one of these calls. Get past fears. Ask your questions. Get inspired! Use this special link: **www .TamaKieves.com/uncertainty-freecall**

SOME POWERFUL EXPERIENCES I RECOMMEND

I always have new programs, workshops, retreats, and free tele-classes and talks going on, so do stay connected to the mothership, my e-newsletter list, for continual content, inspiration, specials, and reminders. Meanwhile, here are three ways to get past fears and take your inspired next steps, via training with me and entering transformative experiences with other conscious, creative individuals.

Join me for a retreat. Don't walk. Run. Fly. Crawl. Get here any way you can. Why not give yourself this experience in your lifetime? The magic is indescribable. See who you become when you enter inspired time out of ordinary life. Or maybe you want to bring me into your group. Let's talk. **www.TamaKieves.com/retreats**

Join my Inspired & Unstoppable Life Tribe right this minute!

Experience continual support to stay in an inspired mind-set and keep taking exceptional steps toward your dreams. It's super affordable! Join me and your worldwide tribe of smart, conscious, loving, creative individuals on two calls a month (also recorded). Time-tested techniques. Wild encouragement. Access to me! **www .TamaKieves.com/inspired-and-unstoppable-life-tribe**

Take A Course in Miracles with me. Join me LIVE or virtually for a program. I'd love to share this phenomenal material with you. I'm a believer in making it real and practical, reverent and irreverent. Check out the ongoing workshops and programs on my website at **www.TamaKieves.com/a-course-in-miracles**. You can also download my e-book *A Course in Miracles for Life Ninjas: 3 Breakthrough Practices to Fiercely Love Your Life* on Amazon.com for just $2.99.

I urge you to dedicate yourself to getting support for your new life, whether it's with one of my programs or anywhere else. We often don't realize how much support can make a difference in helping us think in new ways. Remember: Thriving is a practice. It's a way of living. It's the cultivation of a mind-set that allows you to engage with every minute of your life and make inspired, imperative choices. You have an infinite presence within you that *requires* expression.

Journey well, my extraordinary thriving friend. . . .

SHARE THE MESSAGE

I am *incredibly grateful* that my work and message have spread throughout the world by word of mouth. (Especially because I refuse to market in sticky, fear-based ways.) If you've felt the energy of this work, I'd truly appreciate it if you shared it in whatever way is right for you. Be an inspired ambassador. No gesture is too small or too big. Let's work together to create a world that lives and works from inspired power instead of fear.

SPEAKING/MEDIA

To book Tama Kieves for a speaking engagement, please visit her at **www.TamaKieves.com/speaking**. Contact her by e-mail at **Connect @TamaKieves.com**. Or call toll-free at **(800) 334-8114**.

Would you like to have Tama speak to your group or organization? She can take the messages and techniques of this book and speak about Thriving Through Uncertainty and adapt it to your business or organization as a keynote, one-day presentation, or any other format. She loves speaking to forward-thinking organizations. Her talks are always dynamic, interactive, fun, and life altering.

Or would you like a more creative group experience? Or want to set up a private retreat? Ask us, especially if you live in a particularly beautiful part of the world.

To book Tama for a media interview or story, to review this book or any of her other work, or to check her availability to write/ contribute an article, please contact us at **www.TamaKieves.com/ media**, e-mail **Connect@TamaKieves.com**, or call toll-free at **(800) 334-8114**. Know someone in the media who needs to know about Tama? You know what to do. You know Oprah? Stop reading. Start calling.

WHAT YOU CAN DO RIGHT NOW

Share, share, share. A *Course in Miracles* teaches that when we share ideas, we strengthen them. Share with someone else the concepts from this book that touched you most, especially if you know someone who is in transition. Or please buy him or her a book.

Start a reading and discussion group about this book with your coaching group, networking organization, church, yoga friends, divorce support group, business team, or other group. Or meet with one other person for coffee and thriving weekly. There is magic in joining with others.

Be a thought leader. Write a review of this book on your blog, Amazon, or social media platforms. Pitch an article. Do a talk. Your voice matters. If you're sparked, carry the torch.

Become part of our team. Do you love the message of *Thriving Through Uncertainty* and the work of Tama Kieves? Consider joining us to spread the reach of this work and to lend your genius to this transformation in perpetual progress. We are often looking for bright, amazing souls who are skilled, enthusiastic, and ridiculously competent. **www.TamaKieves.com/work-team-tama**

Got a brilliant idea? Share it with us. Follow the call. Everything wondrous begins with a whisper.

ACKNOWLEDGMENTS

This is not the whole picture. Just snapshots.

Growing up in Brooklyn, I dreamed that maybe someday I could be published by a big publisher in New York City. And as fantastical as that seemed, I don't think I could have ever dreamed of having a publisher as wonderful as Joel Fotinos. Joel, I will be grateful for the rest of my life for the chance I have had to work with you on four books. I have never told you this in person, but your generosity of spirit is like being given a diamond. That said, I'm still happy to accept an advance for another book.

I thank my readers, and all of you on my Facebook page and e-newsletter list who have written to me, telling me that my words helped you find your truth. You may have thought your message ended up in an anonymous pile. But let me tell you that your words have helped me find *my* truth. There are moments when I am completely free inside myself because I know that in my lifetime, I have been received. Wow. May everyone know how incredible this feeling is.

And for each of you brave and brilliant souls in my programs and retreats, you are my family, and I haven't even met some of you. I believe in the power of soul family, and you are that for me. My work isn't just a way to pay the bills. For me, it's a way to finally breathe. Meeting each of you has helped me breathe sweeter air. I'm grateful that my destiny is to serve mavericks, creatives, depth seekers, voices of change, those fumbling toward the light, deciding to go first, powerhouses like you.

Here's a strange acknowledgment. I thank my life for arduous terrain. With my partner Paul's ongoing health challenges and my own fears of not having support in my business and life, plus hormonal roller coasters, I've spent too many nights awake, feeling out of control. But these experiences forced me to let go of control. Strangely, I feel more whole now—and it makes me trust this crazy path even when I don't trust it for a minute. I would not have written this book with the same integrity or conviction without my challenges—challenges that were always buffered by the Presence of Love that comforted me immensely.

And for the Voice within me, which never fails me. Ever. Thank you for choosing me to walk this walk.

And for Marney, who helped me keep winging my life and business like a frisbee in the park, and for bearing witness to my gospel powers. Your love is creative elixir. And SARK for your brilliance and kindness and for showing me how to be on my own and not be lonely and to enjoy the festivity of being alive. And for all my friends, you know who you are and what you mean to me.

And Paul. Oh, Paul. Through it all. I honor your bravery through this journey, your consistent ease and strength even in crazy, heart-wrenching frustration. And for loving me like no other, and for the love in your eyes when I was scared to fly home alone from Rome, and for the love in your depths for all my fears and for setting me free while grounding me. And for our flawed and majestic journey together—of loving and thriving through uncertainty.

ABOUT THE AUTHOR

Tama Kieves, an honors graduate of Harvard Law School, left her law practice in litigation with a large corporate law firm to write and help others discover and express the most meaningful lives they were born to live. She is the bestselling author of *This Time I Dance!: Creating the Work You Love, Inspired & Unstoppable: Wildly Succeeding in Your Life's Work!,* and *A Year without Fear: 365 Days of Magnificence.*

Featured in *USA Today,* the *Huffington Post,* and *Success* magazine, as well as on ABC News, Oprah Radio, and other national media, she is a sought-after speaker and visionary career/success catalyst and coach who has helped thousands worldwide to create extraordinary lives, work, and businesses based in brilliance instead of fear. She is known for her edgy humor, "real-world" spirituality, warm compassion, and the big possibilities she brings out in others. Tama is on the faculty of premier holistic learning institutes such as Omega, Kripalu, and Esalen, and has presented at TEDx. Tama has also taught *A Course in Miracles* for more than twenty-eight years.

Says Tama: I was put on this earth to champion artists, purpose-driven entrepreneurs, organizations and leaders, visionaries, change agents, conscious meaning seekers, and mavericks. You didn't come here just to make it in the world. You're here to remake the world with your creative genius, empowering love, and unparalleled voice and vision. *We need your true gifts. You need to give them.* Join me in an inspired revolution of living from your inspired power instead of from fear.

If you're thinking of contacting her, give in to the urge:

www.TamaKieves.com
Facebook.com/TamaKieves Twitter.com/
TamaKieves